YOUR BETTER SELF

Your Better Self

CHRISTIANITY, PSYCHOLOGY, AND SELF-ESTEEM

Craig W. Ellison, Editor

A HARPER/CAPS BOOK

Published in collaboration with The Christian Association for Psychological Studies
for the series Christian Perspectives on Counseling and the Behavioral Sciences

1817

Harper & Row, Publishers, San Francisco
Cambridge, Hagerstown, New York, Philadelphia
London, Mexico City, São Paulo, Sydney

FIRST EDITION

Library of Congress Cataloging in Publication Data
Main entry under title:

YOUR BETTER SELF.

"A Harper/Caps book."
Includes index.
1. Self-love (Theology)—Addresses, essays, lectures. 2. Self-respect—Addresses, essays, lectures.
I. Ellison, Craig W., 1944-
BV4639.Y64 1982   248.4   82-47742
ISBN 0-06-062237-7

83 84 85 86 87 10 9 8 7 6 5 4 3 2 1

To Sharon and our sons

Contents

Preface to
Harper/CAPS Series

THROUGHOUT much of this past century, Christianity and psychology have been viewed as enemies. Religion has been a taboo topic for most psychologists, with a few notable exceptions such as William James and Gordon Allport. Psychology has been viewed with suspicion and fear by many in the Christian community. Within recent years, however, increasing numbers of individuals with personal commitment to the historic Judaeo-Christian faith have entered the counseling and behavioral science fields. Increasing numbers of ministers have received psychological training.

Several associations involving Christians in psychologically related fields have emerged, including the national Christian Association for Psychological Studies (CAPS). At the same time the American Psychological Association has recognized the legitimate study of psychology and religion with creation of Division 36, Psychologists Interested in Religious Issues. The Society for the Scientific Study of Religion has also blossomed into an international association with nearly 2000 members. Although Division 36 and S.S.S.R. are composed of members with a wide variety of Christian and non-Christian commitments, the trend is clearly toward the legitimizing of the study of psychology/religion relationships. In addition to these associations, several journals have been developed to provide outlets for those wishing to publish theory and research. Within conservative Christian circles are the *Journal of Psychology and Theology,* and the *Journal of Psychology and Christianity* (formerly the *CAPS Bulletin*). Other prestigious journals include the *Journal for the Scientific Study of Religion* and *Zygon.* There is a new willingness and perceived need to consider the ethical implications of research and practice as a result of the new knowledge that has been gained in the behavioral and biomedical sciences. Few behavioral scientists are willing to accept the notion that their research is totally objective, and many clinicians are questioning the validity of the detached, completely objective therapist model.

All of this is not to say that most psychologists are interested in religion, or most Christians are comfortable with psychology. Neither is probably true. However, for a growing number of Christians and non-Christians, the rigorous study of relationships between psychology and religion in general (and Christianity in particular) is an important and legitimate activity.

To date, there has been no systematic publishing outlet for those committed to the Christian belief system wishing to write on a professional level on Christianity/psychology relationships. Among most religious publishers the tendency has been to popularize the writing due to market considerations. Secular publishers have tended to severely downplay or omit any explicit religious dimension. *Christian Perspectives on Counseling and the Behavioral Sciences* is the first series to appear that is both explicitly Christian in orientation, written on a professional level, and yet readable by psychologically educated lay persons. Professionals in counseling and the behavioral sciences will benefit, as will pastors. The books in the Series will be valuable as supplementary texts in upper division undergraduate courses, seminary and graduate programs.

The purpose of the Series is to describe and analyze relationships between psychology and the orthodox Christian belief system. At the same time, the Series will be investigational and exploratory. For example, individual authors will undoubtedly take different views on the basic issue of whether it is even possible to "integrate" Christianity and psychology. The Series will encourage examination of behavioral science findings and their implications for understanding the Christian faith, as well as look at the implications of Christianity for the behavioral sciences. The topics explored will range from more general theoretical concerns to specific phenomena and issues.

Books in the Series do not represent the views of Christian Association for Psychological Studies in any formal way. They reflect the individual authors.

CAPS is a national organization of Christians working in psychologically related fields, including psychology, psychiatry, sociology, counseling and social work. It also encourages participation and membership by members of the ministry. It was begun formally in 1955 in Western Michigan as a predominantly regional group. CAPS holds an annual convention, publishes a quarterly *Bulletin*, sponsors regional meetings throughout the

United States several times each year, and publishes a membership and referral directory. Members are asked to indicate agreement with the basic purposes and statement of faith of the association. Further information can be obtained from the Executive Secretary, 26711 Farmington Road, Farmington Hills, Michigan 48018.

In a time of great concern about personal rights, self-fulfillment, and individual happiness, *Your Better Self* presents an important view: while agreeing that positive self-feelings are vitally important, this volume presents a crucial balance between affirmation of healthy self-esteem and warnings against an unhealthy self-centered and narcissistic preoccupation with oneself. *Your Better Self* also gives an interesting interplay between diverse biblical/theological and theoretical views, while demonstrating the implications of self-evaluation for varying aspects of individual and institutional life.

CRAIG W. ELLISON, Ph.D.
Series Editor

Acknowledgments

IT HAS BEEN a pleasure to work with the contributors to this volume. They have conscientiously responded to necessary guidelines and graciously responded to editorial feedback and requests.

I am especially grateful to Susan Huse Miller, for her superb help in retyping and organizing chapters of the book. At times she probably felt as if she were drowning in a sea of paper, but she quietly and cheerfully kept afloat.

For the continual encouragement and assistance of my editor, Roy M. Carlisle, at Harper & Row San Francisco, I'm most appreciative. Roy's expertise and insight, combined with his kindly manner, made the process a pleasure.

For my dear wife, Sharon, and sons Scott, Timothy, and Jonathan, contributors of much delight and givers of worth in my life, a special word of thanks.

Self-Esteem: An Overview

CRAIG W. ELLISON

SELF-DESCRIPTION and self-evaluation appear to be unique to human beings. No other creatures seem to be capable of viewing themselves as the object of their own thoughts. No other beings give indications of concern about who they are and how they feel about themselves.

As a result, philosophers have attempted to unravel the mystery of self-awareness for centuries. Since the beginning of modern psychology, the nature and impact of self-reflection have been topics of interest. For example, William James distinguished between the material, social, and spiritual selves and suggested that self-evaluation involved a comparison of aspirations with achievements.[1]

Following James, sociologists Cooley and Mead emphasized the interpersonal nature of the self. Cooley introduced the idea of the *looking-glass self,* thereby suggesting that we conceive of ourselves primarily in the terms and tones that other people reflect to us.[2] Mead felt that language was a vital aspect of self-description and self-assessment.[3] He also proposed a distinction between the generalized self and more specific selves that are displayed in particular situations.

Until the late 1940s, comparatively little attention was paid to the study of the self by academic psychology. This was largely due to the preoccupation of mainstream psychology with forming an identity as scientific. In a grand effort to model after the physical sciences, many psychologists tried to avoid issues that could be construed as subjective or philosophical. The major emphasis was on explanation of human functioning in terms of external and physicalistic causes.

Several neo-psychoanalytic theorists who emphasized the role of interpersonal relationships in the shaping of personality touched upon the notions of self-conception and self-esteem, however. Adler's emphasis on the

inferiority complex as the dynamic behind striving for superiority implies
the importance of self-esteem for human behavior.[4] A basic component of
Horney's theory was the need to value one's self and to be valued by others.[5]
Sullivan felt that the self-concept was learned through the reflected apprais-
als of those significant in our lives.[6] Fromm viewed self-love as crucial for
healthy social functioning.[7]

With the development of humanistic psychology and its prominent
theorists, considerable theoretical and therapeutic work has focused on
self-perception. Self is central in humanistic psychology. Along with the
recent waning of more radical forms of behaviorism, which tried to abolish
the concept of self as scientifically useful, has come the resurgence of
cognitive psychology and the development of experimental study of the self
in social psychology.

Coopersmith, Rosenberg, and Ziller[8] have formulated the most explicit
contemporary theories of self-esteem based on empirical studies. Coopersmith believes that self-esteem is determined by an interaction of success,
values, desires, and defenses in each person.[9] He views self-esteem as a
personal assessment of worth that has strong emotions associated with it.
Rosenberg takes a more sociological approach and analyzes the self-concept
in terms of attitudinal structures.[10] He views self-esteem in more topologi-
cal and Gestalt terms, as a buffer between the self and the environment.

THE NATURE OF SELF-ESTEEM

Self-reflection is based upon the cognitive capacities for abstraction,
generalization, and convergent thinking. Characteristics of a variety of
events or stimuli are identified as similar in kind with reference to some
central set of attributes. Wherever such attributes are identified, the event
or object becomes classified and responded to in reference to the conceptual category. Concepts may be more or less general (for example, animal
is more general than dog, which is more general than German Shepherd),
more or less complex (based on few or many dimensions or sets of attributes), and more or less differentiated. Concepts appear to be learned rather
than inherited.

The self-concept as usually discussed has exactly these characteristics. It
consists of behaviors, feelings, and beliefs that can be commonly referred
to the conceptual category of self. The self is seen to be related to a diversity
of events, usually because these events are viewed as somehow originating
with (or would at least seem non-sensical without reference to) a central
factor.

The self-concept, however, has both content and feeling components. It is not only my perception of who I am based on various conceptually interrelated inputs, but how I feel about who I am. Because it also appears to be primarily learned, the self-concept may be considered an attitude. Viewing it as an attitude introduces a dynamic, directing quality that is not readily apparent in use of the notion of concept. Though it is a concept, it is also more. Most definitions of attitude include the suggestion that it guides one's thoughts, feelings, and actions toward classes of events or objects, a predisposition to respond toward an object positively or negatively. As such, the self is not only an *object*, or a set of abstractions expressed in adjectives, but a *subject*, or a directional and selecting force. This perspective is closely related to the symbolic interactionist view based on the sociological writings of Mead and Cooley, which generally hold that an individual's self-concept emerges from social learning and, in turn, guides or influences the subsequent behavior of the individual.[11]

Attitudes, including those about the self, are formed as the result of direct or indirect experience. Direct experience includes self-observation[12] and conditioning. It is interesting to note that the resistance of self-concepts to change may be due to the emotional classical conditioning foundation of many early self-referent experiences. Indirect experience includes information given by others, such as parents, friends, employers, and media. Parents have an extremely powerful early influence on the self-concept because they are both conditioners and also providers and controllers of information reaching the child.

The feeling or evaluation component of self-attitude is what is meant by self-esteem. The most commonly accepted analysis of self-esteem sees it as the result of comparisons between one's perceived self, which combines both the assessments of others and one's private perceptions, and the ideal self, which is both how one feels one would like to be and how one feels one ought to be. The ideal self represents an internalization of values transmitted by significant others and the culture. Individual differences in the ideal self are due to the divergence of values held within various subcultures and the selecting capacity of the self. Self-esteem is generally considered to be measured by the extent of the discrepancy between perceived self and ideal self for any individual. Therefore, the less discrepancy, the higher self-esteem and vice versa. Much work remains to verify empirically and clarify this conception. For example, it is not clear whether how one would *like* to be or how one feels one *should* be affects self-esteem more. It is also not clear whether self-concepts can be changed more or less easily depending upon the forms of feedback that have used to shape both the perceived self and the ideal self, and the timing of particular forms of feedback in the development of the self-concept.

Nevertheless, at least five interrelated trends in the development of the self have been identified.[13] These include: increased ability to evaluate one's self in relation to distinct situations and tasks, rather than in a global, absolute, unqualified way ("I am a good boy"); increasing distinction with age between the perceived self and the ideal self and an increasing view of one's self in terms of several dimensions; increasing tendencies for consistency and stability in one's self-concept, which is related to the growth of abilities for cognitive organization.

THE IMPACT OF SELF-EVALUATION

How we feel about ourselves has been shown to be related to a wide variety of personal and interpersonal characteristics. Because most of the findings are correlational, it is impossible, at this point, to determine directionality of cause. It is likely that self-esteem may serve as both cause and effect, depending upon the person and the characteristic.

Persons higher in self-esteem are more active and expressive in group discussions, not particularly sensitive to criticism, show little anxiety, and are much less afflicted with psychosomatic illnesses than low self-esteem persons. Those with low self-esteem feel isolated, unlovable, too weak to overcome their deficiencies, and unable to defend themselves, as well as afraid of angering others or drawing attention to themselves in any way.[14] In addition, low self-esteem children have been found to have higher anxiety levels and to receive generally more negative reactions from peers.[15] Intelligence and curiosity are positively associated with self-esteem.[16] Those with more positive self-evaluation do significantly better in school,[17] while underachievers are more likely to have negative self-feelings.[18] Finally, those with low self-esteem are more likely to be submissive and dependent, more vulnerable in interpersonal relations, more concerned about what others think of them, and more likely to have their feelings hurt.[19] Self-esteem seems to operate at least partially as a mediating variable[20] that interacts with significant stimulus characteristics in affecting such responses as trust.[21] In general, less self-disclosure,[22] greater field dependence,[23] and vulnerability to delinquency[24] are related to negative self-worth.

THEOLOGY

The biblical roots of positive self-regard may be traced initially to the *creation* account. In contrast to a view of humanity's origins that regards people as a chance mutation or impersonally evolved, the Genesis account suggests that from the beginning people were both very special and highly regarded. God created us in his own image, gave us major responsibility, provided abundantly for our needs, and considered his creation very good.[25] Hardly the picture of a despicable worm! Rather, this is a portrait of a being that the perfect Judge has placed the highest value upon. And yet this is a view of humanity before the Fall, still perfect and not yet God's enemy. Is there a scriptural basis for positive self-esteem after the Fall?

Quite clearly there is. Referring to God's creation considerably after the Fall, the psalmist speaks with awe about both the Lord God and his creation: "What is man that thou are mindful of him, and the son of man that thou dost care for him? Yet thou has made him a little less than God, and dost crown him with glory and honor."[26] The tense used with reference to God's evaluation implies a present, continuing act. Even after the Fall, God continues to evaluate positively, or "crown man with glory and honor."

An even more convincing basis for human worth is found in the act of *redemption*. God did not turn away from us in disgust and consider us worthless once we had sinned. Rather, he sacrificed his Son for us while we were still very much his enemies![27] It might be argued that this simply reflects God's incredible mercy because he loved us when we were worthless. Earlier in this same passage of Scripture, however, we are told that Christ died for the ungodly while we were still *helpless*, not worthless.

This points up an important distinction that perhaps has been misunderstood: to be a sinner is to be helpless, not worthless.[28] God's mercy is expressed both in not destroying humanity and in providing help for the helpless or those unable to meet God's standard of perfection on their own. God distinguishes between ungodliness and worthwhileness, between sin and the placing of positive value upon the human personality or self. Bruce Narramore referred to this when he said:

The first thing I'd like to do is suggest that we need to understand the biblical meaning of the concept of self. . . . The Greek word *ego* means I, the total personality. . . . The ego is the whole man, the total person. . . . The flesh theologically is the rebellious sin principle. . . . We fail sometimes to differentiate between the self and the flesh, or the self and the old sin nature, or the self and the old man. . . . They are distinctly different aspects of the human personality. . . . It's very clear that man has deeply fallen, but we tend to confuse righteousness and value. You see, according to Scripture we can be of immense value and worth to God, and still be very, very sinful. But sometimes we say since we are totally depraved or totally sinful we are, therefore, worthless.[29]

6 YOUR BETTER SELF

The underlying dynamic for our self-esteem, or human worth, is the unconditional love of God, expressed in his redemptive act. "We love, because He first loved us."[30] We not only love God in reciprocation, but we also can love ourselves because God validates our worth simply by loving his creation without conditions attached. Unconditional love does not mean that God has no standards or requirements. Redemption is conditioned upon repentance. Nevertheless, God continues to love us even if we reject him.

The establishing of our self-worth in God's unconditional love suggests two additional concepts important for a biblical understanding and personal experience of self-esteem. The first is that self-esteem is primarily shaped and sustained through social reinforcements. It is developed in an interpersonal context. Biblically, the interpersonal nature of the self is originally implied in the initial creation act ("let us make man in *our* image")[31] and in the creation of a helpmate ("it is not good that man should be alone").[32] It is basic to our nature, then, to require relationships for self-development. Evaluation necessitates a judge-judged relationship. Self-esteem is initially rooted in the evaluations of significant others: "And God saw everything that he had made, and behold, it was very good";[33] "By this we know love, that he laid down his life for us."[34] Eventually it becomes partially internalized so that self-judgments are made, as in the case of Adam and Eve after their sin, but it still continues largely as a function of feedback from others. In contrast to the valuing process of our society, which gives reinforcements, at least for men, on the basis of achievements (that is, conditionally), God's love is unconditional. He continuously values us, so we can value ourselves.

The second implication of God's unconditional love is its unchanging nature. In human relationships, positive feedback from others, which is basic to positive self-esteem, is not always consistent. We don't always achieve sufficiently to win unbroken regard. Those who love us don't love perfectly. God's love is steadfast[35] and therefore provides a stable source of positive regard, which carries us through the vagaries of human relationships and allows us to stand somewhat independently.

While God's love is unconditional and unchanging, our experience of it is not always consistent. The major obstruction, biblically, in our experience of God's love is sin. Likewise, the conditional nature of human valuing processes and much of the struggle to experience positive self-esteem may be traced to the effects of sin.

The original sin was fundamentally a violation of relationship. It was not only a negating of God's authority and truthfulness, but it was also a negating of his character. In the process of God-negation, humanity, which was made in the image of God, negated itself. We could no longer look at ourselves with unconditional self-regard. In violating our relationship with God, we cut off our central source of self-esteem and became self-centered.

Adam and Eve became knowledgeable, but knowing was painful. Their first act was to hide. Ever since that act, the human race has naturally tried to hide what is bad from God and from itself. Ego defenses are fundamentally attempts to guard ourselves from negative truth. In the act of redemption and the continuing process of forgiveness, God's grace allows us to face the truth about ourselves and restore the relationship. Nevertheless, because we are fallen, even the redeemed employ techniques designed to insulate themselves from truth and to hide from God at times.

Intertwined with hiding came blaming and violence. "Passing the buck" started with Adam and Eve.[36] In an attempt to get out from under the painful, bright spotlight of negative self-knowledge and to escape responsibility for breaking the relationship with God, both Adam and Eve tried to place the blame on someone else. The attempt was both to escape judgment and to preserve positive self-regard, even if the preservation was self-delusional. In our day, we characteristically blame parents or circumstances that "determined" the way we are. The irony is that those who rely most heavily on such ego defenses are characterized by extremely low self-esteem or extremely active compensation in the form of arrogance. By blaming others and deluding themselves, they block off the major sources of self-esteem found in positive relationships with God and others.

Cain's murder of Abel demonstrates the lengths to which attempts at self-justification and preservation of self-regard can go. The biblical incident is particularly fascinating in view of studies showing that low self-esteem is associated with delinquency and antisocial behaviors. Apparently, God had established standards regarding offerings. Instead of accepting God's evaluation and changing his offering, Cain viewed Abel as the cause of his rejection. Perhaps he reasoned that if he could remove Abel, God would accept his offering or, at the very least, he would be rid of the painful comparison. Because self-esteem is based in interpersonal feedback, it is customary for people to look for those who are similar to aid in self-evaluation and to avoid or get rid of those who are not similar.[37] Similarity breeds attraction, at least in part because it allows us to receive feedback that confirms our way of thinking, feeling, and behaving. Making, or at least choosing, others in our own image helps us to maintain that self-image.[38]

Another effect of sin is to create depression. (This is not an assertion that all depression is due to sin). Ronald Rottschafer points out that self-esteem and depression are interrelated.[39] The psalmist suggests that lack of integrity, or the covering up of sin, results in depression and, by implication, negative self-esteem.[40] His body groaned, his soul *(psyche)* was cast down, and he was overcome by guilt. The New Testament reminds us that a double-minded person is unstable in *all* his ways.[41] The implication is that people who have not clearly decided their loyalties or who have not been purified of their sin but hide it, will be unstable in their faith, behaviors, and self-perception.

Indeed, the pervasive effects of sin are clearly presented in Romans 3:11–18, where we see that human understanding, motivation, social relationships, behavior, communication, emotions, perceptions, and relationship with God become twisted and negative through the power of sin. The way in which we feel about ourselves and go about trying to establish our self-esteem, as well as the way in which we respond to others' needs are all affected negatively by sin.

Fortunately, God has provided a means whereby the negative effects of sin can be short-circuited. Rather than trying to do away with the notion of sin as pathogenic, or denying the presence of sin, God has established *confession* as the means to intrapsychic and interpersonal healing. Confession brings a sense of emotional cleansing through the release of anxiety and bitterness. It restores relationships and re-establishes interpersonal transparency. Through confession to God and appropriate others,[42] forgiveness is experienced and the confessor is once again able to receive and give the mutual affirmation that is the foundation of self-worth. In the process of confession, the individual is able to accept himself or herself as he or she is, rather than trying to build worth on the basis of denial and self-deceit.

The biblical concept of *servanthood* is another cornerstone for positive self-esteem. Throughout his writings, the apostle Paul repeatedly identified himself as a *doulos,* or bond servant, of the Lord. His primary self-concept was that of God's servant. As a result of such identification, Paul's concern was about God's evaluation rather than about social comparison.[43] He was freed from much of the anxiety and destructive impact of negative evaluation from others because his concern was affirmation by God. His work was

also invested with special purpose and took on a more caring and constructive quality. To the extent that the people of God identify wholeheartedly
with God's purposes and his evaluation as the basis of their lives, self-esteem
will be removed from the more transient and unpredictable feedback of the
social context.

The fifth biblical base of self-worth is that of *community*. Throughout
the New Testament, Paul emphasizes the importance of incarnating
Christ's love. In Colossians 3:12–15, he urged believers to be kind, meek,
compassionate, patient, forbearing, and loving. Not only was this essential
for corporate harmony, but these characteristics are fundamental to the
individual self-esteem upon which corporate conflict or harmony pivots. In
numerous places, Christians are instructed to judge not, to forbear, and to
consider their own sins and weaknesses.[44] Such an orientation is crucial if
a church community is to build and encourage positive self-esteem in its
members. I suspect that the commandment to avoid judgment, or negative
feedback that is provided without a spirit of compassion and caring, is given
for the following two reasons. First, it fosters self-delusion. In Romans 2,
after describing a great deal of wickedness in the previous chapter, Paul
immediately warns the Roman believers not to get puffed up through social
comparison, but to reflect themselves accurately in comparison with the
perfect standard. Second, such judgment lowers the other person's self-
esteem and results in dysfunction within the body. The cycle is definite;
the social-psychological principle is reciprocity. Judgment begets judgment
and conflict; praise elevates esteem and fosters harmony. Judgment brings
out natural ego-defenses that are emotionally employed unless a person is
sufficiently spiritually mature and of high enough self-esteem to identify
with Christ in his or her response rather than imitating the judger. Unfortunately, most of us are not at that level of ego-strength or spiritual experience, and so churches split.

The Christian community, then, is to be a *place of affirmation*. Not only
is it to be a place where love dominates over judgment, but each person
is recognized as having a special place and contribution to make to the
community. The biblical foundation of such valuing is found in the doctrine of spiritual gifts and offices.[45] Scripture makes it clear that there are
a variety of gifts that are given for the common good and that all of the
contributions are important.[46]

The church is also to be a *place of counterculture*, where the primary
emphasis is on acceptance based on Christ's love rather than a conditional

admission based on such criteria as appearance, achievement, articulate-
ness, and affluence.

Ultimately, the most compelling biblical foundation for positive self-
esteem is the person of Jesus Christ. He is the greatest example of true
humility and positive self-esteem.[47] Christ was clearly sinless and therefore
truly humble, but he also asserted who he was without apology. Scripture
does not allow the conclusion that he was arrogant *or* that he belittled
himself. Because of his worth, his servanthood and sacrifice have redemptive meaning. The Bible suggests that Christians are to have the same
servant attitude as Christ[48] and implies that we are expected to love
ourselves properly as Christ did.[49]

SELF-ESTEEM AND PRIDE

Scripture indicates that pride is one of the sins most abhorred by God[50]
and was the root sin behind Lucifer's abortive coup attempt. For this
reason, Christians have been quick to suspect the notion of self-esteem as
a cover-up for arrogance. We are told by many that there is no good in
ourselves and that we must be emptied of self. There is a confusion about
self as personality and self-centeredness as an expression of the flesh or
sin-principle.

In order to understand properly the relationship between self-esteem,
pride, and humility, we must look at the biblical pattern of God-man
interaction, the notions of perfection and goodness, and the concepts of
works and grace.

Pride is characterized by an exaggerated desire to win the notice or praise
of others and the rigid taking of a superior position in which others'
opinions are virtually never regarded as good as one's own. Humility is
characterized by accurate self-appraisal, responsiveness to the opinions of
others, and a willingness to give praise to others before claiming it for one's
self. Biblically, pride is expressed in attempts to claim glory due to God for
one's self and in the attempt to justify one's self in rejection of God's
redemptive process.

From what we know of the components of positive self-esteem, humility
is the biblical counterpart, not pride. The ability to face one's self and to
assess and accept both strengths and weaknesses accurately, while being
responsive to, but not overly dependent upon, social approval are basic
ingredients of nondefensive self-esteem. On the other hand, psychologists
since Adler have associated both pride and excessive self-disparagement,
which some might regard as humility, as indications of basic feelings of
inferiority or low self-esteem.

The biblical position is not that we shouldn't feel good about ourselves, but rather that we should love ourselves,[51] and accurately assess ourselves.[52] The critical distinction is between goodness and perfection. In his act of creating us in his image, God gave us intrinsic capacities that can be developed by human effort, enjoyed, and felt good about. The problem comes when we don't accept God's evaluation or his plan and when, in our attempts to justify ourselves spiritually and morally, we start thinking of ourselves as overly good or as capable of becoming perfect. Pride, then, is based on an unwillingness to accept God's moral judgment of us as imperfect. Its dynamic is rooted in feelings of rejection or inferiority and expressed in overcompensation aimed at becoming so superior that one can delude himself into thinking he is perfect, without God. Pride may not be based on conscious rejection of God, but may arise from a background of rejection and the failure to be exposed to and experience God's unconditional love.

Humility and positive self-esteem are not based upon self-negation or the "emptying of one's self." They are based upon affirmation of God's regard for us and a right relationship with him in which imperfection, weaknesses, and strengths can be accepted or confessed and changed as appropriate. The biblical history of God-man interaction is not one of God manipulating "empty shells," devoid of personality, in robotlike fashion. God doesn't act in place of personality, but *through* personality. Christ's incarnation and human development are affirmations of this. The pattern of interaction is one of mutual influence: God acts and man responds. This should not be too surprising if we take creation in God's image and the Scriptures seriously; if the Old Testament left doubts about God's personality, the incarnation removed those doubts. There is no doubt that Jesus Christ regarded himself positively. He could not have made the assertions he did if that weren't the case. On the other hand, he was marked by perfect humility. The biblical injunctions to "have this mind in you which was also in Christ Jesus"[53] and to "be imitators of God as beloved children"[54] are directed at Christ's whole personality. We are to be marked by humility based on accurate and positive self-appraisal. Christians basking in God's perfect love are able to accept their imperfections more completely, acknowledge their sins, and face themselves free from fear of rejection.[55]

Many Christians, it seems, hold to a false form of humility associated with negative self-esteem in contradiction to the biblical pattern. Associated with this negative self-regard, which is a reversed form of pride in one's badness,[56] are depression and a sense of emotional unbelief or anxiety about eternal salvation.

Comparison of True Humility, Pride, and False Humility

True Humility	Pride	False Humility
1. Based in self-worth.	1. Based in self-doubt.	1. Based in self-deprecation.
2. Accepts both strengths and weaknesses.	2. Denies weaknesses.	2. Rejects strengths.
3. Is open to both positive and negative feedback.	3. Is closed to corrective and negative feedback.	3. Is closed to affirmation and positive feedback.
4. Results in accurate appraisal.	4. Results in unrealistic appraisal (attitude of superiority).	4. Results in unrealistic appraisal (attitude of inferiority).

Whereas pride is inevitably connected with an achievement or power basis of self-esteem, humility frees people from the bondage of striving to gain approval by always looking superior in the eyes of others or themselves. The fundamental dynamic behind humility is grace. The Scripture consistently emphasizes that neither spiritual salvation nor human value are rooted in works. Rather, they are founded upon grace. Fundamentally, there are two ways in which one can gain and maintain self-esteem: the first is through power or achievement; the second is through love and relationship. For the most part, our society socializes us into the former. Grace relieves us of that pressure and, also, of the temptation of pride.

An understanding of grace is essential for humility within the church. One suspects that there is a lot of pride circulating in nonobvious corridors of the church at the same time that self is decried. For example, the use of spiritual gifts seems to be an area where people who negate their self in other areas subtly get involved with pride. When one realizes that the spiritual gifts are not earned but given through grace, the emphasis shifts from how spiritual I am to how I can best use my gift. As a matter of fact, a close look at both the gifts of the Spirit and the fruits of the Spirit reveals that the gifts really don't make any sense, perhaps don't exist, unless they are seen as interpersonal. They are not something privately possessable and conducive to pride, in the sense of a child showing off a new toy, which some other child doesn't have, with an attitude of "I'm better than you."

THEORETICAL ISSUES

One of the characteristic emphases of American social psychologists has been upon the environment. Increasingly, in the study of attitudes, an emphasis on situational factors has emerged. This has been due to the repeated observations of inconsistency between the belief, feeling, and behavioral components of attitudes. Some have gone so far as to suggest that the traditional concept of attitude ought to be abandoned because the consistency upon which the concept is based has not been sufficiently demonstrated, though this is a minority view.[57] At the very least, there seems to be a new recognition of the need to consider situational factors.

Similarly, Wylie questions the assumption that there is a strong general factor in self-evaluation and suggests that self-assessment must include conceptually different dimensions of the self.[58] Kenneth Gergen likewise questions the assumptions that it is both normal and healthy for a person to develop a rigid, unified self-concept.[59] While not arguing that there are no common factors in the self-concept, Gergen presents research indicating the varied and contradictory nature of the self. He suggests the need to investigate the range and complexity of the many selves that each person has rather than reducing a person to one self.

Some measures of self-concept seem to accept this assumption by referring to physical, moral, and social self-concepts.[60] More recent literature also seems to recognize the existence of multiple components of the self.[61] No current self or personality theory, however, systematically identifies the multiple self-concepts and relates them to evaluation.

Such a theory must begin with an empirically derived set of self-concepts. This could include those mentioned above with additional possibilities, such as spiritual self (distinct from moral), occupational or productive self, and familial self or selves (parent, child, spouse, sibling), distinct from general social self. The theory must show how an individual develops his or her self-concept and how this self-concept relates to the individual's overall perceived self (if the concept remains meaningful) and ideal self. The theory must account for the process of evaluation, empirically showing whether evaluation takes place at the level of each distinct self-concept through an equation between, for example, perceived social self and ideal social self, or at the level of a generalized self, based on some summation or interaction of the components, or both. Further, if the assumption is that self develops from social/environmental feedback, the theory must account for nonisomorphic relationships between social feedback and one's perceived self. That is, it appears that high self-esteem people and very low self-esteem people are relatively independent of what feedback others give them, *once they have internalized their evaluations.*[62] Baron's SRS Model may provide some suggestions regarding this.[63] Finally, an adequate theory must account for internalization of values in the ideal self and for the process by which the individual chooses to value each self-concept component. For example, why do some people evaluate themselves primarily in terms of their occupational success while others judge themselves most centrally in terms of their social or spiritual selves? As we will discuss further, the general society, one's subculture, and the family all serve to influence these value choices.

Some investigators feel that, apart from specific issues of agreement regarding one's self, self-acceptance and social acceptance are inextricably intertwined.[64] This is certainly consistent with evidence showing that low self-esteem people assume the greatest amount of social distance,[65] are less people-oriented,[66] and are members of societally rejected groups.[67]

The roots of the social self can be found in the need to survive. Survival requires constant evaluation and feedback from one's environment. In many instances, this cannot be gained objectively. Because we are interdependent beings, we must then look to others for feedback regarding our functioning.[68] As a matter of fact, it is given to us anyway by virtue of our initial, interdependent relationship with caretakers, usually in the form of parents. Erikson has suggested that the first year of development forms the basis of both self and other orientation of trust or mistrust.[69] Trust and mistrust reflect acceptance or rejection by significant others as expressed through their concrete caring responses. Acceptance-rejection is the basis of self-evaluation because it reflects others' evaluations of basic worth, prior to the child having had an opportunity to earn either. As the child develops, and throughout life, that human being is part of various reference groups that provide evaluative feedback.[70] Human existence is inevitably social, and self-esteem is at least partially a mirror of social relationships.

Baron's SRS Model provides an empirically useful way of demonstrating and understanding the social reinforcement/self-concept relationship, though the predictive value of the model remains to be clearly shown. Baron argues that "a person's self-concept represents an SRS of SRS's. That is, it may be argued that a person's self-concept is derived as an integration of his reinforcement experiences in a number of different behavior domains, each with its separate SRS. . . . One's self concept is probably determined by, and in turn is a determinant of, one's responsivity to different types and levels of reinforcement."[71] The SRS Model combines the notions of reinforcement history and schedules with social interaction concepts such as social exchange and self-presentation. It assumes that an individual's past social reinforcement history produces an internal standard that is objectively related to the actual evaluations of others and against which present reinforcements are judged. The model assumes that the SRS is a preferred region around which the individual seeks reinforcement and that the standards act to reduce interpersonal uncertainty and help the individual to coordinate behavior with unknown others. In addition, the model makes several assumptions confirmed by research about the effects of present reinforcement that is different from the SRS. These will be considered in our subsequent discussion about changing self-esteem.

Although social reinforcement history is obviously important to the self-concept, and the evaluative nature of the SRS can be related to notions of the ideal self and self-esteem, it is not clear that SRS is the same as self-concept, or how it is related. Neither is it clear, as discussed earlier, that the self-concept or SRS is as objectively related to feedback from others as is assumed by the model. Finally, Baron does not explain why people would accept feeling negatively about themselves, though he does explain resistance to change, whether one's SRS is positive or negative. If negative feelings about one's self can be considered aversive, then an adequate model must explain why there is not more effort to change from negative to positive. That may, of course, involve one's perceived power to influence the outcomes from one's behavior.[72] Nevertheless, the SRS model potentially ties the rather fuzzy notions of self-development into an empirically rigorous conceptual framework and does help account for the resistance of the self to change, as we shall see later.

Another empirically oriented theory of the self is that of Rosenberg.[73] He suggests that attitudes toward the self involve *content, direction* (positive or negative), *intensity, salience* (importance or centrality), *consistency, stability, clarity, accuracy,* and *verifiability.* While basing the self-concept solidly in social identity and experience, Rosenberg suggests the need to distinguish between self-confidence (the feeling of being competent and actively operating on one's life) and self-esteem (which is based more on reflected social appraisal). Viewed in this manner, self-confidence contributes to self-esteem, but is not identical with it.

CHANGING SELF-ESTEEM

If positive self-esteem is so important for healthy psychological, interpersonal, and spiritual functioning, it seems critical that we identify some of the factors or strategies that might be used to make one's self-esteem more positive.

The first strategy would be to increase the level of approval or acceptance expressed toward an individual. This would have to be done in relation to realistic, objective assessment, if it is approval of achievements or performance, and must be done genuinely and not too abruptly, if it is the expression of affection and acceptance. Baron theorizes that large deviations in social reinforcement from an individual's SRS, whether positive or negative in direction, results in negative feelings.[74] The perception of substantial discrepancies will lead initially to behaviors on the part of the individual to reduce the difference. The behaviors may include such things as avoidance of the reinforcing agent, attempts to bring the agent under control, and increases or decreases in behaviors that have typically brought reinforcement, depending upon the positive or negative discrepancy currently being experienced. If the feedback received from others continues to deviate substantially from the SRS over a prolonged period, Baron hypothesizes the person will change his SRS (self-concept). In addition, Baron suggests that more moderate discrepancies in a positive direction will produce positive affect. Initial research results have tended to confirm these predictions.

⁜ The implication is that the Christian community can have an important role in changing self-concepts through the medium of acceptance, but that care must be taken not to overwhelm initially and to be genuine in the use of such reinforcement. The Christian has a powerful change message that should speak to the millions who feel negatively about themselves. The directional dynamic shifts the primary basis of positive esteem from the stresses and uncertainties of seeking approval from others to that of pleasing God and receiving his perfect evaluation of well-done, as well as his noncontingent reinforcement of grace. This is certainly, in part at least, the thrust of Colossians 3:17, 23–24, and the experience of Paul, who experienced so much disapproval from others but centered his esteem in God's approval, as in 2 Timothy 4:7–8. Not only is the message that God unconditionally loves and will make a new creature out of the person,[75] with behavioral and self-evaluational effects, but the medium is that of a caring community that extends specific positive reinforcements over an extended period of time in the context of caring interpersonal relationships.[76]

Another strategy that can be used within the general church community, small groups, or in one-to-one relationships is to change the basis of evaluation. As we have mentioned already, the values espoused by the society, which are used as content for self-concepts and the basis of evaluation, are mainly power- or achievement-oriented. This is in radical opposition to the biblical standard of self-esteem, though the Bible certainly makes ample use of contingent reinforcement.[77] The church community ought to be a cross-cultural reinforcement center, where individuals are reinforced for shaping their ideals and self-images counter to the culture if those values conflict with biblically understood values. If the church can begin to reject some of the materialism and success/achievement-orientation that it seems to have quietly accepted during this century, it will become both an alternative for the culture at large and a dynamic supporting community for its members. Such a position will inevitably lead to conflict with the culture at large and may lead to the effects of social comparison and change-attempt that Jesus experienced when he tried to move the basis of accept-ance from achievement to love. Nevertheless, consistent with Scripture, individuals accepting and supported in such values will experientially verify the reality of God's love and the benefits of positive self-esteem based on stable sources.

On a more individual scale, we can assist others by helping them to choose more appropriate social comparison standards. People who think poorly of themselves because they cannot play sports like professional athletes will be helped, for example, to change their evaluation standard to other nonprofessionals of their age or, even more effectively, to enjoyment of the activity and awareness of other, more effective means than that to gain self-esteem. In addition to changing the social comparison standard, we can help in the selection of more appropriate evaluation criteria. It is not necessary, for example, to do everything perfectly in order to receive positive reinforcement. The perfectionist must be aided in adopting a more realistic criteria. This may involve systematic social reinforcement for other than perfection, conversation, or even specific forms of therapy in the extreme.

Finally, on a practical level, we can concentrate on helping individuals acquire new skills or improve old ones. Through the process of competency acquisition, confidence will increase, new efforts (which will in turn bring reinforcement) will be tried, and self-esteem will be elevated. Within the church community, older members of the congregation could be very positive influences upon adolescents in the acquisition of various occupa-tional or professional skills, for example. A given church or churches might sponsor adult education nights aimed at the sharing of practical skills for

members, within the general context of the caring Christian community
and without the usual negative correlates of education based on achievement and evaluation stresses.

NOTES

1. W. James, *Principles of Psychology*
(New York: Henry Holt, 1890), vol. 1.
2. C. H. Cooley, *Human Nature and the
Social Order* (New York: Charles
Scribner's Sons, 1902).
3. G. H. Mead, *Mind, Self and Society*
(Chicago: University of Chicago Press,
1934).
4. H. Ansbacher and R. Ansbacher, *The
Individual Psychology of Alfred Adler*
(New York: Basic Books, 1956).
5. K. Horney, *Neurosis and Human
Growth* (New York: W. W. Norton,
1950).
6. H. S. Sullivan, *The Interpersonal Theory
of Psychiatry* (New York: W. W. Norton, 1953).
7. E. Fromm, *The Sane Society* (Green-
wich, Conn: Fawcett, 1955).
8. R. Ziller, "A Developmental Study of
the Self-Social Constructs on Normals
and the Neurotic Personality," *Journal
of Clinical Psychology* 23: 15–21.
9. S. Coopersmith, *The Antecedents of
Self-Esteem* (San Francisco: W. H.
Freeman, 1967).
10. M. Rosenberg, *Conceiving the Self*
(New York: Basic Books, 1979).
11. J. W. Kinch, "A Formalized Theory of
the Self-Concept," *Symbolic Interaction,*
eds. J. G. Manis and B. N. Meltzer (Boston: Allyn and Bacon, 1967). Also, H.
Blumer, *Symbolic Interactionism: Perspective and Method* (Englewood Cliffs,
N. J.: Prentice-Hall, 1969).
12. D. J. Bem, "Self-Perception Theory,"
*Advances in Experimental Social Psy-
chology,* ed. L. Berkowitz (New York:
Academic Press, 1972), vol. 6, pp. 1–62.
13. B. R. McCandless and E. D. Evnas,
*Children and Youth: Psychosocial Devel-
opment* (Hinsdale, Ill.: Dryden Press,
1973).
14. S. Coopersmith, "Studies in Self-

Esteem," *Scientific American* 218
(1968): 96–106.
15. D. W. Felker, "The Relationship Between Anxiety, Self Ratings, and Ratings by Others in Fifth Grade Children," *Journal of Genetic Psychology*
115 (1969): 81–86.
16. W. H. Maw and E. W. Maw, "Self Concepts of High and Low Curiosity Boys,"
Child Development 41 (1970): 123–129;
T. A. Ringness, "Self-Concept of Children of Low, Average and High Intelligence," *American Journal of Mental
Deficiency* 65 (1961): 543–561.
17. James B. Ousek, *Adolescent Development and Behavior* (Palo Alto, Calif.:
Science Research Associates, 1977), p.
330.
18. Ibid., p. 331.
19. P. W. Luck, "Social Determinants of
Self-Esteem," *Dissertation Abstracts International 30 (1969) / 2-A: 810.*
20. J. O. Lugo and G. L. Hershey, *Human
Development* (New York: Macmillan
Publishing Company, 1974).
21. C. W. Ellison and I. J. Firestone, "Development of Interpersonal Trust as a
Function of Self-Esteem, Target Status,
and Target Style," *Journal of Personality
and Social Psychology* 29 (1974) / 5:
655–663.
22. S. M. Jourard, *The Transparent Self*
(Princeton, N.J.: Van Nostrand, 1964);
L. M. Vosen, "The Relationship Between Self-Disclosure and Self-Esteem,"
Dissertation Abstracts 27B (1967) 8-B:
2882.
23. B. M. Mossman and R. C. Ziller, "Self-
Esteem and Consistency of Social Behavior," *Journal of Abnormal Psychology*
73 (1968): 363–367.
24. W. C. Reckless and S. Dinitz, "Pioneer-
ing with the Self-Concept as a Vulnerability Factor in Delinquency," *Journal of*

Criminal Law, Criminology and Police Science, 58 (1967): 515–523. It should be noted that some studies (such as G. F. Jensen, "Delinquency and Adolescent Self-Conceptions: A Study of the Personal Relevance of Infraction," *Social Problems* [Summer 1972]: 84–102) contest the self-concept and delinquency relationship found by Reckless and his colleagues in several studies. A host of other factors, including parent-child and marital relationships support the self-concept notion indirectly, though.

25. Genesis 1:26–28, 1:31, 5:1. This and other biblical references are from the Revised Standard Version.

26. Psalm 8:4–5.

27. Romans 5:8, 10.

28. Romans 5:6.

29. Remarks made in his presidential address for the Western Association of Christians for Psychological Studies, Westmont College, May, 1975.

30. 1 John 4:19.

31. Genesis 1:26.

32. Genesis 2:18.

33. Genesis 1:31.

34. 1 John 3:16.

35. Psalm 36:5–10.

36. Genesis 3:11–13.

37. L. Festinger, "A Theory of Social Comparison Processes," *Human Relations* 7 (1954): 117–140.

38. It is not clear that this holds for those with extremely negative self-images. In fact, these individuals tend to introject blame and may look for others who are more dominant and dissimilar to help them maintain their poor self-image.

39. R. H. Rottschafer, "Self-Esteem and Depression," *Self-Esteem,* ed. C. W. Ellison (Oklahoma City, Okla.: Southwestern Press, 1976).

40. Psalm 32:1–5; Psalm 38.

41. James 1:8, 4:8.

42. Matthew 5:23–24; 1 John 1:9.

43. 2 Timothy 4:7–8.

44. Colossians 3:12–14; Matthew 7:1; Ephesians 4:2–3; Galatians 6:1–2.

45. Romans 12:5–8; Ephesians 4:11–13.

46. 1 Corinthians 12:4–31.

47. Philippians 2:6–7.

48. Philippians 2:5.

49. Luke 10:27; Ephesians 5:1–2.

50. Proverbs 6:16–17; James 4:6–7.

51. Mark 12:31; Ephesians 4:28–29.

52. Romans 12:3; Galatians 633–4.

53. Philippians 2:5.

54. Ephesians 5:1.

55. 1 John 4:18.

56. Presidential address, Western Association of Christians for Psychological Studies, Westmont College, May, 1975.

57. M. Fishbein and I. Ajzen, *Belief, Attitude, Intention, and Behavior* (Menlo Park, Calif.: Addison-Wesley, 1975).

58. R. Wylie, "The Present Status of Self Theory," *Handbook of Personality Theory and Research,* eds. E. F. Borgatta and W. W. Lambert, (Chicago: Rand McNally, 1968).

59. K. J. Gergen, "The Healthy, Happy Human Being Wears Many Masks," *Psychology Today* (May, 1972).

60. W. H. Fitts, *Manual, Tennessee Self-Concept Scale* (Nashville, Tenn.: Counselor Recordings and Tests, 1965).

61. J. O. Lugo and G. L. Hershey, *Human Development.*

62. P. N. Middlebrook, *Social Psychology and Modern Life* (New York: Alfred A. Knopf, 1974), pp. 91–93.

63. R. M. Baron, "Social Reinforcement Effects as a Function of Social Reinforcement History," *Psychological Review* 6 (1966): 529–539.

64. R. C. Ziller, J. Hagey, M. D. C. Smith, and G. H. Long, "Self-Esteem: A Self-Social Construct," *Journal of Consulting and Clinical Psychology* 33 (1969) 1: 8495.

65. M. P. Fitzgerald, "Self-Disclosure and Expressed Self-Esteem, Social Distance and Areas of the Self Revealed," *The Journal of Psychology* 56 (1963): 405–412.

66. D. A. Taylor, and L. Oberlander, "Person Perception and Self-Disclosure: Motivational Mechanisms in Interpersonal Processes," *Journal of Experimental Research in Personality* 4 (1969): 14–28.

67. B. R. McCandless and E. D. Evans, *Children and Youth*, pp. 399–405.
68. L. Festinger, "Theory of Social Comparison Processes," pp. 117–140.
69. E. H. Erikson, *Childhood and Society* (New York: Norton, 1963).
70. P. N. Middlebrook, *Social Psychology*, pp. 82–90.
71. R. M. Baron, "The SRS Model as a Predictor of Negro Responsiveness to Reinforcement," *Journal of Social Issues* 26 (1970) / 2: 61–81.

72. R. Epstein, and S. S. Komorita, "Self-Esteem, Success-Failure, and Locus of Control in Negro Children," *Developmental Psychology* 4 (1971): 2–8.
73. M. Rosenberg, *Conceiving the Self*.
74. W. H. Fitts, *Manual*; L. Festinger, "Theory of Social Comparison Processes."
75. 2 Corinthians 5:17; Ephesians 4:22–24.
76. Colossians 3:12–17; Ephesians 4:1–19.
77. Ephesians 2:10; James 1:12.

PART I

Analysis

SECTION I:
THEOLOGICAL PERSPECTIVES

Introduction

FOR THE Christian community, the relationship between self-esteem and the Scriptures is fundamentally important. Historically, there has been a strong emphasis on self-negation that has seemed at times to counsel psychological self-destruction. Sin is closely related to self-centeredness, so that getting rid of self has seemed to be one of the ways to achieve victory over sin. On the other hand, there are those who have emphasized that God does not work with hollow people, that he uses the self as expressed in personality. The need is not self-destruction, but the rightful relationship of self-desiring and self-will in subordination to God.

Both Anthony Hoekema and Franklyn Wise indicate that encounter with God has profound effects upon self-esteem. Though Hoekema stresses the impact of conversion more strongly than Wise, both suggest that the ordering of values and the perception of self in relation to God are substantially changed at that point. It is in regards to postconversion fluctuations in that relationship and their resultant effects that their theologies differ most significantly.

Hoekema deplores the experiential overemphasis upon depravity and the negative self that has characterized Calvinistic circles. In essence, he agrees with Wise's analysis that positive self-esteem is most satisfactorily and stably established in a relationship of surrender with God. He then deals with the theological and experiential issues of conflict and fluctuating self-esteem, which Wise suggests are greatly reduced by a second work of grace. Through detailed exegesis of Romans 7 and 8, Hoekema concludes that positive self-image of a sustained nature must be based upon a decisive act of conversion in which the old is transformed into the new. While not denying conflicts with sin and its effects after conversion, he argues that this is an exception. Every set of actions under the influence of the "old man" goes contrary to one's true being. The fact that the Holy Spirit has indwelled, however, moves the conflicts from the arena of defeat and despair to the arena of victory and positive self-regard. Progressive renewal for Hoekema is similar to sanctification for Wise in that the focus shifts from one's self to the building up of others, to giving rather than receiving. He does not, however, concern himself with a second crisis and second work of grace that frees one. Rather, Hoekema finds conversion is the point of freedom.

Wesleyan theology, according to Wise, suggests that one is moved away from self-centered orientation at the point of salvation. However, Wise believes that the process of sanctification, including a second crisis of total commitment, is essential for self-esteem. As the Holy Spirit brings one to the point of total commitment and loss of self, individuals are paradoxically able to find themselves. They gain a new basis of self-acceptance that is stable and conflict-free because it is established in God's view of them, rather than in the views of others or self. The highest levels of self-esteem are reached when the individual affirms values that transcend themselves and their surroundings in the process of surrender to God.

Dennis Voskuil first examines the basic assumptions of those who are helping to develop a theology of self-esteem and then sounds some warning signals about this movement. He is concerned that sin should be regarded seriously and explicitly as utter perversity rather than emotional weakness. He also cautions against viewing the gospel as a psychological means to the end of mental health, an overfocus on the self, and a psychologized gospel. In essence, Voskuil warns against excessive focus on our selves, lest it promote our natural bent toward self-deification.

The Christian Self-Image:
A Reformed Perspective

ANTHONY A. HOEKEMA

In Reformed or Calvinistic circles, we often have a self-image that over-accentuates the negative.[1] We tend to see ourselves through the purple-colored glasses of our depravity. We have been writing of our continuing sinfulness in capital letters and of our newness in Christ in very small letters. We tend to believe in total depravity so strongly that we think we have to practice it, while we hardly dare to believe in our newness.[2]

It is, however, not only among Calvinists that this morbid preoccupation with sin and depravity is found. It would seem that Jean-Paul Sartre is particularly caricaturing Roman Catholics when in his play, *The Flies,* he has a man fall on his knees saying, "I stink! Oh, how I stink! I am a mass of rottenness. . . . I have sinned a thousand times, I am a stink of ordure, and I reek to heaven." After this pretty little speech, Zeus, the character who stands for God, comments, "O worthy man!"[3] Here Sartre, the athe-ist, is telling us: this is how I see Christians, as always groveling in the dust because of their sins—and the more they do this, the more their God is pleased. The only way for people to acquire an adequate self-image, Sartre implies, is for them to get rid of the last vestiges of their Christian faith, since all Christianity ever does for people is take away their self-respect.

It is precisely this point that I wish to challenge. I would like to explore the resources of the Christian faith for the cultivation of a positive self-image. When properly understood and taken in its totality, the New Testa-ment repudiates this kind of negative self-image. For what the New Testa-ment writers emphasize is that the Christian is a *new creature*—who, to be sure, continues to struggle against sin during this life, but does so as one who is more than a conqueror through Christ.

Before summarizing direct scriptural teachings on this subject, I would like to approach my subject in an indirect way. The apostle Paul, though deeply conscious of his sinful past and of his continuing imperfection, still had a predominantly positive self-image. It will be helpful for us to look first at Paul's self-image, as an illustration of what a Christian self-image can and ought to be.

Paul often saw himself as a great sinner. He never described himself as a sinner, however, without at the same time referring to the grace of God, which forgave his sins, accepted him, and enabled him to be useful in God's kingdom.[4] In other words, whenever Paul thought about his sin, he thought about the grace of God. In 1 Timothy 1:15, for example, he calls himself the chief or foremost of sinners, but he does this in a context in which he is describing the salvation Christ came into the world to bring. The point of Ephesians 3:8 is the contrast between Paul's feeling of unworthiness and the privileged position to which God has called him. In 1 Corinthians 15:9–10, Paul expresses his deep regret at his having once been a persecutor of the church; yet he maintains a positive self-image because of what the grace of God has done for him: "For I am the least of the apostles, unfit to be called an apostle, because I persecuted the church of God. But by the grace of God I am what I am, and his grace toward me was not in vain. On the contrary, I worked harder than any of them, though it was not I, but the grace of God which is with me."[5] Without detracting from the gravity of his past sins, Paul did not continue to brood over these sins (Phil. 3:13).

We may say, then, that though Paul had a very deep sense of sin, he also had a positive self-image. Yet his confidence was not so much in himself as in God, who enabled him to do his task. Because Paul often made positive statements about himself, he is sometimes accused of pride. I cannot agree with this judgment. Whenever Paul spoke of his achievements, he always gave God the praise.[6] In fact, in 2 Corinthians 11:30, he said, "If I must boast, I will boast of the things that show my weakness." Paul's point was this: the secret of his apostleship and the dynamic of his life was not to be found in his own strong personal qualities, but rather in the fact that he was and continued to be a man empowered by Christ. "I will all the more gladly boast of my weaknesses, that the power of Christ may rest upon me" (2 Cor. 12:9).

Yet, while giving God all the glory, Paul did not simply brush aside his considerable achievements with a wave of the hand—a procedure sometimes considered a mark of piety among Christians. Paul dared to say, "I worked harder than any of them [the other apostles]" (1 Cor. 15:10). And as his life was nearing its end, he wrote to Timothy, "I have fought the good fight, I have finished the race, I have kept the faith" (2 Tim. 4:7).

Paul realized that he had not yet attained perfection. In spite of this fact, he dared to say, on more than one occasion, to the Christians who received his letters, "Be imitators of me" (1 Cor. 4:16, 11:1; Phil. 3:17; 2 Thess. 3:7). Most of us would much rather say to our children, students, parishioners, or friends, "Do as I say, but not as I do." These passages certainly do reveal a positive self-image. Conscious of the fact that he was not perfect and that whatever good there was in him was due to God's grace, Paul was yet so confident that the Holy Spirit would continue to empower him to do God's will that he had the courage to say to others, "Be imitators of me."

THREE PROBLEMS OF INTERPRETATION

The Struggle Against Sin

I would like to consider three problems related to the issue of the self-image. The first concerns the interpretation of Romans 7:13–25. Does this passage describe the struggle against sin, which is typical of the daily life of the regenerate person? Or does it describe the struggle to keep the law, which is characteristic of the unregenerate person? I agree with Herman Ridderbos that these verses describe the unregenerate person who is trying to fight sin through the law alone, apart from the renewing strength of the Holy Spirit.[7] This is a picture of the unregenerate person seen through the eyes of a regenerate person, since Paul wrote these words after his conversion. Despite the present tense and the dramatic first-person form in which this material is cast ("for I do not do the good I want"), the passage appears to be describing the unregenerate person—the one who is not, or not yet, in Christ.

My reasons for interpreting the passage in this way are as follows:

(1) Romans 7:13–25 reflects and elaborates on the condition pictured in 7:5. In the previous verse (7:4), Paul has just stated that believers have died to the law because they have been crucified with Christ. Since they are now one with Christ, not only in his death but also in his resurrection, they have now been made to belong to Christ—to be married to him, as it were— that they might bear fruit for God. In Romans 7:5, however, Paul continued, "While we were living in the flesh, our sinful passions, aroused by the law, were at work in our members to bear fruit for death." Obviously, what is here being described is a state previous to conversion, a state of being "in the flesh" rather than "in the Spirit." Those who are in this state,

Paul asserted, are not keeping God's law, but find that the law arouses their sinful passions in such a way that they bear fruit, not for God (as in v. 4), but for death.

This is precisely the state of those being described in Romans 7:13–25. Verse 13 describes again, though in slightly different words, the situation of those pictured in verse 5: "Did that which is good, then, bring death to me? By no means! It was sin, working death in me through what is good, in order that sin might be shown to be sin. . . ." What follows, from verse 14 on, is introduced by the word *for* and is a further elaboration of this condition: "For we know that the law is spiritual; but I am carnal, sold under sin" (ASV). The rest of the chapter dramatically portrays the state of the person described in verses 5 and 13—the person who is living "in the flesh." While such a person remains in this state, he or she may be able to delight in the law, in a certain sense, but cannot and does not keep it.

(2) One finds no mention of the Holy Spirit or of the strength it provides for overcoming sin in Romans 7:13–25. In comparison, there are at least sixteen references to the Holy Spirit in chapter 8. This fact cannot be without significance.

(3) The mood of frustration and defeat that permeates Romans 7:13–25 does not comport with the mood of victory in terms of which Paul usually describes the normal life of the Christian. When Paul said that he saw in his members another law at war with the law of his mind (Rom. 7:23) which made him captive to the law of sin, he certainly did not seem to be picturing the same situation as that which he described in Romans 8:2: "For the law of the Spirit of life in Christ Jesus has set me free from the law of sin and death." Further, the main thrust of Romans 6 is that because the believer has been crucified with Christ, he or she is no longer a slave of sin.

(4) Many commentators have called attention to these unusual words found in Romans 7:25: "So then, I of myself serve the law of God with my mind, but with my flesh I serve the law of sin." The words "of myself" are emphatic. They suggest that Paul was indeed describing a person who tries to "go it himself" or "go it alone"—to live the obedient life in his own strength, instead of in the strength of the Spirit.

(5) As has already been suggested, there is an abrupt change of mood as we go from Romans 7 to Romans 8. Romans 8:2 tells us that we have obtained freedom from the law of sin and death through the law of the Spirit of life in Christ Jesus. Paul used the word *law* in various ways; in this verse, he meant law in the sense of *principle* or *power*. The power of sin and death, described in the latter part of Romans 7, was what Paul had been experiencing during his unregenerate state. But the power of the

Spirit set him free from this enslavement. What Paul says in 8:2, therefore, is actually a restatement of what he had said in 7:6: "But now we are discharged from the law, dead to that which held us captive, so that we serve not under the old written code but in the new life of the Spirit." These words obviously describe, not the unregenerate person who is still "living in the flesh," but the regenerate person who has been delivered from the slavery of sin. The rest of chapter 7, beginning with verse 7, is a kind of interlude, elaborating on the condition pictured in 7:5. Chapter 8 takes up again where 7:6 left off.

Therefore, Romans 7:13–25 may be seen as a vivid description of the inability of people to serve God obediently in their own strength with only the law to help them. This description was particularly addressed to the Pharisaical Jews among Paul's readers who set great stock by the law and who thought that the way to salvation was through law-keeping rather than through faith in Christ. It would be possible for regenerate people to slip into the type of life described in the latter half of Romans 7, if they stopped walking by the Spirit and tried to keep God's law in their own strength. But I do not believe, for the reasons given above, that this passage describes the typical life-style of regenerate believers.

This understanding of Romans 7 has important implications for our view of the Christian's self-image. To understand the passage in this way does not imply that the Christian does not need to struggle against sin; it only implies that Romans 7:13–25 does not describe that struggle in its usual form. There is struggle in the Christian life, to be sure; but that struggle is not to be carried on in an atmosphere of constant defeat. People like the individual described in the second half of Romans 7 seem doomed to perpetual frustration; they desire to keep God's law but cannot do so. They never do the good they want to do, and they always do the evil they hate. A self-image based exclusively on this passage would be negative indeed.

The person described in Romans 8, however, is one who, strengthened by the Spirit, is (at least, in principle) fulfilling the just requirement of the law, is putting to death the deeds of the body, is setting the mind on the things of the Spirit, and is more than a conqueror through the One who loved us. It is Romans 8, not Romans 7, that pictures what the normal Christian life is like. Accordingly, the biblical view of the Christian's self-image should be drawn, not from Romans 7, but from Romans 8.

The Issue of Sinless Perfection

A second problem related to the self-image concerns the question of whether sinless perfection is possible for the Christian in this present life.

Some claim that it is possible for those who have been born again to live totally without sin in this life, pointing particularly to a passage like 1 John 3:9: "No one born of God commits sin; for God's nature abides in him, and he cannot sin because he is born of God." At first glance, this text does seem to teach not only the possibility but even the likelihood that those who have been "born of God" will no longer commit any sin.

To understand fully what John meant by these words, however, we must look at some other passages from the same epistle. For example, in 1 John 1:8–9, we read, "If we say we have no sin, we deceive ourselves, and the truth is not in us. If we confess our sins, he is faithful and just, and will forgive our sins. . . ." In 2:1, we read, "My little children, I am writing this to you so that you may not sin; but if anyone does sin, we have an advocate with the Father, Jesus Christ the righteous." Since John was writing to Christians, these verses clearly teach that any Christians who claim to have no sin whatever and who reject the need for continuing to confess their sin are deceiving themselves. Obviously, then, when John said that the born-again person cannot sin, he did not mean that such a person can live a life completely free from sinning. Let us now take a closer look at 1 John 3:9. In this verse, the tenses that are used to describe the kind of sinning that the regenerate person cannot do are present, and the present tense in Greek indicates continued or habitual action. Literally translated, this verse would read as follows: "No one who has been born of God continually lives in sin . . . and he is not able to keep on living in sin because he has been born of God." What this passage teaches, therefore, is that regenerate people do not and cannot continue to live in sin, in the sense that they enjoy it and give themselves up to it.

In 1 John 2:1, however, the tenses used to describe the kind of sinning regenerate people can still do are aorists. The aorist tense in Greek commonly indicates snapshot or momentary action. A literal translation of this verse, therefore, might read somewhat as follows: "My little children, I write these things to you so that you may not commit sin; and if anyone does commit a sin, we have an advocate with the Father." What John is here teaching us is that regenerate people can indeed still fall into sin, but that when they do so they should not despair, since they have an Advocate with the Father through whom they may obtain forgiveness. Putting all these passages together, we find John saying something like this: the regenerate person may still *fall* into sin, but he or she cannot *live* in sin.

The perfectionist, therefore, who claims that the believer can live totally without sin in this life, cannot find support for that position in John's First Epistle. On the other hand, I do find John militating against the rather common notion that sin in the believer's life ought to be looked upon as the usual thing. As a matter of fact, sin is no longer the atmosphere in which believers live; if a person has been born again, it is impossible for that person to continue to live in sin. If, then, it happens that a Christian does fall into sin, he or she ought not to be completely demoralized, but ought to be a little bit surprised.[8]

The Tension of Already and Not Yet

A third problem I should like to take up is this: how does the tension between the "already" and the "not yet" affect our self-image? That there is such a tension in the believer's life has been stressed by such writers as Herman Ridderbos and Oscar Cullmann.[9] Jesus Christ has come, and therefore the decisive victory over sin, the devil, and the flesh has been won. However, the victory is not yet complete. We live, as Cullmann puts it, between D-day and V-day; though the enemy has been decisively defeated, there remain pockets of resistance, there are still guerrilla troops to be defeated, there are still battles to be fought. In one sense, we already possess salvation; in another sense, we still look forward to our salvation. We *already* have the new life; we do *not yet* have perfection.

Paul often made this point. In Philippians 3:7–8, Paul asserted that what he experienced in Christ was so tremendous that he willingly gave up everything that was gain so that he might know Christ. Yet a few verses further he said, "Brothers, I do not consider myself yet to have taken hold of it [perfection]. But one thing I do . . . I press on toward the goal . . ." (vv. 13–14, NIV). Probably the most triumphant chapter in the entire Bible is Romans 8; yet in the midst of the triumph, Paul has to say, "And not only the creation, but we ourselves, who have the first fruits of the Spirit, groan inwardly as we wait for adoption as sons, the redemption of our bodies" (v. 23).

Our self-image, then, must be seen in the light of this tension between the "already" and the "not yet." We are in Christ, to be sure, and therefore we share his decisive victory over the powers of evil. But since we are still on this side of the Parousia, we do not yet enjoy the totality of Christ's victory. Our self-image must leave room for eschatology. What we have now is only the beginning; the best is yet to come. The Christian, in other words, is *genuinely* new, but not yet *totally* new.

BIBLICAL CONCEPTS OF THE PERSON

Having looked at Paul's self-image and at some problems of interpretation related to the question of our self-image, the next question is, "What should the Christian's self-image be?" Several biblical concepts are important in shaping a proper answer.

The Forgiveness of Sin

Nothing contributes more to a negative self-image than feelings of guilt. When people are obsessed by guilt feelings, they despise themselves, feel utterly worthless, and are likely to plunge into the depths of depression. What do the Scriptures teach about guilt? The first thing we should note is that the Bible deepens the problem and makes our guilt a much more serious matter than we might have thought it was. The Bible teaches us that when we do wrong, we sin, not just against other people, but against God himself. After deepening the problem of guilt, the Bible goes on to show how God has provided a way whereby we can be delivered both from guilt and from guilt feelings. Christ took away our guilt when he died for us on the cross. In 2 Corinthians 5:21, we read: "For our sake he made him to be sin who knew no sin, so that in him we might become the righteousness of God." Christ identified himself with human sin so that each one of us is subsequently able to identify with the righteousness of God—that is, so that we might now stand before God as perfectly righteous because we are one with Christ.

The result of this is that those who believe in Jesus Christ and are truly one with him should no longer be troubled by feelings of guilt, at least as far as their relation to God is concerned. Such people, having confessed their sins to God and having asked for forgiveness on the basis of the work of Christ, are assured by Scripture that their guilt has been taken away. When any such person does wrong to someone, he or she should of course apologize and make restitution, if necessary. But feelings of guilt toward God are meant to be done with forever. The confident appropriation of our forgiveness, the exhilaration of knowing that God accepts us and loves us in spite of our shortcomings and failures, is the foundation for a positive self-image. Because God has accepted us, we can now also accept ourselves.

"Old Man" and "New Man"

It has been rather commonly held by Christians that the believer is both an "old man" and a "new man"—or both an old and new person. According to this view, the old person and the new person are distinguishable "parts" of the believer. Before conversion, the believer was only an old person; at the time of conversion, he or she is said to put on the new person —without, however, totally losing the old person. This understanding of the old and new, needless to say, can easily lead to a very negative self-image —particularly for those who think of themselves as primarily old and only secondarily new.

It must be seriously questioned, however, whether this view of old and new is the right one. I believe that, according to the New Testament, the believer has put off the old person and has put on the new person; hence we must now think of the believer as a new person, though a new person not yet made perfect. Professor John Murray, in his *Principles of Conduct*, states that it is just as wrong to call the believer both a new person and an old person as it is to say that he or she is both regenerate and unregenerate.[10] Murray goes on to say:

> The believer is a new man, a new creation, but he is a new man not yet made perfect. Sin dwells in him still and he still commits sin. He is necessarily the subject of progressive renewal. . . . But this *progressive* renewal is not represented as the putting off of the old man and the putting on of the new, nor is it to be conceived of as the progressive crucifixion of the old man. It does mean the mortification of the deeds of the flesh and of all sin in heart and life. But it is the renewal of the "new man" unto the attainment of that glory for which he is destined, conformity to the image of God's Son.[11]

Old and new person ought not to be seen as *parts* of the believer, both of which are still somehow present in that individual. How, then, should we understand these concepts? Professor Murray suggests that the " 'old man' is a designation of the person in his unity as dominated by the flesh and sin."[12] If this is so, it is obvious that the regenerated person is no longer an "old man." Paul says in Romans 6:6, "Knowing this, that our old man was crucified with him, that the body of sin might be done away, that so we should no longer be in bondage to sin" (ASV). When Christ died on the cross, our old persons—that is, our total persons as enslaved by flesh and sin—were put to death with him. This means that we who have been united with Christ through faith are no longer the old persons we once were.

What happened when Christ was crucified, however, has also been subjectively appropriated by us. This is taught by Paul in Colossians 3:9–10: "Lie not one to another, seeing that ye have put off the old man with his doings and have put on the new man that is being renewed unto knowledge after the image of him that created him" (ASV). After the analogy of what has just been said about the "old man," we conclude that the "new man" must mean the person in his or her unity ruled by the Holy Spirit. In this passage, therefore, Paul appeals to his readers not to lie to each other because they have, once and for all, put off the old persons they used to be and have, once and for all, put on the new persons they now are in Christ. Our self-image, therefore, must reflect this definite and decisive change.

Does the fact that Christians are new persons in Christ mean that we have attained our goal? Not at all. Note that, according to Colossians 3:10, the new person we have put on is being continually renewed (the Greek participle is in the present tense, and this tense describes continuing action). In other words, believers are far from what they ought to be and still have a great deal of growing to do. Still, though not yet perfect, they are indeed new persons.

Does this mean that for believers the struggle against sin is over? No. The New Testament is full of the language of struggle. The Christian life is called a battle, a race, and a wrestling against evil spirits; we are told to be good Christian soldiers, to fight the good fight of the faith, to resist the devil, to take heed lest we fall, and to put on the whole armor of God. Moreover, in this struggle, we do not always win; we do not resist every temptation. The point is, however, that when we do fall into sin, we are momentarily living according to the old persons we have repudiated. We are then living contrary to what we really are in Christ. We are then inconsistent new persons.

But the fact that this does happen does not mean that we must therefore revise our self-image as having to include both old person and new person. For—and this is a most important point—when we slip into the old way of living, we are living contrary to our true selves; we are denying our true self-image. Paul says in Romans 6:11, "So you also must consider yourselves dead to sin and alive to God in Christ Jesus." We must consider ourselves to be new persons in Christ, who have once and for all turned our backs upon the old person and who therefore refuse to be identified with it any longer. In the strength of the Spirit, we must try to make our life-styles consistent with the new selves we have put on.

Spirit and Flesh

What does Paul mean by "flesh" and "Spirit"? We must not see in these two concepts a contrast between two aspects of man's nature, a "fleshly" aspect and a "spiritual" one. Rather, we must see in these terms a description of two contrasting power-spheres associated with the two ages distinguished from each other through the coming of Christ. Apart from Christ, man is by nature under the domination and enslavement of the flesh. Flesh in this sense refers, it must be emphasized, not to man's physical nature alone, but to his whole being as it is under the power of sin. When Christ came, however, he ushered in a new way of living, which is called "life in the Spirit."

According to Romans 8:9, believers are no longer "in the flesh," but are now "in the Spirit." This means that they are no longer slaves of the flesh, but have now been brought under the liberating regime of the Spirit. Again what emerges is a positive self-image.

But, one may ask, is there not a continuing struggle in the Christian life between the flesh and the Spirit? There is, but the New Testament indicates that this struggle is to be engaged in, not in an atmosphere of defeat, but in the confidence of victory. Note how Paul describes this struggle in Galatians 5:16: "But I say, Walk by the Spirit, and ye shall not fulfill the lust of the flesh" (ASV). In the original Greek, the second clause is not a prohibition but a strong negation; it really amounts to a promise: if you walk by the Spirit, you shall not in any way fulfill the lust of the flesh. Believers must still do battle against fleshly impulses, to be sure, but they are promised victory in the strength of the Spirit.

After listing the works of the flesh and the various facets of the fruit of the Spirit, Paul goes on to say, in verse 24, "And those who belong to Christ Jesus have crucified the flesh with its passions and desires." It is therefore not correct to say that Christians are part flesh and part Spirit. They are in the Spirit and have decisively repudiated the way of living called the flesh. When they do "gratify the desires of the flesh," they are going contrary to what they really are.

The New Creature

As we continue to ask what the Bible teaches us about the Christian self-image, let us see what light is shed on this question by the New Testament concept of the new creation. A primary passage is 2 Corinthians 5:17: "Therefore, if anyone is in Christ, he is a new creation; the old has passed away, behold, the new has come." Translations vary in the way they render the Greek word *ktisis* here: some have "creation," while others have "creature." The primary meaning of the passage is probably that the person who is in Christ is to be seen as a member of God's new creation. He or she belongs to the new age that was ushered in by Christ—a new age that will culminate in the new heavens and the new earth from which all the consequences of sin will have been removed and in which God will be all in all. Yet the translation "new creature" is not totally wrong. Since believers now belong to Christ's new creation, we are to see ourselves as new creatures in Christ. The text does not simply predict that we shall be new creatures some time in the distant future; Paul says that if we are in Christ, we are new creatures now—not yet *totally* new, but *genuinely* new.

The Christian life does not merely involve believing something about Christ; it also involves believing something about ourselves. Having a proper Christian self-image, therefore, is an aspect of our Christian faith. Conversely, failing to see ourselves as new creatures in Christ is tantamount to a denial of our faith.

Honest Appraisal

The question has been raised whether a biblical expression like "counting others better than ourselves" (Phil. 2:3) implies a sort of negative self-image. Does this injunction tell us that, in order to be good Christians, we must run ourselves down and think of ourselves as inferior to others?

I do not think so. Phillips, I believe, has effectively captured the spirit of Philippians 2:3 when he translates, "Never act from motives of rivalry or personal vanity, but in humility think more of each other than you do of yourselves." The point is not that we must demean ourselves. The point is rather that we must not seek our own honor at someone else's expense and that we must be more concerned to honor or praise others than we are to have others praise us. One is reminded of Romans 12:10, "Outdo one another in showing honor."

What this means is that we must be more eager to see others get honored than we are to be honored ourselves. This does not imply that we need to despise ourselves or to deprecate ourselves. As a matter of fact, it requires a pretty healthy kind of self-esteem for us to be more concerned for the other person's honor than for our own. It is precisely the person with a negative self-image who is inclined to run other people down in order to bolster his or her own ego.

Paul approached this problem in another way in Romans 12:3: "For by the grace given to me I bid every one among you not to think of himself more highly than he ought to think, but to think with sober judgment, each according to the measure of faith which God has assigned him." To think more highly of ourselves than we ought to think is pride. To think less highly of ourselves than we ought to think is false modesty. To think soberly ("with sober judgment") about ourselves is to think realistically, to take stock of the talents and abilities God has given us, and to make an honest appraisal of ourselves. Such an honest appraisal, however, will immediately bring us back to the question that makes the shoe pinch: how well are we using our abilities in the service of the Lord and for the advancement of his kingdom?

Progressive Transformation

This leads us to the consideration of a final biblical concept: that of progressive transformation. Our self-image must not be static but dynamic. We may feel good about ourselves, but we may never be satisfied with ourselves; we must always be pressing on toward the goal.

Though we are to think of ourselves as new persons in Christ, the new persons we have put on are being continually renewed in knowledge after the image of our creator (Col. 3:10). This progressive renewal involves personal responsibility. Paul insists that Christians play an important part in perfecting their own holiness: "Since we have these promises, dear friends, let us purify ourselves from everything that contaminates body and spirit, perfecting holiness out of reverence for God" (2 Cor. 7:1, NIV). A similar point is made in Romans 12:2: "Do not conform any longer to the pattern of this world, but be transformed by the renewing of your mind" (NIV). The word *transformed* means not just outward change, but inner transformation: new motives, new values, and new goals.

At the same time, however, this progressive renewal is ultimately the work of God within us. The same transformation that is called our task in 2 Corinthians 7 and Romans 12 is ascribed to God's Holy Spirit in 2 Corinthians 3:18: "And we, who with unveiled faces all reflect the Lord's glory, are being transformed into his likeness with ever-increasing glory, which comes from the Lord, who is the Spirit" (NIV).

We are now new creatures. Some day our newness will be complete. "Beloved, we are God's children now; it does not yet appear what we shall be, but we know that when he appears we shall be like him, for we shall see him as he is" (1 John 3:2).

NOTES

1. When I say this, I am not thinking primarily about what is found in Calvinistic creeds or in the writings of Calvinistic theologians. I grant that the concept of the positive Christian self-image (believers are new persons in Christ) is to be found in these writings. I am thinking, however, about the self-image we Calvinists commonly seem to grow up with, about the kind of psychological and spiritual "climate" in which we ordinarily live. It is my impression that this "cli-

mate" is often far more chilly than the Bible warrants.

2. This is in spite of the clear statement made in Question and Answer 8 of what is probably one of the most popular Calvinistic creeds, the *Heidelberg Catechism*, "But are we so corrupt that we are totally unable to do any good and inclined toward all evil? Yes, unless we are born again by the Spirit of God."

3. In *No Exit and Three Other Plays* (New York: Vintage Books, 1948), pp. 77–78.

4. Paul, in other words, exemplified the attitude of believers who, without minimizing their sins, refuse to be constantly hypnotized by them. My former professor of New Testament, the late Professor Henry Schultze, used to put it this way: "You cannot think too seriously about your sins, but you can think too exclusively about them."

5. Unless otherwise noted, all Scripture quotations are from the Revised Standard Version.

6. "It was not I, but the grace of God which is with me" (1 Cor. 15:10). "Such is the confidence that we have through Christ toward God. Not that we are sufficient of ourselves to claim anything as coming from us; our sufficiency is from God" (2 Cor. 3:4–5). "But we have this treasure in earthen vessels, to show that the transcendent power belongs to God and not to us" (2 Cor. 4:7).

7. See Hermann Ridderbos, *Aan De Romeinen* (Kampen: Kok, 1959), pp. 153–171. This view of Romans 7:13–25 is also defended in his more recent book, which has been translated into English, *Paul, an Outline of his Theology* (Grand Rapids, Mich.: Eerdmans, 1975), pp. 126–130.

8. We could summarize John's teachings on this point as follows: believers must always remember two things about themselves: (1) their new lives as born-again persons, and (2) their continuing imperfection on this side of the Second Coming. But what John emphasizes is the new life.

9. Hermann Ridderbos in *Paul;* Oscar Cullmann in *Christ and Time* (Philadelphia: Westminster, 1950). See also, A. A. Hoekema, *The Bible and the Future* (Grand Rapids, Mich.: Eerdmans, 1979), pp. 68–75.

10. John Murray, *Principles of Conduct* (Grand Rapids, Mich.: Eerdmans, 1957), p. 218.

11. Ibid., p. 219.

12. Ibid., p. 218.

BIOGRAPHICAL SKETCH

ANTHONY A. HOEKEMA was professor of systematic theology at Calvin Theological Seminary in Grand Rapids, Michigan, until his recent retirement. He received an M.A. in psychology from the University of Michigan, a Th.B. from Calvin Theological Seminary, and a Th.D. from Princeton Theological Seminary. Prior to his teaching career, he served as pastor of three Christian Reformed Churches. He has contributed to a variety of professional and religious periodicals, including *The Reformed Journal* and *Christianity Today*. He is the author of *The Four Major Cults, What About Tongue-Speaking?, Holy Spirit Baptism, The Bible and the Future,* and *The Christian Looks at Himself. The Christian Looks at Himself,* published by Eerdmans in 1975, is an expanded version of this chapter and was dedicated to the Christian Association for Psychological Studies.

Wesleyan Perspectives on Self-Valuing

F. FRANKLYN WISE

RECENT movements in psychology as represented by the works of Collins,[1] Koteskey,[2] and Mowrer[3] remind us that theology and psychology both focus on the same subject—humanity. Each discipline utilizes its own methods of conceptual thinking and perception, as well as developing its peculiar technical jargon. Unfortunately, the end results may be confusion, tunnel vision, and deprivation of insight.

But what the more sophisticated scientist is now in the process of learning is that though he must disagree with most of the answers to religious questions which have been given by organized religion, it is increasingly clear that the religious questions themselves—and religious quests, the religious yearnings, the religious needs themselves—are perfectly respectable scientifically, that they are rooted deep in human nature, that they can be studied, described, examined in a scientific way, and that the churches were trying to answer perfectly sound human questions.[4]

When various psychological and theological perspectives are surveyed, one can easily be blinded to the fact that people and their adjustments to physical, social, political, and psychological environments are the object of scrutiny. As each theoretical approach is propounded, the observer easily loses sight of the fact each cognitive appraisal is but a partial answer to the puzzle of humanity.

Thus it is with a discussion of self-valuing. Each psychological approach and each theological perspective has something to contribute to the whole body of knowledge. None has the complete total answers to all of the questions.

The self-valuing activity is an inescapable aspect of human functioning. Psychology is intensely interested in it because the resultant self-concept and self-esteem so vitally affect the adjustment functions and behaviors of the individual. One's whole life-style, successes, failures, social interactions are influenced strongly by the process.

Theology is also concerned with self-valuing. Biblical theology especially is concerned because its postulates of revealed truth inject an additional parameter to the self-valuing process that psychology by its very nature does not. One's concept of oneself is derived from the faith postulates one holds about God's expectations for humanity, and humanity's rebellion against God, the possibilities available to one through the redemptive mission of Jesus Christ, and the promised empowerment of the Holy Spirit in one's daily living.

Theology itself cannot encompass all of this biblical plan into one compact system. In fact, some truths seem so beyond full human understanding that on the surface they may appear to be contradictory, or at least incompatible. The traditional Calvinist-Arminian discussions are a case in point.

It is not the purpose of this chapter to attempt to resolve these questions in the theological-psychological examination of self-valuing function. Rather, this discussion is to present the Wesleyan perspective for due consideration as one way of looking at the human predicament.

PERSPECTIVE

In contrast to much emphasis in current psychological theorizing on self-fulfillment as a result of self-actualization and self-realization, Wesleyan theology strongly asserts such efforts are inadequate. While it is true that one's self-concept is a vital element in one's adjustments in life's changing situations, Wesleyan theologians insist that the work of the Holy Spirit in his forgiving, sanctifying, and enabling roles must be added to this.

Support for this insistence is found in Paul's writings: "The unspiritual man does not receive the gifts of the Spirit of God, for they are folly to him, and he is not able to understand them because they are spiritually discerned."[5] This "unspiritual man" is also described as a "natural man," or as the "animal man" by John Calvin.[6]

By the *animal man* he does not mean (as is commonly thought) the man that is given up to gross lusts, or, as they say, to his own sensuality, but any man that is endowed with nothing more than the faculties mature.[7]

Thus the "natural man" Paul referred to is not necessarily a grossly corrupt, sexually promiscuous, wicked person, but a person—man or woman—who is totally insensitive to the influences, truths, and activities of the Holy Spirit. Such a person may or may not engage in many such immoral activities, but may seem to be quite self-accepting, to have a relatively healthy self-concept, and an expected, consistent positive self-esteem.

Spiritual things are foolishness to the natural man, for such a man lives as if the totality of life were in physical things; he lives only for this world. His values are based on the material and physical, and he judges everything in the light of these terms. Such a man simply cannot understand spiritual things.[8]

Unfortunately, the natural person's self-concept and self-esteem are inadequately based since they are derived from a materialistic, humanistic basis solely. They do not take into account God's design. Psychologically, such a person may be declared healthy; biblically, that person would be appraised as unspiritual. Paul insisted that "all have sinned and come short of the glory of God."[9] Sin has invaded the human race and "there is none righteous, no, not one."[10] As a result, we are born with an inclination toward self-centeredness, the antithesis of an adequate, truly healthy self-concept, according to Wesleyan theology.

While the natural person may, by human and psychological assessments, be declared to have a healthy self-concept and positive self-esteem, such a person's self-valuing omits God's expectations. The biblical goal for all humanity is that each person should "be holy, as He is holy."[11] That expectation involves two extremely demanding constraints that are impossible to achieve solely on the basis of human effort—complete cleansing from the inherited distortions of original sin and complete, unreserved commitment of one's whole self to God and his will. These two expectations are achieved by means of divine grace and faith, not human activity.

At first glance, the self-fulfilling, self-actualizing inclined advocate may view such a goal as self-defeating. How can one surrender one's self to God, lose one's basic self-drives in God's will, and still retain any trace of personal identity, uniqueness, or self-direction? Does the goal of holiness of heart and life destroy the selfhood of person?

The natural person says yes. The demand of God that all shall be holy is excessive, impossible, and beyond reason. On the surface, the charge seems supported. However, the very basic premise of the natural person is self-oriented. A positive self-concept, according to that perspective, is the result of self-effort, determining to become what one decides to become.

On the other hand, it is this very concept that Wesleyan theology, as well as other theological positions, addresses. Wesleyan theology views such self-efforts as limited in potential. Self-willing cannot release a person from the self-preoccupation, self-will, and self-centeredness that dominate his or her life. Adam's sin tainted the human hereditary processes so that we seem to have a propensity to regard ourselves as the controllers of our own fates, limited only by imagination and determination.

To the natural person, such subjugation of the personality's powers to God involves the loss of identity, the destruction of the selfhood. To Wesleyan theologians, the exact opposite is true. Loss of egocentricity and total self-domination is the avenue to self-actualization and self fulfillment. A fuller, more complete, stabler self-concept emerges along with a heightened self-esteem.

How can all this come about? How does the Wesleyan perspective on humanity and salvation come to terms with and describe the processes of self-valuing that bring healing and wholeness to people? If natural people, though humanistically described as having a healthy self-concept, have such self-value on inadequate bases, how can they move to a self-concept and self-esteem that resolves the tension between God's assessment and humanistic expectations?

The Self

While a full discussion of Wesleyan theology is beyond the scope of this chapter, some attention must be given to a key concern in Wesley's concept of person—the self. John Wesley felt keenly that the natural person was focused upon self, not God. He described this condition:

Man was created looking directly to God, as his last end; but falling into sin, he fell off from God, and turned into himself. Now, this infers [sic] a total apostasy and universal corruption in man; for where the last end is changed, there can be no real goodness. And this is the case of all men in their natural state. They seek not God but themselves. . . . Whithersoever they move, they cannot move beyond the circle of self. They seek themselves; they act for themselves; their natural, civil, and religious actions, from whatsoever spring they come, do all run into, and meet in this dead sea.[12]

Present-day writers in the Wesleyan tradition reiterate that theme:

But man has turned from his true *esse* to himself as the false end of his existence. This his existential plight is one of false self-centeredness. The self which was made for God now seeks to exist for itself, in reality becomes a god to itself.[13]

Perhaps the Wesleyan position is summed up best in the postulate that sin and self are frequently seen as synonymous terms.[14] E. Stanley Jones summarizes the problem as follows: "The question of what happens to the self is central in religion."[15] This is not to say that God's grace destroys the selfhood of a person, but to emphasize that when the natural person is turned in upon the self and becomes very self-oriented, that person seeks to gratify his or her desires without any reference to God and this expectation of holiness. Wholeness is found by surrendering the whole self to God; this brings one to holiness.

TRANSFORMATION

How can the natural person resolve this conflict? Several options are accessible. Such a person may live life in a humanistic shell, insensitive to God's expectations, denying the reality of spiritual need, and maintaining tunnel vision. In this case, self-valuing is based on the amount of or deprivation of extrinsic social symbols of status and acceptance received: socioeconomic rewards, achievements, acclaim, rather than upon one's intrinsic being. Whatever degree of healthy self-concept may evolve, it is inadequate from the Christian perspective.

Or, the natural person may make another response. He or she may abandon the natural state and seek a fully integrated life through Jesus Christ, becoming sensitized by the Holy Spirit. This movement involves two rites of passage. The first is generally proclaimed by most evangelical churches as conversion, accepting Christ, believing in Christ, or being born again. The second is more specifically described in Wesleyan theology as sanctification. Many theological positions espouse the same goal as Wesleyan theology does. They may use such terms as the committed life, the deeper life, or the spirit-filled life. All of these are consistent with what Wesley saw as the ultimate expectations for the Christian life. Wesleyan theology would differ mainly in its description of the process by which this passage is made.

Conversion

These acts of "becoming" involve self-valuing by the person. Such self-valuing experiences bring the individual to a point of drastically altered self-concept. For example, conversion begins in conviction. Conviction by the Holy Spirit is the process by which God breaks through the complacency, insensitivity, and unexamined self-concept of the natural person. The feeling tone accompanying such awareness may take any one of many forms—discontent with one's self, sense of guilt for actions for which one assumes responsibility, and feelings of emptiness and worthlessness. However, such emotional responses differ from self-devaluating feeling and loss of self-worth that accompany a deeply entrenched poor self-image. The

Holy Spirit induces such destruction of the self-concept by creating an awareness of the possibility of a better life-style. The "have-not" feeling is accompanied by "can-have," not merely a sense of lack.

Jesus introduced the constitution of his kingdom by proclaiming, "Happy are the poor in Spirit: for theirs is the kingdom of heaven."[16] In this present context, one could say, "Blessed or happy are those whose self-concept as self-sufficient persons has been shattered and they sense their lowered self-esteem for they are then able to come into the kingdom of God." Utter despair and self-destruction may result when such self-valuing is done in isolation from the hope of salvation. But in the Christian context, such discontent with one's self is always cast in the context of hope and God's love for the person.

This constructive self-valuing is analogous to that of people who voluntarily seek therapeutic counseling. Such individuals do not seek such help until they come to the point where self-concept and self-esteem have been confronted, and their inadequate coping with life admitted. Until such self-confrontation is honestly and realistically undertaken, these people will continue to live emotionally deprived, unsatisfactory lives. Their lack of motivation will continue as long as they continue to deny reality and refuse to engage in honest self-valuing.

There is a difference, however, between the person who seeks therapeutic counseling and the person who seeks spiritual restoration. The psychotherapist, of necessity, deals on the human level of behavioral functioning. The individual responding to the Holy Spirit's sensitization is seeking at-one-ment with God's design for life. Should the therapist be also committed to religious values, both aspects of assistance will be utilized.

When individuals whose self-concepts have been shattered by the Holy Spirit "believe in Christ," a miraculous event occurs—their self-concepts are restored into a new pattern. As a consequence, they feel joy, confidence, and peace because inner personality has been united into a more fully effective functioning whole.

Is it possible that Lewin's field theory of personality psychologically described this first eventual passage? He described the inner personality as having regions within the life space. These regions within the inner personality are theorized as having nearness-remoteness, firmness-weakness, and fluidity-rigidity characteristics. To the degree that the barriers between the regions are weak or firm, near or remote, and the medium of the region fluid or rigid, the regions are isolated or integrated, changeable or persistent, influenced or uninfluenced by facts of the environment.[17]

The natural person may be psychologically described as one whose inner personality has the region in which the knowledge of God posited is remote, its boundaries firm, and the medium of the region rigid. The fact of God and his demands upon the person are isolated and do not influence the personality at all.

Conviction by the Holy Spirit may be thought of as the process by which the Spirit brings the region of God near to the other regions, softens the boundaries of the self-concept, until they are pliable, and the region itself becomes fluid. At that point, the individual may believe God and experience conversion because the involved regions have resulted in both locomotion and communication.[18] Theology may describe such changes as conversion; psychology, as restructuring the life space.

Up to this point, the discussion has focused on the conscious level of cognitive functioning. The person's self-valuing procedures have initiated the personality changes about which the person is aware, though the detailed psychological and spiritual changes have been unknown. It is at this point that Wesleyan theology develops its own unique descriptions of self-valuing. Its concern is how the unconscious factors of the human personality and the conscious self are brought into a harmoniously functioning whole.

Sanctification

Some theological positions feel conversion accomplishes this result. Others feel it is either impossible to achieve or unnecessary to fulfill God's expectations for the self. Wesleyan theology holds this unification to be of paramount importance. John Wesley in a conference in June, 1747, described such an experience as being "wholly, entirely" sanctified.[19] This moment of sanctification comes "subsequent to regeneration."[20] It is espoused by all evangelical, conservative churches that believe in John Wesley's position.

Obviously, such a position cannot be unquestionably proven or disproven because it arises out of certain premises. As any theory of the behavioral sciences is assayed on the basis, not of truth or falsity, but usefulness or unusefulness, logical consistency, and predictive capability,[21] so must theological positions be evaluated.

Wesley formulated his concepts of "entire sanctification," Christian perfection, or perfect love from his understanding of Scripture, his experience, and his observations of other persons' spiritual pilgrimages. He identified with Paul's professed conflict, "I find then a law, that when I would do good, evil is present with me. For I delight in the law of God after the inward man. But I see another in my members, warring against the law of my mind, and bringing me into captivity to the law of sin which is in my members."[22] To him, this meant that, after conversion, there was yet in the convicted person a force or inclination that was out of harmony with God's will. This tension seemed to him to be out of harmony with Christ's call, "Be ye perfect, as your heavenly Father is perfect,"[23] and "Be ye holy for I am holy."[24]

Many other Scriptures support this goal and possibility for humanity. Describing converted Christians, Wesley said:

Now they see all the hidden abominations there, the depths of pride, self-will, and hell; yet having the witness in themselves, "Thou art an heir of God, a joint heir with Christ, even in the midst of this fiery trial"; which continually heightens both the strong sense they then have of their inability to keep themselves, and the inexpressible hunger they feel after a full renewal in His image, in "righteousness and true holiness."[25]

E. Stanley Jones puts the same concept in more modern terms:

When we speak of the cleansing of the heart, we usually mean cleansing from the impurity of sex. It does mean that; but it means much more—it means cleansing from all inner conflict and division. The pure heart is the undivided heart.

We now know that the center of our inner conflict is between the conscious and the subconscious minds. Psychology tells us that about one tenth of the mind is conscious and about nine tenths is subconscious . . . [so that] whatever controls the subconscious controls us.

The subconscious has been so interpreted by some modern psychologists that it leaves a sense of determinism—we are determined by the subconscious. . . . Man is enslaved—unless the subconscious can be redeemed, cleansed, and controlled. . . .

The question of questions for religion is: Can the subconscious mind be redeemed? If it cannot, then religion will deal with the conscious motives and leave unredeemed the depths. . . .[26]

These perceptions of human experience seem analogous to the observations of Freud when he described the human personality in terms of the id, ego, and superego, the unconscious and the conscious aspects. Whenever the id (which functions largely on the unconscious level, but is nonetheless influential in behavior), the ego, and the superego are in goal conflict, tension develops.

It is easy to show that the ego ideal answers to everything that is expected of the higher nature of man. As a substitute for a longing for the father, it contains the germ from which all religions evolved. The self-judgement [sic] which declares that the ego falls short of its ideal produces the religious sense of humility to which the believer appeals in his longing. . . . The tension between the demands of conscience and the actual performances of the ego is experienced as a sense of guilt.[27]

Jung also describes man as being "in a split condition"—"that evil, without man's ever having chosen it, is lodged in human nature, then it bestrides the psychological stage as the equal and opposite partner of good."[28]

Lewin's concept of personality does not preclude the possibility that the various areas of the inner personality core retain rigidity, remoteness, and weakness. Thus the personality may have various conflicting valences that must be resolved. Is it beyond reason to assume that the peace and productivity, the adequate functioning of the human person, is directly proportionate to the degree of open communication and ease of locomotion among the various perceptual-motor segments of the person?

It is to this end that Wesley felt the experience of entire sanctification brought persons who sought it. Those who were converted, who "walked in the light," and who consciously pursued communication with the Holy Spirit's assessment of their behavior, emotions, thoughts, and motives would discover this "dualism," "the evil within," "the inner conflicts between obedience to God and self-centeredness," and they would find their self-esteem and self-concept constantly vacillating. At times, they would enjoy God's approval, but at other times they would be dismayed by their inner compulsion for evil, self-indulgence, self-seeking, and self-will.

 To resolve this conflict, Wesley joined Paul and other biblical authors in calling for a full surrender of the self to God. Paul described such a full yielding as "being crucified with Christ."[29] Jesus himself talked about the necessity of "a corn of wheat" falling into the ground and dying if it is to become fruitful.[30] A psychologist stressed the same principle and wrote, "In our present Protean environment the principle still holds: *every significant step in human existence involves some inner sense of death.*"[31] Another observed, "There are two ways to try to get rid of yourself—one is by self-expression and the other is by self-surrender leading to self-dedication."[32]

As believers evaluate themselves honestly, they develop an awareness of this inner conflict, they must "lose" themselves, completely abandon themselves to God and thus find new, cleansed, harmonious transcendent selves. Such a change cannot take place without the aid of the Holy Spirit in the self-valuing process. Neither can it be effected by a partial surrendering of the individual. It requires the "all-or-none" decision. Under the sensitizing function of the Holy Spirit, all areas of the unconscious ego that have been alienated must now be admitted and brought into consciousness. Just as the therapist insists upon complete honesty and openness on the part of the client in order for healing to take place, seekers for wholeness, sanctification, holiness must face themselves in similar terms. "Paradoxically, self-expression requires the capacity to lose one's self in the pursuit of objectives not primarily referred to the self."[33]

Another condition seekers for wholeness must meet in the process is a forfeiting of autonomy. All claims to self-rights and self-will must be surrendered, as Paul urged in the great Kenosis passage.[34] Seekers must pledge themselves to unquestioned and unswerving obedience to God's will.

When they have done this with the aid of the Holy Spirit, they can rest in faith in God's word that the *psyche* has been cleansed, the self has been made into a harmonious whole, and their love has been made complete. According to Wesleyan theology, they have been sanctified.

Psychologically, such persons may be described as having moved to the level of self-actualization in Maslow's model. "Self-actualization means experiencing fully, vividly, selflessly, with full concentration and total absorption."[35] The other characteristics of such persons discussed by Maslow are very similar to Wesleyan theological descriptions.[36] Sanctification and peak-experiences seem to be describing essentially similar experiences.[37]

In reviewing Jung's analytic psychology, Hall and Lindzey observed:

The self is life's goal, a goal people constantly strive for but rarely reach. Like all archetypes, it motivates human behavior and causes one to search for wholeness especially through avenues provided by religion. True religious experiences are about as close to selfhood as most humans will ever come. . . ."[38]

Sanctification launches believers on the road toward mature religion, a religion of

dynamic organization of cognitive—affective—conative factors . . . [with its] . . . feelings of wonder and awe, a sense of oneness with the All, humility, elation, and freedom; . . . that pervades the individual's whole spectrum of . . . personal and interpersonal relationships, including such spheres as morality, love, work, and so forth.[39]

For some people, losing themselves in such an experience means literally to "lose themselves." But for other people, this losing of self means to find and gain a larger, more comprehensive sense of self. If this can happen, we say the self-transcendence is beautiful.[40]

Becoming Mature

The self-valuing process does not cease with the mobilization of the total personality around the core experience of conversion and sanctification. These experiences are but critical, decisive, life-changing moments. According to theology, there is no "instant maturity" but a continual process of becoming. "But as many as received him, to them gave he power [right, or privilege] to become the sons of God."[41]

This process is never-ending in this life. As Christians live out their lives, the Holy Spirit is a spiritual cybernetic system, constantly providing feedback as to how well they are implementing God's call to purity of thoughts, motivations, and behaviors in daily encounters. The Holy Spirit is commissioned specifically to "guide . . . [us] into all truth"[42]—the truth about ourselves and about God's potential for us.

The more Christians cultivate a sensitivity to that feedback, the keener skills of self-valuation and spiritual discrimination they acquire, the more authentic, wholly integrated their lives become. They are growing in grace —constantly engaging in self-valuing.

Distinctive Terms

Wesley used some terms in connection with his theology that have frequently been misunderstood and misused. He talked about "perfect love" and "Christian perfection." His use of perfection did not imply the Christian had reached the point at which no further progress in loving God and others was possible. He used the term in the sense of completion and wholeness. The Christian's love for God and commitment to God had been fully consummated. This love had been singularly directed toward God so the Christian could love him completely.

In answer to the question, "What is Christian perfection?" Wesley replied, "The loving of God with all our heart, mind, and soul, and strength. This implies that no wrong temper, none contrary to love, remains in the soul; and that all the thoughts, words, and actions are governed by pure love."[43]

Does not such a lofty concept deny the limitations of the human personality? Such a level of living seems unrealistically idealistic. Wesley answered this misapprehension when, about 1742, he wrote,

Perhaps the general prejudice against Christian perfection may chiefly arise from a misapprehension of the nature of it. We willingly allow, and continually declare,

48 THEOLOGICAL PERSPECTIVES

there is no such perfection in this life as implies either a dispensation from doing good, and attending all the ordinances of God, or a freedom from ignorance, mistake, temptation, and a thousand infirmaties necessarily connected with flesh and blood.[44]

CONCLUSION

Humanity is the focus of psychology and theology. Both disciplines seek to help persons find wholeness, to enable them to achieve a healthy self-concept, a positive rewarding self-esteem. God's plan for wholeness is reflected in both approaches, though each discipline has its own jargon.

Just as psychology has been unable to comprehend in one theoretical description the complexities of human personality; theology has not been any more successful. Wesleyan theology is but one such approach. Its focus is upon the subconscious level of human behavior, stressing the brokenness of individuals while at the same time pointing them to restoration, and centering upon the indispensable enablement of the Holy Spirit. Wesleyan theology has brought healing and joy to many whose honest self-valuing makes them "saints under construction," constantly valuing themselves and re-evaluating their intra- and interpersonal relationships.

NOTES

1. Gary R. Collins, *The Rebuilding of Psychology* (Wheaton, Ill.: Tyndale House Publishers, 1977).
2. Ronald L. Koteskey, *Psychology from a Christian Perspective* (Nashville, Tenn.: Abingdon Press, 1980).
3. O. Hobart Mowrer, *The Crisis in Psychiatry and Religion* (Princeton, N.J.: D. Van Nostrand Co., 1961).
4. Abraham H. Maslow, *Religions, Values, and Peak Experiences* (Columbus: Ohio State University Press, 1964), p. 18.
5. 1 Corinthians 2:14. This and other biblical references are from the King James Version.
6. John Calvin, *Commentary on the Epistle of Paul to the Corinthians,* trans. Rev. John Pringle (Grand Rapids, Mich.: Wm. B. Eerdmans Publishers, 1948), vol. 1, p. 115.
7. Ibid.
8. Donald S. Metz, *Beacon Bible Commentary* (Kansas City, Mo.: Beacon Hill Press, 1968), vol. 8, p. 327.
9. Romans 3:23.
10. Romans 3:10.
11. 1 Peter 1:16.
12. John Wesley, *The Works of John Wesley* (Kansas City, Mo.: Nazarene Publishing House, n.d.), vol. 9, p. 456.
13. Dr. William Greathouse, in a personal letter to the author, dated March 5, 1971.
14. Peter Wiseman, *Scriptural Sanctification* (Kansas City, Mo.: Beacon Hill Press, 1951), p. 41.
15. E. Stanley Jones, *Conversion* (New York: Abingdon Press, 1959), p. 51.
16. Matthew 5:3.
17. Calvin S. Hall and Gardner Lindzey, *Theories of Personality,* 3rd ed. (New York: John Wiley and Sons, 1978), pp. 392–400.
18. Ibid.
19. John Wesley, *Plain Account of Christian Perfection* (Chicago: The Christian Witness Co., n.d.), p. 33.
20. Church of the Nazarene, *Manual* (Kan-

sas City, Mo.: Nazarene Publishing House, 1980), p. 31.
21. Hall and Lindzey, *Theories of Personality*, pp. 10–11.
22. Romans 7:14–23.
23. Matthew 5:48.
24. 1 Peter 1:16.
25. Wesley, *Plain Account of Christian Perfection*, p. 23.
26. E. Stanley Jones, *The Way to Power and Poise* (New York: Abingdon Press, 1949), pp. 99–100.
27. Sigmund Freud, *The Ego and the Id*, trans. Joan Riviere and ed. James Starchey (New York: W. W. Norton and Co., 1960), p. 27.
28. C. G. Jung, *The Undiscovered Self*, trans. R. F. C. Hall (New York: New American Library, 1958), p. 110.
29. Galatians 2:20.
30. John 12:24.
31. Robert J. Lifton, *The Life of the Self: Toward a New Psychology* (New York: Simon and Schuster, 1976), p. 149.

32. Jones, *The Way to Power and Poise*, p. 109.
33. Gordon Allport, cited in Jones, *The Way to Power and Poise*, p. 108.
34. Philippians 2:5–11.
35. Abraham H. Maslow, *The Farther Reaches of Human Nature* (New York: The Viking Press, 1971), p. 45.
36. Ibid., pp. 45–50.
37. Maslow, *Religions, Values and Peak-Experiences*, pp. 59–68.
38. Hall and Lindzey, *Theories of Personality*, p. 124.
39. Otto Strunk, Jr., *Mature Religion: A Psychological Study* (New York: Abingdon Press, 1965), pp. 144–145.
40. John H. Brannecke and Robert G. Amick, *The Struggle for Significance* (Beverly Hills, Calif.: Glencoe Press, 1971), pp. 288–289.
41. John 1:12.
42. John 16:13.
43. Wesley, *Plain Account of Christian Perfection*, pp. 40–41.
44. Ibid., p. 25.

BIOGRAPHICAL SKETCH

F. FRANKLYN WISE is professor of Christian education at Olivet Nazarene College in Kankakee, Illinois. He holds a B.A. at Eastern Nazarene College, and an M.Ed. and a Ph.D. at the University of Pittsburgh. His articles have appeared in *Psychology and Theology, Religious Education, Bulletin of C.A.P.S., Herald of Holiness, Edge,* and *Church School Builder.* He has contributed to *Self Esteem, Exploring Christian Education,* and *Developmental Psychology: A Holistic Approach.* And, finally, he has served as dean at Canadian Nazarene College and dean of students at both Malone College and Trevecca Nazarene College, he has been a pastor for thirteen years, and he has spent twenty-four years as a college teacher.

The Theology of Self-Esteem: An Analysis

DENNIS VOSKUIL

EVEN IN this electronic era, it is possible to learn a great deal about American culture by examining our most popular books. A survey of the best-seller lists during the past two decades reveals that we have been intensely interested in self-fulfillment through such avenues as individual success, power, and happiness. In a nation that has consistently glorified individualism, recent concern for self is certainly no aberrant theme, but the current emphasis seems to be more vigorous and unchallenged than in the past.

Most of us have read one or more of the intriguing books that supposedly lay bare the personal and interpersonal mysteries of life—*Games People Play, I'm OK—You're OK, Breaking Free, Winning through Intimidation, Your Erroneous Zones, Looking Out for #1*. These and similar best-sellers have essentially been popularized and simplified versions of the diverse strains of self-theory propounded by eminent humanistic psychologists such as Erich Fromm, Rollo May, Abraham Maslow, and Carl Rogers. Reacting against behaviorism and Freudianism, especially where it comes to an understanding of human nature, these theorists have written of the reality of individual freedom, responsibility, and potential for self-actualization.

The self movement in psychology has been buttressed by numerous studies which have indicated that mental adjustment and personal happiness are directly related to favorable self-esteem. According to researchers, feelings of inadequacy, unworthiness, inferiority, isolation, guilt, depression, and shame are among the wide range of psychological disorders experienced by those who have low self-esteem.[1] Such findings have encouraged psychologists like Nathaniel Branden to conclude that a person's self-evaluation is "the single most significant key to his behavior."[2]

Considering such widespread interest in self-fulfillment, and the psychological evidence for the importance of self-esteem, it is not surprising that Christians have also become keenly interested in this issue. As John Stott notes, "a whole new literature" has sprouted up in support of Christian self-affirmation.[3] Christian writers are imploring us to love ourselves almost as a moral and theological duty. Certain that you are out of practice, Cecil Osborne demonstrates *The Art of Learning to Love Yourself,* Walter Trobisch tells you simply to *Love Yourself,* and Bryan Jay Cannon insists that you must *Celebrate Yourself.* First cousins of these celebrations of the self are a large offering of self-help books that promise evangelical readers various forms of fulfillment—happy marriages, weight loss, financial prosperity, and peace of mind. As Nathan Hatch puts it, "What seems to be in the works today is a convenient marriage of evangelical piety and self-help."[4]

The dean of the success gospellers is Robert Schuller, host of religious television's upbeat "Hour of Power" and the inspiration behind the nationally recognized Crystal Cathedral. No one associated with American evangelicalism has done more to promote the twin-edged message of success through positive self-esteem and possibility thinking. Like his mentor, Norman Vincent Peale, Schuller has been more concerned with practice than theory. Most of his books focus on the way to gain peace, power, and prosperity. These include *God's Way to the Good Life, Peace of Mind through Possibility Thinking, Move Ahead with Possibility Thinking,* and *You Can Become the Person You Want to Be.* Because he is primarily interested in the mass market, Schuller has produced little that could be called serious theology. Occasionally, however, his inchoate theology of self-esteem has surfaced in various articles and in sections of an early book, *Self-Love: The Dynamic Force of Success.* Schuller is apparently now working on a systematic theology of self-esteem that will undoubtedly serve as the foundation for a new movement in American theology.

Until such a full-fledged theological treatment appears, whether it is contributed by Schuller or others, an analysis of the theology of self-esteem must be based upon the reconstruction of a scattering of writings that have been produced by evangelical thinkers. Perhaps the most thoughtful and balanced treatment of the self is Anthony Hoekema's *A Christian Looks At Himself,* a book that Schuller has explicitly endorsed.[5] Drawing upon what Hoekema, Schuller, and others have contributed to this discussion, I will, first, describe the essential themes of the theology of self-esteem and, second, analyze the relationship of this movement to the broad spectrum of evangelical thought.

COMMON THEMES

The diverse confederation of Christians who have made contributions to the emerging theology of self-esteem seem to share three basic sets of beliefs. First, there is the common assumption that *high self-esteem is a positive personality trait.* All are aware of the psychological studies which indicate that persons with a weak self-image are less likely to be as happy, creative, poised, fulfilled, and successful as those with a strong self-image. Like Adler, Brandon, and other psychologists who have insisted that self-image is the drive wheel of our being, a growing number of Christian apologists have begun to express concern that the gospel facilitate high self-esteem, and therefore emotional health.

The second common presupposition is that *evangelical Christians too often have an unhealthy negative self-image* because they have been besieged by a relentless message of sin and guilt. It is generally agreed that evangelical pulpiteers have battered the self with repeated sermons on willfulness, original sin, and human depravity. Reinforced by hymns that have urged Christians to loathe and abhor themselves, these sermons have effectively communicated the message of human worthlessness. Certain that far too many preachers have shared the sentiments of the clergyman who stated, "I feel I've preached an effective sermon when I've left my congregation feeling guilty," Hoekema warns that unless it is backed by the biblical message of forgiveness, affirmation, and renewal, "such preaching may indeed create in the hearers a negative self-image which may take years to erase."[6]

This leads directly to the third underlying principle (here the Christian and non-Christian psychologists of the self part company): the identification of *the gospel as the ultimate resource for building positive self-esteem.* While none of the evangelical proponents of the self would deny the radical fallenness of humanity, they would certainly agree that the true biblical doctrine of humanity has been too often misunderstood and distorted— with far too much emphasis placed upon sin and guilt and far too little emphasis placed upon redemption and renewal. Providing a corrective for Christians who stress human worthlessness and wretchedness, the supporters of the movement argue that the gospel is more truly a message of self-dignity and self-worth. "We have been writing our continuing sinfulness in capital letters and our newness in Christ in small letters," says

Hoekema. "When the Christian faith is accepted in its totality, that faith brings with it a predominantly positive self-image."[7]

The doctrines of creation and redemption are pivotal for the theology of self-esteem. Humans were made in the image of God, the pinnacle of creation, and though this image was distorted by the Fall, God has neither abandoned his wayward creatures nor counted them as worthless. Indeed, God so valued us that he sent his own son to suffer and die on the cross that we might be redeemed and renewed. As Schuller puts it, God's acceptance of us in Christ is "the ultimate capstone around which self-esteem is really wrapped."[8] Because God loves us, we are able to love ourselves.

Schuller has taken this premise to its logical extreme, using the cross as the foundation upon which to build a program of self-help through possibility thinking. Pronounced worthy by God, human beings are freed from crippling guilt and low self-esteem, and thereby given a green light to pursue their grandest dreams of success, power, and fulfillment. Through possibility thinking, we can become the persons we want to be. Schuller invites the Christian to indulge in self-love—because of Christ. According to him, "The Cross sanctifies the ego-trip."[9]

WARNING SIGNALS

In assessing the Christian self movement, one must acknowledge that it has generated a wholesome and beneficial discussion in the evangelical churches. At its best, the theology of self-esteem is simply a reorchestration of the symphony of salvation. We have been created in God's image, and even as fallen creatures we are never worthless, however unworthy we are of God's love. The cross of Christ sets us free from guilt and recreates us for sacrifice and service. As Hoekema reiterates again and again: "The Christian believer should have a basically positive self-image."[10]

The comments that follow, then, do not challenge the biblical and theological integrity of the movement. But I do wish to raise a few warning signals, for there are some dangerous turns on the highway of self-esteem.

Sliding over Sin

The evangelicals who tell us to celebrate ourselves do not dispute the biblical doctrine of sin. But there does seem to be a tendency to move too quickly from creation to redemption without coming to grips with the consequences of human fallenness. This inclination to slide over sin seems to be inherent in a movement that seeks to provide Christian resources for self-esteem. After all, does it not seem counterproductive, even before an encounter with Christ, to strip away private pretenses of self and to look deeply into our sinful souls? It is a fatal blow to our self-esteem. Interested in preserving precarious self-esteem, Schuller counsels pastors to avoid preaching about sin because such a message merely reinforces a negative self-image. "Don't tell them they're sinners. They'll believe you—and you'll reinforce this self-image! You'll set this negative impression firmly in their minds and their conduct will only prove how right you were."[11] Certain that people who are afflicted with low self-esteem already know that they are miserable creatures, Schuller insists that it is insulting and slanderous to tell them that they are wretched sinners. Such an approach, he tells us, "produces a destructive strategy of evangelism."[12]

Taken in this direction, the theology of self-esteem contradicts the critical biblical principle that repentance precedes conversion, that we must give up the old self before putting on the new. Calvin writes that we must undergo a radical self-examination, for such knowledge "will strip us of all confidence in our ability, deprive us of all occasion for boasting, and lead us to submission."[13] It was Wesley who claimed that we must confront Christ as sinners "inwardly and outwardly destroyed."[14] Nathan Hatch, reminding us that the majestic Reformation doctrine of grace followed a doctrine of human depravity, reiterates the paradox of the gospel: "That it must crush self-righteousness before uplifting the contrite; that it must root out self-centeredness before offering consolation; that it must kill off self-will before unveiling the power to live by."[15] A gospel that does not point to the depth of human misery and deceit cannot bring us to the height of grace.

Sin as Low Self-Esteem

There is a tendency among some of the Christian advocates of self-worth to identify the essence of sin with negative self-esteem, which is understood as weakness rather than utter perversity. The cure for such a condition, of course, is the raising of self-esteem. This is a matter that strikes at the very heart of the Christian understanding of human depravity. It is Schuller's position that Adam's and Eve's sin of self-will and rebellion is to be distinguished from the "original sin" to which all of us are subject, and that this basic sin is that of an insufficient self-esteem. Adam and Eve had a choice, and they willfully rebelled against God. They knew better, but their children (and we are all their sons and daughters) were "born in the bushes, in hiding, and it's not fair to pick on those kids and preach to them as if they were the same as the parents. Those kids never had a choice . . . so you take the positive approach . . . one that has some strokes in it."[16] For Schuller, human pride (or self-centeredness) is nothing more than a negative fruit of the Fall, a "defense mechanism" triggered by an insecure ego. Our sinfulness is not rooted in strength, but in weakness; it is a symptom of our fallen condition rather than its cause.

Few advocates of self-esteem want to embrace Schuller's rather Pelagian understanding of the nature of sin—denying original sin and holding that humanity has perfect freedom to do either right or wrong. Still, it raises a critical question for the movement as a whole, "What is the relationship between sin and low self-esteem?"

Of course, many of us *are* afflicted with low self-esteem, and self-pride *is* often a defense mechanism that covers up our insecurities and weaknesses. But excessive self-will is the essence of our sinfulness. However we define it—self-glorification, self-deification, self-pride—this basic sin is one we share with all human beings, including our spiritual parents. It is this vibrant pride that causes us, again and again, to rebel against the Lord our God. It is because we have loved ourselves too much, not too little, that we have, as Paul writes, "exchanged the glory of the immortal God for images resembling mortal man" (Rom. 1:23). It is not out of weakness that we rail at God, but out of strength, and it is this that leads to self-destruction.

Those who claim that the basic human problem is inadequate self-esteem are misinterpreting Scripture and misreading the human heart. As Augustine insisted, pride or self-deification is the essential sin. "What is pride but undue exaltation? And this is undue exaltation, when the soul abandons Him to whom it ought to cleave as its end and becomes a kind of end in itself."[17] Calvin understands us well when he writes that there is "nothing that man's nature seeks more eagerly than to be flattered," adding that "blind self-love is innate in all mortals."[18]

Recent studies of psychologists seem to support the notion that we are blinded by self-love.[19] People are affected by a strong self-serving and self-justifying bias. These biases, I believe, are basic to our human condition and not simply a disguise for essential weakness or low self-esteem. Sin is much more deeply entrenched and indelibly etched upon the human condition than we would like to admit.

The Prudential Gospel

We must beware of understanding the Christian faith as a mere means to an end. Such a tendency has always been apparent within the Christian tradition, but a theology of self-esteem is so dangerously vulnerable to utilitarianism. If persons come to Christ expecting to gain self-esteem, hoping to find the key to success, happiness, and peace of mind, they have misunderstood the call to conversion and commitment. The call of Christ is to brokenness and suffering and service, not to other-worldly or this-worldly fulfillment. Religious utilitarianism must be challenged even as it relates to the question of self-esteem. Psychologist Andre Godin warns against using Christianity as "a means of assuring mental health."

God is never a *means*, but an end. And the religion that keeps us in a living relationship with the Divine presence should never be regarded as a means or as if it were to be used for the acquisition of restoration of a human balance. To consider it so would be to deprive religion of its deepest meaning.[20]

A self-seeking faith is an utterly misdirected faith. A relationship of trust that is a gift from God (Eph. 2:8), faith is never to be embraced "in order that" our ends might be served. Neal Plantinga warns against this "cash and carry" Christianity. "We are intended to please *God*—not the other way around—and the idea that Christianity is something we adapt for what it will pay us in happiness and personal mastery is an idea which must be explicitly discouraged."[21]

Self-Obsession

The interest in self-esteem among Christians is simply one indication of the recent obsession with the self in America. The popularity of self-help and success manuals in Christian bookstores reveals that there is more than a whiff of Christian narcissism circulating today. It is ironic that this tendency should infect the Christian community, for Christ spoke so ex-plicitly and strongly to this very point: "If any man would come after me, let him deny himself and take up his cross and follow me. For whoever would save his life will lose it and whoever loses his life shall save it." (Matt. 16:24–25).

Karl Barth once observed that the greatest freedom we can experience is freedom from the self.[22] Isn't this the gospel promise? Not that we are freed by Christ to love ourselves, but that we are free from self-obsession. Not that the cross frees us *for* the ego trip, but that the cross frees us *from* the ego trip. What a refreshing message! In removing our sin of self-centeredness, in enabling us to forget the self, Christ frees us to focus our attention upon God and those around us. Rather than sanctifying narcis-sism, Christ negates it.

The Psychologized Gospel

It is revealing that most of those who have contributed to the discussion on self-esteem have close ties to psychology. To make such a connection is not to indict anyone, certainly not in the context of a book sponsored by the Christian Association for Psychological Studies. I fully support the uneasy truce between psychology and Christianity which has been so mutually beneficial.

I do wonder, however, whether the theology of self-esteem is not really a psychologized interpretation of the gospel. And this leads to the basic question of whether biblical terms and psychological terms are interchangeable. Nathan Hatch claims that the recent union of evangelicalism and self-help has been based upon the assumption that it makes little difference if we replace the biblical concepts of moral poverty, selfish blindness, and spiritual nakedness with the more fashionable psychological notions of fear, frustration, and anxiety.[23] Those who claim that this is simply a matter of putting traditional ideas into modern idiom in order to update the gospel make a valid point, but I'm afraid that something important is lost in the translation. When the biblical notion of willful human pride becomes the psychological equivalent, at least for some, of a defense mechanism to cover insecurity, I feel it is necessary to raise warning signals.

Christians must be very careful about psychologizing the gospel. Paul Vitz probably overstated this case in his searing book, *Psychology as Religion: The Cult of Self-Worship,* but Wayne Joosse was certainly on target when he wrote that "much of popular Christian psychology unwittingly incorporates considerable humanistic ideology, only slightly camouflaged with a veneer of God-talk and a scattering of Scripture."[24] It is important to encourage and nurture the present-day reapproachment between psychology and Christianity, remembering that while psychology can tell us about the essential human condition, it does not study man in relationship to God. Psychology, then, is inherently anthropocentric. Christianity is enthusiastically theocentric.

CONCLUSION

The theology of self-esteem has made some important contributions to the contemporary church. First, it has served as a biblical counterbalance to the theology of self-negation that has persisted in certain strains of American evangelicalism. There is little doubt that many evangelicals have distorted the basic Christian message by accentuating human guilt and depravity rather than divine redemption and recreation. Second, the self movement has demonstrated that, despite the consequences of the Fall, the Christian possesses immediate resources for a positive self-image. After all, the promise of the gospel is that we become new beings in Christ (2 Cor. 5:17). Affirmed, forgiven, and renewed, we are authentically free to love God, neighbor, and self. Third, the Christian self movement, in a general way, has identified psychological dimensions to the gospel, thereby accelerating evangelical interest in psychological studies. The recent dialogue between theologians and psychologists is essentially healthy and certainly long overdue. Hence, the warning signals that I have raised are not meant to inhibit the movement, but to serve as caution lights—blinking reds (stop before proceeding) or blinking yellows (proceed with care). Such signals warn against the tendency to slip into an excessive focus upon the self. Because our basic sin is that of self-deification, we are persistently prone to serve and glorify ourselves rather than God. Howard Chandler Robbins reminds us that even the act of worshipping God can be diverted into self-centeredness.[25] A theological movement that places such heavy emphasis upon self-worth inevitably runs the risk of taking a detour down the dangerous highway of self-worship. Proceed, yes, but proceed with caution.

NOTES

1. Some of these studies are cited by W. Glenn Wilder, "The Search for Self-Esteem," *Journal of Psychology and Theology* 6 (Spring, 1978): 183.
2. Nathaniel Branden, *The Psychology of Self-Esteem* (New York: Bantam Books, 1969), p. 110.
3. John R. W. Stott, "Must I Really Love Myself?" *Christianity Today* 22 (May 5, 1978): 34.
4. Nathan Hatch, "Purging the Poisoned Well Within," *Christianity Today*, 23 (March 2, 1979): 15. See Cynthia Shaible's exploration of the evangelical self-help market, "The Gospel of the Good Life," *Eternity* 32 (February, 1981): 21–27; and Dennis Voskuil, "Mountains into Goldmines: Robert Schuller's Gospel of Success," *Reformed Journal* 31 (May, 1981): 8–14.
5. See Robert H. Schuller, "Why Bob Schuller Smiles on Television," *Leadership* 2 (Winter, 1981): 30.
6. Anthony A. Hoekema, *The Christian Looks at Himself* (Grand Rapids, Mich.: Eerdmans, 1975), p. 16. See also William M. Counts, "The Nature of Man and the Christian's Self-Esteem," *Journal of Psychology and Theology* 1 (January, 1973): 38–44.
7. Hoekema, *The Christian Looks at Himself*, pp. 18, 23.
8. Robert H. Schuller, "Self-Love: How Far? How Biblical? How Healthy?" (Panel Discussion), *Eternity* 30 (February, 1979): 23.
9. Ibid., p. 21.
10. Hoekema, *The Christian Looks at Himself*, p. 23.
11. Robert H. Schuller, *You Can Become the Person You Want to Be* (Old Tappan, N.J.: Revell, 1973), p. 123.

12. Schuller, "Self-Love," p. 23.
13. John Calvin, *Institutes of the Christian Religion*, ed. John T. McNeill and trans. Ford Lewis Battles (Philadelphia: Westminsters, 1960), vol. 2, sections 1, 2, p. 242.
14. Quoted in Hatch, "Purging the Poisoned Well Within," p. 15.
15. Hatch, "Purging the Poisoned Well Within." p. 15.
16. Schuller, "Why Robert Schuller Smiles," p. 30.
17. Saint Augustine, *City of God*, XIV, 13. Quoted in Reinhold Niebuhr, *The Nature and Destiny of Man* (New York: Scribner's, 1941), vol. 1, pp. 186–187, footnote 1.
18. Calvin, *Institutes of the Christian Religion*, pp. 242–243.
19. See David G. Myer, *The Inflated Self: Human Illusions and the Call to Biblical Hope* (New York: Seabury Press, 1980),

pp. 32–120; David G. Myer and Jack Ridl, "Can We All Be Better Than Average?" *Psychology Today* 13 (August, 1979): 89, 95, 96, 98.
20. Andre Godin, "Mental Health in Christian Life," *Religion in Medicine*, ed. David Belgum (Ames: Iowa State University Press, 1967), p. 143.
21. Neal Plantinga, "Schullerism and Church Growth," *The Banner*, 111 (March 26, 1976): 5.
22. Karl Barth, *Final Testimonies*, ed. Eberhard Busch and trans. Geoffrey W. Bromiley (Grand Rapids, Mich.: Eerdmans, 1977), p. 37.
23. Hatch, "Purging the Poisoned Well Within," p. 15.
24. Wayne Joosse, "Reflections on Narcissism," *Eternity* 30 (February, 1979): 22.
25. Cited in Viktor Frankl, *The Will to Meaning* (New York: New American Library, 1969), p. 143.

BIOGRAPHICAL SKETCH

DENNIS N. VOSKUIL, assistant professor of religion at Hope College, received his Ph.D. from Harvard University. His articles have appeared in *Fides et Historia*, *The Reformed Journal*, and *The Reformed Review*. He has a newly published book, *Mountains Into Gold Mines: Robert Schuller and the Gospel of Success*.

SECTION II:
THEORY AND RESEARCH

Introduction

UNDERSTANDING the Scriptures inevitably involves the development of an interpretative framework based upon internal consistency and context, as well as upon experiential information. Similarly, psychological theories provide interpretative and integrative orientations in which to understand empirical data. Theories describe, organize, and, at their best, provide predictions. In order for either theologies or psychological theories to have significance and value, there must be the opportunity for testing in experience.

In this section, we turn to a more explicit consideration of the factors in social development and interaction which affect self-esteem.

Sociologist David Moberg examines the relational basis of self-esteem and laments the minimal study of religious reference groups in the formation and evaluation of self-concepts. Moberg points out the prophetic nature of the self-concept, which is both fed by and influences social feedback. Moberg then points out that religious beliefs and conversion have significant, though varied, impact upon self-concepts. Religious orientation expands one's frame of reference to include conception of the self in relation to the cosmos, and the result may be either positive or negative self-esteem, depending on perceived harmony with God. Conversion produces new perceptual, valuing, and motivational patterns, or a new self-concept. The act is encouraged typically by a sympathetic community that reinforces the new creation. Moberg links self-esteem with the cultivation of spiritual well-being, expanding the person's sense of self and filling it with broader meaning that enhances self-esteem.

Psychologist C. Markham Berry also sees the development of a healthy self-concept as a function of early interaction with parents. His primary focus, however, is on disturbances in the formation of the self. Two clinical patterns that reflect a failure to distinguish between self and not-self in a manner which allows adult intimacy are narcissism and the borderline personality. Narcissism involves the psychological swallowing up of others to serve one's own self-centered needs and desires so that genuine relationships are impossible. The diffusion of self or borderline personality refers to an inability to form a coherent and relatively stable self-image that is maintained at least somewhat independently of circumstances and situations. Berry traces the development of these pathological processes to the early life of the infant and specifically to the failure to successfully accomplish *separation-individuation*. Further, he sees parental empathy in the emotional environment as crucial to positive self-esteem and to the avoidance of narcissism.

David Myers critically and creatively analyzes what he calls the "self-serving bias" from a social psychological perspective. While admitting the benefits of positive self-esteem, Myers argues that, for most, the problem is one of arrogance rather than inferiority. He argues persuasively that pride is a pervasive part of our psychological and cognitive functioning, and he points out seven "streams of data" that illustrate the human twist toward self-centeredness. Myers then considers several objections to this data and concludes with an appeal for humility that is not self-contempt.

Our ability to talk meaningfully about the development, maintenance, and change of self-esteem requires valid and reliable measures of the phenomenon. John Gartner scrutinizes the role of values in the construction of self-esteem tests and suggests that most of the current tests available contain subtle, antibiblical assumptions that distort the interpretation of such tests when taken by Christians. Gartner isolates six types of questions commonly used in self-esteem measures and shows how the assumptions underlying these questions run contrary to Christian values. He then proposes the theoretical and theological basis for revising these assumptions and developing a test of self-esteem that would not only be free of anti-Christian bias but would also be harmonious with biblical conceptions of the self.

Paul Clement approaches the change of self-esteem from a behavioral perspective. He sees the need for a more exacting analysis of the functional meaning of self-esteem in order to bring about effective change through the detailed specification of goals and change methods. He proposes techniques for self-evaluation and self-regulation that can be self-administered and are therefore not as dependent on the behavior of others in order for change to occur. Identifying four categories of self-regulation methods for changing one's own behavior, Clement provides a detailed analysis of each set of methods and shows how each can be used to promote self-efficacy.

The Social Nature of the Self

DAVID O. MOBERG

SEVERAL years ago I was sensitized to a deeper concern for self-esteem by the amazed question of a Jewish social worker, "Don't you Protestants have any concept of self-love in your religion?" Subsequent observations and reflections have reminded me of Jesus' summary of ethical responsibility: we should love our neighbors as we love ourselves (Matt. 22:39). This is often countered in evangelical Protestantism by the biblical perspectives that all have sinned, that none can save oneself, and that self-love is easily debased into avarice, envy, greed, and other works of the flesh that are contrary to the fruit of the Spirit (Gal. 5:16–26). Perhaps there is a pendulum-like alternation in such groups between an emphasis upon "total depravity" and the dignity of human beings as created in the image of God, kept as the apple of God's eye (Ps. 17:8), and crowned with kingly glory and honor to be ruler over all things (Heb. 2:5–8; Gen. 1:28).

Recently a "sacralization of selfhood" has made self-realization central to many philosophies, psychologies, and theologies. The stress upon self-affirmation, subjectivity, self-consciousness, individualism, narcissism, personal freedom, and autonomy of the self has occurred at the expense of social integration, cohesion, stability, and responsibility.[1] The first and greatest cultural commandment today is, "Thou shalt love thyself," and almost every interpersonal problem is thought to be caused by someone's low self-esteem.[2]

According to the spirit of this decade, the ultimate sin is no longer the failure to honor God and thank him but the failure to esteem oneself. Self-abasement, not God-abasement, is the evil.[3]

Self-concepts, then are related to the well-being of both individuals and society. Let us examine some aspects of their development and significance, along with associated correlates and consequences.

THE DEVELOPMENT OF SELF-CONCEPTS

The self-concept of a person is whatever one means to oneself, whether the assumptions made are accurately consistent with the objective situation and are consciously expressed or not.[4] "The self-concept is thus the individual's fundamental frame of reference, the foundation on which almost all his actions are predicated."[5]

Each takes his personal identity so much for granted that he does not realize the extent to which his life is structured by the working conception he forms of himself. The things that a man does voluntarily, and in some cases even involuntarily, depend upon the assumptions he makes about the kind of person he is and about the way in which he fits into the scheme of things in his world. . . . A man is able to act with reasonable consistency in a wide variety of situations because of the relative stability of his self-conception.[6]

Despite this stability, the self-concept is never rigidly fixed; gradual modifications and occasionally sudden changes continue throughout life, for the self is an active coping agent, not an inert, passive object determined solely by external influences.[7]

The conception one has of oneself is formed so largely on the basis of relationships with others that Cooley described it as the "looking glass self." This involves a person's beliefs about what others see when they observe him or her, the imagination of their evaluation of such observations, and the resulting self-feeling of some form of either pride or abnegation.[8] To be sure, we are selective in our responses; we "couldn't care less" about what some people think. Certain people who are "significant others" to us have the greatest impact upon our self-concepts and behavior, and even among them some have more influence than others. Those who count the most are likely to be the members of our reference groups who think highly of us and maximize our self-esteem.[9] Self-conceptions thus develop through interaction with other people.

People who define themselves and their actions by supernatural reference groups, in addition to their earthly ones, believe themselves to have the endorsement of divine support as well as of significant others, so religious orientations may modify their self-definitions. One then may

define himself as having a destiny unbounded by earthly restriction, . . . as being an important cog in an eternal scheme of things. . . . When God is defined as ultimate and eternal there can be no higher reference.[10]

On the other hand, religious orientations may lead to viewing oneself as out of harmony with God's will, thus incurring God's disapproval, rejected by Deity as well as by people. The influence of religion upon self-concepts hence is not simply a consequence of ritualistic practices, sacraments that provide one with a religious group identity, and participation in the worship and other activities of a congregation. The intentions, expectations, and internalized meanings of participants in the same or similar groups may vary widely, so the impact of Christian practices upon self-definitions differs among the various Protestant denominations and their subgroups as well as along the Protestant-Catholic-Orthodox dimension.[11]

The devout person who is oriented toward an all-inclusive sacred philosophy of life surely has a different type of interiorized self-concept from the individual whose thinking is completely secular. The unspiritual person cannot comprehend that which is spiritually discerned (1 Cor. 2:6–14). The meanings and quality associated with religious practices are related in turn to their social context, including theologically oriented ideals.

Thus practice is not conceived in Christianity as an abstract activity of man, but as a worship in which he offers his whole person, his body in living sacrifice, holy and acceptable to God. (Rom. 12:1)[12]

Despite the probable importance of religious identity, beliefs, and behavior to self-concepts, there has been very little study of the subject. Variables that deserve consideration for such research include diverse theological conceptions and related ritualistic and other behavior pertinent to doctrines like the nature and scope of salvation, predestination, worldliness, human nature, the kingdom of God, and evangelism and the theodicies and paradoxes associated with love and justice, sin and righteousness, and heaven and hell. Problems of semantics would be considerable in such research, for certain words have almost diametrically opposite meanings, emotional connotations, and symbolic implications in different groups.

THE SIGNIFICANCE OF SELF-CONCEPTS

Everything that people do can be viewed from the perspective of their self-concepts. They live to a considerable extent in an unseen world of meanings, imaginations, and mental response patterns as they relate themselves to others. Pictures in their minds[13] (of themselves, of "objective reality" or "facts," and of other people) significantly influence the ways in which they act. There is a wide variety of patterns by which people maximize their self-assertions or self-denials and weave together varying fabrics of life-affirmations and life-negations.[14] They respond attitudinally and behaviorally to themselves, others, God, and the world in terms of their socially shaped self-images.

Because of the straining for consistency in most people, the process of self-development includes a self-fulfilling prophecy. Once one has labeled or defined oneself negatively as evil, sinful, inferior, or inadequate, one tends to behave in a corresponding manner, and the same occurs when one has positive self-definitions as good, righteous, superior, or competent. The behavior, in turn, reinforces responses of other people in the same direction; this further strengthens efforts to behave consistently with the self-definition. The symbolic environment of verbally and nonverbally communicated expectations and meanings among interacting persons exerts a powerful impact upon self-conceptions, constituting a circular pattern of reinforcement. Whatever one believes oneself to be, he or she is rapidly becoming.

The drive for self-preservation includes far more than organic survival; it is oriented considerably toward protecting one's self-conception, which in turn is sustained by social interaction. People struggle for self-respect as well as for social status; this typically involves gratifications from living according to accepted standards, which usually are the standards of their society.[15] Even Rokeach, who emphasizes rationality as the dominant human characteristic, acknowledges that "consistency with self-esteem is probably a more compelling consideration than consistency with logic or reality."[16] Self-esteem is so important that when it is threatened by events leading to development of negative self-images, mental illness may result. Self-depreciation or "psychological self-mutilation" is a major link in the chain of causes that operate in a pattern of circular reinforcement to produce a neurosis.[17]

The fact that probably more research has been devoted to self-esteem than to all the other aspects of the self-concept combined . . . is no doubt attributable to the great relevance of self-esteem for emotional disturbance. . . .[18]

Possibly the most important single objective of the various psychoanalytic defense mechanisms (rationalization, projection, compensation, displacement or scapegoating, reaction formation, repression, etc.) is to defend self-conceptions and especially to protect self-esteem.[19] Self-delusion sometimes may seem the only alternative to complete apathy, depression, or suicide. Maintaining the integrity and value of the self at the cost of partial loss of contact with reality can be viewed as a form of "adjustment" that separates a person from the stark reality of a life situation in which there can be no self-satisfying action to bring some degree of recognition by others.[20]

People who lack access to the means for satisfying and significant life goals may lapse into the condition of normlessness and breakdown of societal values known as anomie.[21] Societal conditions thus influence self-orientations. Alienation (estrangement from oneself, other people, and God) similarly is related to societal conditions and associated self-orientations.[22]

The conviction that one has received divine attention and approval through a special call, vision, gift of healing, endowment of abilities, or other supernatural experience or sanction inevitably affects one's self-feelings.[23] It often provides a major part of the legitimation for charismatic leaders of religious, political, or other groups.[24]

Many "holy wars" have resulted, at least in part, from the conviction of a tribe, subcultural group, or nation that it has been anointed by God to eliminate his enemies. The semireligious "manifest destiny" of the United States, which has aimed to save the entire world for democracy and from Communism, reflects a national self-concept that is reflected in the minds of many citizens. The flaws of cultural imperialism, which often was linked with the Christian foreign missions movement, are thus related to self-concepts.

SELF-CONCEPTS AND CONVERSION

Conversion includes the development of new self-concepts. This is consistent with the biblical theme of being "born again," for at birth a new person is brought into the world. Whether it is gradual or sudden, Christian conversion ideally changes one from self-centeredness to thinking about the well-being of others, from vague belief to awareness of the presence of the Living God, from feelings of inadequacy to recognition that one has abilities or "gifts."[25] The convert views himself or herself as a different person ("a new creation," as described in 2 Cor. 5:17). The new self-concepts are reinforced by a new set of significant others who provide sympathetic support for the new outlook on one's self and the world.[26]

The social situation also changes. The convert may withdraw from or redefine the old environment with the help of new significant others. Testimonies of converts are replete with descriptions of how different the world looks since their experience. The process is not limited to Christian conversion; conversion to cults and the deprogramming process of reversing such conversions reflect similar processes.[27] Social influences are significantly involved in the spiritual experiences associated with conversion both before and after the event.[28] God seldom, if ever, works in the conversion process apart from the medium of people.

The expectation by either a convert or acquaintances that perfection of behavior is the result of conversion, seen as movement from the status of "sinner" to that of "saint," has contributed to many charges of hypocrisy against Christians and to feelings of doubt and insecurity about the reality of the conversion experience. The mistaken notion that saints are no longer sinners make many adopt a "holier-than-thou" attitude toward outsiders, demonstrating their "Christian love" only to those "brethren" who maintain a clear "separation from the world." Actually, the conversion experience is but the beginning of growth toward spiritual maturity. The narrower the scope of a group's definition of conversion and expectations of its consequences, the narrower will be the consequences of conversions among its constituency.

Conversion is three-dimensional. It is intellectual inasmuch as it regards our orientation to the intelligible and the true. It is moral inasmuch as it regards our orientation to the good. It is religious inasmuch as it regards our orientation to God. The three dimensions are distinct, so that conversion can occur in one dimension without occurring in the other two, or in two dimensions without occurring in the other one.[29]

Conversion may have additional dimensions as well, at least in terms of its consequences. Its many implications for social ethics may not be fully covered by the "moral," and it has experiential and emotional components. Christians, especially evangelicals and fundamentalists, need to ask themselves whether a person who is converted in but one dimension of life is truly converted in the biblical sense of the term. Perhaps so much attention has been given to the self-feelings and God-man aspects of justification that other highly significant dimensions have been overlooked. Misleading group interpretations of who are "the saved" spill over into individuals' self-concepts. The worldview of "from what" and "for what" one can be redeemed varies widely from one religious group to another.[30] There is much vagueness, confusion, and double-talk about the meaning and nature of conversion,[31] so there is much disagreement about the definition, goals, methods, and anticipated outcomes in behavior and self-concepts of evangelism.[32] The different answers among religious groups are both an interactive cause and consequence of other observable differences evident in our pluralistic society.

CORRELATES AND CONSEQUENCES OF RELIGIOUS SELF-IMAGES

Wholesome self-images can insulate people against delinquent behavior.[33] The most important explanation for the unusually high level of success of the Teen Challenge program in resocializing drug addicts, criminals, juvenile delinquents, prostitutes, alcoholics, and other deviants is the change in self-concept that occurs as training center students realize that they are whole persons with inherent worth. The inner change produces a feeling of success and a realistic self-image.[34]

The therapeutic implications of wholesome self-concepts are evident also in the human potential movement, which simultaneously treats the psyche and the soma.[35] Social worker Larry Renetzky has gone even further in his marriage and family counseling; to the biological, psychological, and sociological dimensions of life, he adds "the Fourth Dimension," which centers around such components as meaning, purpose, and fulfillment, the will to live, and faith in self, others, and a power beyond self. He concludes that "the Fourth Dimension embodies, and even directs, much of the successful counseling that is done. . . . [O]ne's spiritual well-being directly or indirectly affects all of his or her life . . . with a rippling effect."[36]

In our era of relatively high rootlessness, religious affiliation is one of the major sources of personal identity for many people, particularly those in the more orthodox, sectarian, and evangelical religious groups.[37] That may be why research shows that

Quality of life, as measured by self-esteem and spiritual well-being, was [found to be] consistently related to those doctrinal, liturgical, devotional and organizational beliefs and behaviors which emphasize God's affirmation and acceptance of the individual, personal communion with God that is positive, and a sense of being in a caring community (koinonia). [38]

Elkind has concluded that religious self-identity passes through three distinct stages during childhood. Beginning with a global, nominal, undifferentiated impression of denominational identity as a kind of family name, it moves into a more concrete and clear-cut functional conception of religious identity based upon what people do (such as, going to church) without an awareness of why they do it, and finally into a stage more like that of adults in which the religious identity is an inner, subjective reality and not merely an objective, outward form.[39] The stages of faith development, which Fowler is developing, may share some common elements,[40] and the "transcending process" related to spiritual well-being during the later years of life can provide a person with an area of ascendance when other domains of experience decline.[41]

Cultivation of the spiritual life through the exercises of St. Ignatius Loyola has a significant integrative effect on the self-systems of Jesuit novices.[42] It is likely that the same results occur among other populations as well, even though the relationship has not yet been tested. We know, for example, that religious faith and practices make significant contributions to the sense of well-being among the elderly, so we can hypothesize that they relate to self-esteem as well.[43] Similarly, among Catholic adolescents from five different cultures, a positive relationship has been found between several measures of religiosity and self-esteem.[44]

Hence we can predict that where levels of spiritual well-being are high, self-esteem also will be high, and vice versa. Meaning in life is a linking concept, correlating with both.[45] The exhilaration associated with spiritual well-being can take a person out of himself or herself, shedding self-concern in social and spiritual union with others and in the "spiritual intoxication" of the assurance of salvation.[46] Even in a complex, urbanized, pluralistic society of "symbolic migrants"—people who lack a single, overarching collectivity to command their allegiance, uprooted and displaced by the absence of an abiding moral universe or a recognized religious world—it is possible for one to cultivate an interiorized spiritual life that has the integrity "of acting rather than merely reacting, of being a source, an origin, an initiator" and that is characterized by joy, satisfying solutions to questions of identity and meaning, and "a sense of being bound by symbols which enrich as well as express his life."[47]

CONCLUSION

The self never exists in isolation from other people. It is developed through socialization processes and continually modified and shaped throughout the entire life span in relationships with other people. Self-concepts are highly dependent upon the symbolic interaction that occurs in social contexts. A person's religious experiences and perspectives are to a considerable extent a consequence of social influences, but they also are among the sources of self-images, whether of esteem or degradation. All of the piecemeal evidence available to date suggests that cultivation of spiritual well-being is one of the most important means for enhancing self-esteem.

Three proverbs summarize some of the most important principles about self-concepts.[48] First, "For as [a man] thinketh in his heart, so is he" (Prov.

23:7). That is, our conception of self makes us what we are; outward appearances are often less important than inner orientations. Second, "Keep thy heart with all diligence; for out of it are the issues of life" (Prov. 4:23). In other words, our integration of self flows from holding proper values. And third, "As in water, face answereth to face, so the heart of man to man" (Prov. 27:19). Which means simply that our conditioning of self is influenced by others.

NOTES

1. For a sociological interpretation of these perspectives, see Hans Mol, *Identity and the Sacred* (Agincourt, Canada: Book Society of Canada Ltd., 1976), especially pp. 142–165.
2. John Piper, "Is Self-Love Biblical?" *Christianity Today* 21 (August 12, 1977): 1150–1153.
3. Ibid., p. 1150.
4. Tamotsu Shibutani, *Society and Personality* (Englewood Cliffs, N.J.: Prentice-Hall, 1961), pp. 230–234.
5. Morris Rosenberg, *Conceiving the Self* (New York: Basic Books, 1979), p. 59. This is the most comprehensive survey and interpretation of research findings on self-concepts.
6. Shibutani, *Society and Personality*, p. 215.
7. Rosenberg, *Conceiving the Self*, pp. 193, 259. See also Anselm Strauss, "Transformations of Identity," *Human Behavior and Social Processes*, ed. Arnold M. Rose (Boston: Houghton Mifflin Co., 1962), pp. 63–85.
8. Charles Horton Cooley, *Human Nature and the Social Order* (New York: Charles Scribner's Sons, 1922), pp. 183–185.
9. Rosenberg, *Conceiving the Self*, pp. 83–98.
10. Glenn M. Vernon, *Sociology of Religion* (New York: McGraw-Hill, 1962), pp. 97, 99.
11. Roger Mehl, *The Sociology of Protestantism* trans. James H. Farley (Philadelphia: Westminster Press, 1970), pp. 110–121.

12. Mehl, *The Sociology of Protestantism*, p. 135.
13. Walter Lippman, *Public Opinion* (New York: Macmillan, 1922).
14. Fascinating autobiographical sketches illustrating these are in Donald and Walter H. Capps, eds., *The Religious Personality* (Belmont, Calif.: Wadsworth Publishing Co., 1970).
15. Shibutani, *Society and Personality*, pp. 465–466.
16. Milton Rokeach, *Beliefs, Attitudes and Values* (San Francisco: Jossey-Bass, 1968), p. 164.
17. Arnold M. Rose, "A Social-Psychological Theory of Neurosis," *Human Behavior and Social Processes* ed. Arnold M. Rose (Boston: Houghton Mifflin Co., 1962), pp. 537–549.
18. Rosenberg, *Conceiving the Self*, p. 55.
19. Ibid., pp. 55–57, 260; Shibutani, *Society and Personality*, pp. 438–447.
20. Rose, "A Social-Psychological Theory of Neurosis," p. 548.
21. Dorothy L. Meier and Wendell Bell, "Anomia and Differential Access to the Achievement of Life Goals," *American Sociological Review* 22 (April, 1959): 189–202. See also J. Milton Yinger, "On Anomie," *Journal for the Scientific Study of Religion* 3 (April, 1964): 158–173.
22. Merton P. Strommen, "Alienation and Gratification in Religious Education," *Social Compass* 17 (1970): 439–443.
23. Vernon, *Sociology of Religion*, p. 195.
24. Max Weber, *The Theory of Social and Economic Organization* (Glencoe, Ill.: Free Press, 1964), pp. 358–359.

25. William S. Hill, "The Psychology of Conversion," *Pastoral Psychology* 6 (November, 1955): 43–46.
26. Shibutani, *Society and Personality,* pp. 141–142. See also Kurt and Gladys E. Lang, "Collective Dynamics: Process and Form," *Human Behavior and Social Processes,* ed. Arnold M. Rose (Boston: Houghton Mifflin Co., 1962), pp. 340–359, especially pp. 354–355.
27. See, for example, Donald Stone, "New Religious Consciousness and Personal Religious Experience," *Sociological Analysis* 39 (Summer, 1978): 123–134; Byong-suh Kim, "Religious Deprogramming and Subjective Reality," *Sociological Analysis* 40 (Fall, 1979): 197–207; V. Bailey Gillespie, *Religious Conversion and Personal Identity* (Birmingham, Ala.: Religious Education Press, 1979).
28. Cf. James T. Duke and D. Wayne Brown, Jr., "Three Paths to Spiritual Well-Being among the Mormons: Conversion, Obedience, and Repentance," *Spiritual Well-Being: Sociological Perspectives,* ed. David O. Moberg (Washington, D. C.: University Press of America, 1979), pp. 173–189.
29. Bernard Lonergan, S. J., *Doctrinal Pluralism* (Milwaukee: Marquette University Press, 1971), p. 34.
30. Max Weber, *From Max Weber: Essays in Sociology,* eds. and trans. H. H. Gerth and C. Wright Mills (New York: Oxford University Press, 1946), pp. 280–282.
31. Paul B. Maves, "Conversion: A Behavioral Category," *Review of Religious Research* 5 (Fall, 1963): 41–48.
32. David O. Moberg, *The Great Reversal: Evangelism and Social Concern,* rev. ed. (Philadelphia: Lippincott, 1977), pp. 67–85.
33. Walter C. Reckless, Simon Dinitz, and Barbara Kay, "The Self Component in Potential Delinquency and Potential Non-Delinquency," *American Sociological Review* 22 (October, 1957): 566–570; Michael Schwartz and Sandra S. Tangri, "A Note on Self-Concept as an Insulator against Delinquency," *American Sociological Review* 30 (December, 1965): 922–926.
34. LeRoy Gruner, "Phasic Progression of Self-Esteem in Teen Challenge—Cross Culturally," paper presented at the annual meeting of the Society for the Scientific Study of Religion, San Antonio, Tex., October 26–28, 1979.
35. Herbert A. Otto, "Toward a Wholistic Psychotherapy, Counseling, and Social Work Treatment Program," *Dimensions in Wholistic Healing,* eds. Herbert A. Otto and James W. Knight (Chicago: Nelson-Hall, 1979), pp. 125–140.
36. Larry Renetzky, "The Fourth Dimension: Applications to the Social Services," *Spiritual Well-Being: Sociological Perspectives,* ed. David O. Moberg (Washington, D.C.: University Press of America, 1979), pp. 215–228 (quotation from p. 227).
37. See Mol, *Identity and the Sacred;* Hans Mol, ed., *Identity and Religion* (Beverly Hills, Calif.: Sage Publications, 1978); Roland Robertson and Burkart Holzner, eds., *Identity and Authority* (New York: St. Martin's Press, 1979).
38. Craig W. Ellison and Tom Economos, "Religious Experience and Quality of Life," paper presented at the annual meeting of the Christian Association for Psychological Studies, San Diego, Calif., April, 1981, p. 16.
39. David Elkind, "Age Changes in the Meaning of Religious Identity," *Review of Religious Research* 6 (Fall, 1964): 36–40.
40. James W. Fowler, *Stages of Faith* (San Francisco: Harper & Row, 1981).
41. Earl D. C. Brewer, "Life Stages and Spiritual Well-Being," *Spiritual Well-Being: Sociological Perspectives,* ed. David O. Moberg (Washington, D.C.: University Press of America, 1979), pp. 99–111.
42. Howard L. Sacks, "The Effect of Spiritual Exercises on the Integration of Self-System," *Journal for the Scientific Study of Religion* 18 (March, 1979): 46–50.
43. See David O. Moberg, *Spiritual Well-Being: Background and Issues* (Wash-

ington, D.C.: White House Conference on Aging, 1971); and Robert M. Gray and David O. Moberg, *The Church and the Older Person*, rev. ed. (Grand Rapids, Mich.: Eerdmans, 1977), pp. 75–120.

44. Christopher B. Smith, Andrew J. Weigert, and Darwin L. Thomas, "Self-Esteem and Religiosity: An Analysis of Catholic Adolescents from Five Cultures," *Journal for the Scientific Study of Religion* 18 (March, 1979): 51–60.

45. See Larry M. Hynson, Jr., "Spiritual Well-Being and Integration in Taiwan," *Spiritual Well-Being: Sociological Perspectives*, ed. David O. Moberg (Washington, D.C.: University Press of America, 1979), pp. 281–289.

46. Harold Fallding, "Spiritual Well-Being as a Variety of Good Morale," in David O. Moberg (ed.), *Spiritual Well-Being: Sociological Perspectives* (Washington, DC: University Press of America, 1979), pp. 23–40.

47. Carroll J. Bourg, "Individuation, Interiority, and Spiritual Traditions," *Spiritual Well-Being: Sociological Perspectives*, ed. David O. Moberg (Washington, D.C.: University Press of America, 1979), pp. 15–22 (quotations from pp. 17, 22).

48. These quotations are from the King James Version; other translations vary, particularly on the first, but they illustrate the same principles.

BIOGRAPHICAL SKETCH

DAVID O. MOBERG is a professor of sociology at Marquette University in Milwaukee, Wisconsin. He received his Ph.D. in sociology from the University of Minnesota. He is the author of *The Church as a Social Institution, The Great Reversal: Evangelism and Social Concern, Inasmuch: Christian Social Responsibility in the Twentieth Century, Spiritual Well-Being: Background and Issues, The Church and the Older Person* (with Robert M. Gray), and he is the editor of *Spiritual Well-Being: Sociological Perspectives*. He has published about 300 articles in professional journals, books, and periodicals in the fields of sociology, religion, gerontology, and related areas. He is president of the Religious Research Association and a former president of the Association for the Sociology of Religion and the Wisconsin Sociological Association.

Narcissism and Loss of Self-Worth

C. MARKHAM BERRY

ANY consideration of the idea of self-esteem presupposes that we know what we mean when we say "self." The question, "Who am I?" is asked by children. It is repeated by teenagers. Young adults echo it when they are first seeking a career, and mature individuals face it with a renewed urgency again at mid-life. The reader has already found in preceding discussions in this book that even a definition of "self" can become difficult to pin down precisely. As the analyst Lynd has said, "The terms 'self' and 'ego' slide around like shiny balls under glass in a child's puzzle, which, no matter how the board is tilted, refuse to stay lodged in any particular hollows."[1]

There does seem though, to be an inner consciousness of ourselves in all of us—as a body, as a series of sensations and thoughts, as a part of many communities, and as a being of meaning and purpose. How clear this self is, how much it is fleshed out with specific details so that we can really know ourselves is another matter. Erik Erikson has taught us to look at our identity as a process that continues, more or less stepwise, throughout our life.[2] This has certainly been the experience of most of us who are older.

Everyone, then, has some sense of self. However, the form that this self takes seems to vary greatly from person to person. When we deal with people in depth, as in therapy, we find that distortions and confusions are common. Many seem to have vague and fluctuating concepts of their innermost selves. Others see themselves very unrealistically. In either case, we can be confident that the patient has a serious problem with self-esteem.

It is in the particular context of a patient in therapy that psychoanalysts make their observations. In recent years, much of their attention has been focused on the self and disturbances in its formation. Their research has been extremely fruitful in many ways, but also has stirred up a good deal of controversy. The purpose of this chapter is to add to our discussion of self-esteem some of the rich insights that have come out of this thinking.

The term generally used for this field of research has been "object relations theory." A good place to start will be to define this particular expression. "Objects" refer in psychoanalytic thought to the internal mental models we have of people and things. In ordinary language, objects would refer to inanimate things and not people, but because we manage both in our heads in a similar way, the term has become useful when applied to persons.

Healthy adults should form clear mental images of the people they know. The "internal object" is a reasonably accurate facsimile of the "external object," or the real person in his or her own place. There is a clear separation between the "self-object" and the object formed of another. Mature adults should have a capacity to "see," rather clearly, both themselves and others from some distance, allowing both integrity and respect.

This ability to know oneself in much the same way as we know others is the basis of what is called *introspection*. Mature introspection will allow us to feel our own feelings and yet, at the same time, see ourselves, to some extent, as others see us.

In addition, mature adults have the capacity to be separate from, and yet relate to, these internal other-objects. Others should not be viewed as extensions of the self, objects subsidiary to it, but as individuals of separate identity, which are valued as such. This ability to know another in much the same way one knows himself is the basis of *empathy*. To empathize, one feels to some degree how things affect another.

With these definitions in mind, let's go back to the patient on the analyst's couch. In recent years, more and more people seek help for problems stemming from serious disturbances in the formation and manipulation of these internal objects. These disorders seem to fall in two related but distinguishable syndromes, or symptom patterns.

The first of these syndromes involves a marked imbalance that tilts the whole object world toward the self. There is difficulty in allowing others, particularly important others, to have a respected, distinct integrity. The "I" becomes the very center of existence, and others are extensions in one way or another. Instead of being able to see oneself as a member of a larger body (say, a marriage or a family), others are bent and distorted to serve one's own needs and desires.

This self-centered pattern is referred to as *narcissism*. The word comes from the mythological Narcissus, who fell in love with his own image.[3] As handy as this label is for descriptive purposes, it erroneously implies an overabundance of self-love. Actually, narcissistic people have as much trouble loving themselves as others. It is more useful to understand the process in terms of disturbed object relations.

When we think about this, though, we realize that all of us struggle with self-centeredness. To this extent, narcissism can be considered a normal part of being human. Therapists, however, ordinarily save the term for those in whom the centering process has become serious enough to disturb relationships with those in intimate circles of life.

The second pathological pattern in disturbed object formation, commonly seen in therapy of any kind, is the inability to form stable, even moderately coherent images of the self and others. Instead of a "me" inside, there is a big question mark. Without such a center, one is forced to identify himself or herself by more superficial things, such as appearance, accomplishments, roles, and masks. Who such people feel themselves to be, then, is determined largely by the treatment they receive, the success they attain, or even their appearance. Such people would then find their self-objects varying from one circumstance to another, from one time to another. Even more painfully, who one is, will be determined largely by others. Failures in performance, or even mild insults, become a threat to identity itself. This is the basis of the sensitivity to being put down or controlled which is characteristic of narcissism.

As it works out, the self in these patients tends to be experienced in two very different ways. On the one hand, there is a grandiose self who is attractive, clever, and successful. Alternately, there is another self who is ugly, dumb, awkward, and fearfully waiting for someone to discover these shortcomings. This tendency to see oneself and others as good and bad, as unrealistically grand and also as worthless, is called *splitting*.

Again, if we are honest, most of us would admit to having to struggle with this tendency also, at least on occasion. Any kind of emotional disturbance tends to increase a tendency toward splitting, but where it persists and is serious enough to prevent the formation of more realistic images, it becomes an earmark of what is called the *borderline personality*. Most of us are not really pure black or white, but fall into some shade of gray. Gray is a hard color for the borderline person to identify.

People with borderline and narcissistic personality disorders, then, in the first place, tend to find intimate relationships difficult or impossible to form. Everyone is disconcertively shifting and chameleonlike. They see themselves and others as wearing various masks or taking on different roles. They are like the Greek God Proteus, who assumed so many forms (wild boar, lion, dragon, fire, and flood, to name a few) that he was unable to commit himself to the one most his own and carry out his prophetic function.[4] They are insecure, tense, and lonely. Largely for these reasons, they suffer from a primitive and profound loss of self-esteem.

EARLY DEVELOPMENT

How do these pathological processes develop in the person of narcissistic or borderline personality—what goes wrong that allows this to happen? To attempt to answer these questions, we must make a previous decision as to what forces shape any of us into what we are. Psychoanalysts see adult pathology as rooted in a complex of influences in the very early life of the infant and child. Adult problems come from *arrests* (hang-ups) or *regressions* to earlier developmental phases. It is assumed that, should we provide an adequate emotional environment or "good enough" mothering,[5] these steps of development will precede in an orderly fashion without hitches. To understand the narcissistic or borderline adult, then, we will need to identify those early infantile processes that are played back in the adult. Further, we will need to point to influences that cause a given individual to arrest or regress in this way. On the basis of these, then, a logical approach to helping them can be suggested.

There are two sources of investigation that have greatly illuminated for us the early life of the infant. The first of these has been from ethology and a group of researchers who view the human infant much as they would any other animal. They tend to see instinct as the primary molding force at work. They have shown us the infant's need for the physical touch of the mother, for cuddling and play.[6] They describe attachment bonds that emotionally support and stimulate the child to grow beyond this dependency.[7]

Other groups of investigators have studied in great depth very disturbed, psychotic children. From these observations, a picture has been pieced together of what the experience of the infant must be like. Margaret Mahler pictures this eloquently and rather completely, bringing together the thinking of many others who preceded her.[8] She describes the initial encounter of the infant with life as being "oceanic," without differentiation. Out of this homogenous mist, certain events, sensations, and emotions begin to form and be remembered. These fragments then tend to coalesce as part-objects. She sees this process occurring under tremendous tension from those powerful primitive drives identified by Freud as love-sex (or *libido*) and aggression. Attempts to form objects in this turbulent, charged brew proceed along two axes: one, a good-bad distinction, or pleasure and unpleasure, and the other, the object distinction of mother and self. For a period then, there will be partially formed objects of good-mother, bad-mother, good-me, and bad-me. As the infant's complicated neurological system develops, he gradually stabilizes these fragments into constant self-object and other-objects, which are realistic mixtures of good and bad. To actually accomplish this, there must be a warm emotional environment that is supportive enough to develop a foundation of confidence and competence. A mother who enjoys the infant's dependency, but also encourages early efforts of independence, shows her child that she has confidence in and appreciates him or her. It is in this nurture that the seeds of self-esteem are planted.

Later this "good enough mother" will permit limited frustrations and tolerate early aggressions from the infant. These, in turn, enable the child to draw clear boundary lines between the two objects. The self-respect and empathy of the primary caregiver encourages the child to discover that important vantage point, outside of self and sensations, from which he or she can introspect and empathize.

This process is generally called one of *separation-individuation.* The goal is to raise a child who is aware of his or her separateness, but free to relate intimately with those close to him or her. A failure in separation leaves hampering residuals of the earlier fusion state. These tend to make relationships that are alternately too sticky or too cold. In one, the mother is an extension, subservient to the child; in the other, a distant relationship forms where there is a fear of intimacy. Intimacy threatens these latter individuals both with a fusion-dependency and with a loss of what freedom and identity has already been developed.

This process normally moves gradually from a universal self-centeredness toward a balanced, realistic view of self and others. When objects stabilize and a moral structure is added to the system, the person has laid down a constant and predictable foundation from which he or she can proceed through the further developmental challenges of life.

The narcissistic pathology described earlier, then, can be seen as a regression to these early experiences in which stable and clear objects were being formed. We enjoy a young child who loves passionately, who is furious when he is frustrated, and regally grandiose. We recognize these as precursors of adult self-confidence. But we must grow away from this childishness. Unrealistic idealization and self-centeredness in the adult is a mark of illness.

We still have not discussed why things go wrong in the development of the narcissistic personality. What is the nature of the psychopathological process?

PATHOLOGY

Analysts recently tend to divide into two camps on this question, each of the two camps describing a different aspect of growth. Both groups understand normal development similarly, but each emphasizes a different aspect as being most important.

The first of these views is more traditionally Freudian in its view and centers around drives. It emphasizes the vicissitudes of libido and aggression. In therapeutic work, analysts with this view preferentially focus on the intrapsychic defenses of the ego in handling drives. Freud, in *On Narcissism: An Introduction,* described this early developmental state, or state of *primary narcissism,* in dynamic terms in this way:

Thus we form the idea of there being an original libidenal cathexis of the ego, from which some is later given off to objects, but which fundamentally persists and is related to the object-cathexis much as the body of an amoeba is related to the pseudopodia which it puts out.[9]

It is the withdrawal of these investments of libido from external objects and their reinvestment in the self-object that produces the "hypercathexis of the self," or the tilt toward the self-object of *secondary narcissism.*

Freud sees further that our efforts to channel these high voltage currents are the primary source of difficulty, and he also offers us a handle for helping the person:

We have recognized our mental apparatus as being first and foremost a device designed for mastering excitations which would otherwise be felt as distressing or would have pathogenic effects. Working them over in the mind helps remarkably toward an internal draining away of excitations which are incapable of direct discharge outwards, or for which such a discharge is for the moment undesirable.[10]

These efforts at mastery are usually thought of as *defense mechanisms.* Defenses are necessary for our internal peace, but in one way or another they distort reality. Many of these distortions can be clearly seen in the narcissistic personality.

In this lively contemporary discussion, Otto Kernberg has added to Freud's original insight light from his own observations and a great body of psychoanalytic thought which has been published since the turn of the century.[11] He, for example, works out in great detail how the primitive idealization, omnipotence, and grandiosity, as well as the denials, introjections, and projectiòns that are seen in narcissism, are actually efforts to maintain defensive operations. Splitting is primarily defensive and is seen in combination with many of these other defense mechanisms. Kernberg makes his case compellingly and supports it broadly and clinically.

The other school of thought also originates in Freudian insight. In my opinion, however, it makes a significant deviation from it, at least in emphasis. In recent years, this position has been stated in somewhat esoteric language, but nonetheless forcefully, by Heintz Kohut of Chicago.[12] Kohut focuses our attention on the early formation of objects as described above. He particularly emphasizes the idealization and grandiosity associated with these early good-mother/good-self part-objects. He further shows how failures in this maturation process distort adult relationships, especially the relationship between the patient and therapist. This is the center of his psychoanalytic work. Kohut has also shed light on the role of empathy in the developing infant, in the mother, and in the therapist. Insufficient empathy in the emotional environment of the infant is seen as the major source of the deficiencies of self-esteem in the adult. Psychoanalytic work, then, would center on the transference, interpreting to the patient the distortions that occur in the way the patient sees the therapist.

My own work has also focused on deficiencies of empathy and introspection in the psychopathology of narcissism and self-esteem.[13] My concern has been with attempting to understand the influence of inborn defects in the capacity of the individual to sense and identify these experiences. There is a striking correlation between one's empathic and introspective abilities and the amount of narcissism one struggles with. A similar but inverse correlation exists between these two and self-esteem. A lack of empathy within the emotional environment of the infant, which is also frequently present in narcissism, tends to augment this deficit rather than cause it.

However we approach it, it is clear that self-esteem, which at first glance seemed simple, actually depends on very complex developmental and experiential mechanisms. All views seem to teach us that our self-esteem develops in the warm and subtle give-and-take of communication with those who are intimate. With or without success before the outside world, an underlying confident sense of self as competent and worthy of love comes from those close to our hearts. The restless efforts we make to heal the defects we feel in this esteem by making ourselves grand and worthy before the crowd are for the most part fruitless.

Therapy for low self-esteem, then, would logically be aimed at healing and deepening these close relationships. Treatment turns out to be difficult and prolonged under the best circumstances, but seems to proceed as long as we maintain a focus on the effective communication of thoughts and subtle feelings. As patients become more skilled at defining precisely and clearly their own feeling responses, and hear more accurately those responses of others, their narcissism decreases and their level of self-esteem escalates.

NOTES

1. H. M. Lynd, *On Shame and the Search for Identity* (New York: Harcourt Brace, 1958).
2. E. H. Erikson, *Identity and the Life Cycle* (New York: International Universities Press, 1959).
3. H. Spotnitz, "The Myths of Narcissus," *Psychoanalytic Review* 41 (1954): 173–181.
4. R. J. Lifton, "Protean Man," *Archives of General Psychiatry* 24 (1971): 298–304.
5. D. W. Winnicott, *The Child and the Outside World* (New York: Basic Books, 1957).
6. R. A. Spitz, *The First Year of Life* (New York: International Universities Press, 1965).
7. J. Bowlby, *Attachment* (New York: Basic Books, 1969).
8. M. Mahler, *The Psychological Birth of the Human Infant* (New York: Basic Books, 1975).
9. Sigmund Freud, "On Narcissism: An Introduction" [1914], *The Standard Edition* (London: Hogarth Press, 1957), pp. 14–85.
10. Ibid.
11. O. Kernberg, *Borderline Conditions and Pathological Narcissism* (New York: Jason Aronson, 1975).
12. H. Kohut, *The Analysis of the Self* (New York: International Universities Press, 1971).
13. C. M. Berry, "Narcissism," *Christian Association for Psychological Studies Bulletin* 6 (1980): 1–7.

BIOGRAPHICAL SKETCH

C. MARKHAM BERRY is currently assistant professor of psychiatry at Emory University School of Medicine. He is also a therapist at the Atlanta Counseling Center and a staff psychiatrist in the Department of Psychiatry at Grady Memorial Hospital in Atlanta, Georgia. He received his B.S. in medicine at Emory University and his M.D. from Emory University School of Medicine. He has been published in *CAPS Journal, Journal Psychology and Theology* (contributing editor), *Journal of the American Scientific Affiliation, Christian Medical Society Journal,* and *Atlanta Medicine.* He has been chairman of the Northwest Georgia Regional Health Advisory Council, president of the Christian Medical Society, and is certified by the American Board of Psychiatry and Neurology.

A New Look at Pride

DAVID G. MYERS

Poised somewhere between sinful vanity and self-destructive submissiveness is a golden mean of self-esteem appropriate to the human condition.

—STANFORD LYMAN[1]

OF THE benefits of high self-esteem, there is little doubt.[2] Those with positive self-image are happier, freer of ulcers and insomnia, less prone to drug and alcohol addictions. Researchers have also found that people whose egos are temporarily deflated—say, by being told that they did miserably on an intelligence test—are more likely then to derogate other people or even express heightened racial prejudice. More generally, people who are negative about themselves also tend to be negative about others. Low self-esteem can feed contemptuous attitudes.

Of the benefits of "positive thinking," there is also little doubt. Those who believe they can control their own destinies—who have what researchers in more than a thousand studies have called "internal locus of control" —achieve more, make more money, are less vulnerable to being manipulated.[3] Believe that things are beyond your control and they probably will be. Believe that you can do it, and maybe you will.

Knowing such to be true may encourage us not to resign to bad situations, to persist despite initial failures, to strive without being derailed by self-doubts. But as Pascal taught, no single truth is ever sufficient, because the world is not simple. Any truth, separated from its complementary truth, is a half-truth. That high self-esteem and positive thinking pay dividends is true. Equally true, though more often forgotten, are the pitfalls of pride. So let us examine social psychology's new version of ancient wisdom about the pervasiveness of pride.

THE SELF-SERVING BIAS

It is popularly believed that most of us suffer the "I'm not OK—you're OK" problem of low self-esteem. As Groucho Marx put it, "I'd never join any club that would accept a person like me." Carl Rogers described this low self-image problem when objecting to Reinhold Niebuhr's idea that original sin is self-love and pretension. To the contrary, declared Rogers, "the central core of difficulty in people as I have come to know them . . . is that in the great majority of cases they despise themselves, regard themselves as worthless and unlovable."[4] The evidence, however, now indicates that Niebuhr was much closer to the truth. As writer William Saroyan put it, "Every man is a good man in a bad world—as he himself knows." Researchers are debating the reasons for this phenomenon of "self-serving bias," but they now generally agree that the phenomenon is both genuine and potent. Eight streams of data merge to form a powerful river of evidence.

Stream #1: Accepting More Responsibility for Success Than Failure

Time and again, experimenters have found that people readily accept credit when told they have succeeded (attributing the success to their ability and effort), yet attribute failure to such external factors as bad luck or the problem's inherent "impossibility."[5] Similarly, in explaining their victories, athletes have been observed to credit themselves, but are more likely to attribute losses to something else: bad breaks, bad officiating, the other team's super effort.[6] And how much responsibility do you suppose car drivers tend to accept for their accidents? On insurance forms, drivers have described their accidents in words such as these: "An invisible car came out of nowhere, struck my car, and vanished"; "As I reached an intersection, a hedge sprang up, obscuring my vision and I did not see the other car"; and "A pedestrian hit me and went under my car." Situations that combine skill and chance (such as games, exams, and job applications) are especially prone to the phenomenon: winners can easily attribute their success to their skill, while losers can attribute their losses to chance.[7] When I win at Scrabble, it is because of my verbal dexterity; when I lose, it is because, "Who could get anywhere with a Q but no U?"

Michael Ross and Fiore Sicoly at the University of Waterloo observed a marital version of the self-serving bias.[8] They found that married people usually gave themselves more credit for such activities as cleaning the house and caring for the children than their spouses were willing to give them credit for. Every night, my wife and I pitch our laundry at the bedroom clothes hamper. In the morning, one of us puts them in. Recently she suggested that I take more responsibility for this. Thinking that I already did so 75 percent of the time, I asked her how often she thought she picked up the clothes. "Oh," she replied, "about 75 percent of the time."

Stream #2: Constructing Favorably Biased Self-Ratings

It appears that on nearly any dimension that is both subjective and socially desirable, most people see themselves as better than average. For example, most American business people see themselves as more ethical than the average American business person.[9] Most community residents see themselves as less prejudiced than others in their communities.[10] Most Americans perceive themselves as more intelligent than their average peer.[11] Most French people perceive themselves as superior to their peers in a variety of socially desirable ways.[12]

The College Board recently invited the million high school seniors who took its aptitude test to indicate "how you feel you compare with other people your own age in certain areas of ability."[13] Judging from the students' responses, it appears that America's high school seniors are not wracked with inferiority feelings. While 60 percent reported themselves as better than average in "athletic ability," only 6 percent felt themselves to be below average. In "leadership ability," 70 percent rated themselves as above average, 2 percent as below average. In "ability to get along with others," *o percent* of the 829,000 students who responded rated themselves below average, 60 percent rated themselves in the top 10 percent, and 25 percent saw themselves among the top 1 percent!

Note how radically at odds these findings are with the notion that most of us have low self-esteem. We are, to be sure, strongly motivated to maintain and enhance our self-esteem, and therefore we will welcome nearly any message that helps us do so. But most of us are not grovelling about with feelings that everyone else is better than we are. To paraphrase Elizabeth Barrett Browning, the question seems rather to be, "How do I love me? Let me count the ways."

Stream #3: Believing Phony Compliments

The "Barnum effect" was named in honor of P. T. Barnum, who said that "there's a sucker born every minute" and that a good circus has a "little something for everybody." Consider the following, which is intended to be a description that fits most people:

You have a strong need for other people to like you and for them to admire you. You have a tendency to be critical of yourself. You have a great deal of unused energy, which you have not turned to your advantage. While you have some personality weaknesses, you are generally able to compensate for them. Your sexual adjustment has presented some problems for you. Disciplined and controlled on the outside, you tend to be worrisome and insecure inside. At times, you have serious doubts as to whether you have made the right decision or done the right thing. You prefer a certain amount of change and variety and become dissatisfied when hemmed in by restrictions and limitations. You pride yourself on being an independent thinker and do not accept other opinions without satisfactory proof. You have found it unwise to be too frank in revealing yourself to others. At times, you are extroverted, affable, sociable, while at other times you are introverted, wary, and reserved. Some of your aspirations tend to be pretty unrealistic.

In many experiments, B. R. Forer, C. R. Snyder, and others have shown people such descriptions, drawn from statements in horoscope books.[14] Told, as were you, that the information is true of most individuals, people usually indicate that it fits so-so. But if told that the description is designed specifically for them on the basis of their psychological tests or astrological data, people usually say the description is very accurate. Moreover, people see these "Barnum descriptions" as more true of themselves than of people in general, *especially* when the description is positive. If favorable, the description will be readily believed by most people, regardless of whether it is said to come from an experienced clinician, their fellow students, a psychological test, or a horoscope. Do people ever distinguish between credible and nontrustworthy sources? Yes—when the feedback is negative.[15]

So here is more evidence of a self-serving bias. Within reason, the more favorable a phony personality description is, the more people believe it and the more likely they are to perceive it as uniquely theirs.[16]

Stream #4: Revising One's Past to Fit the Present

We also maintain favorably biased ideas of ourselves by remembering our past in ways consistent with our current attitudes. For example, in research at the University of Waterloo, Michael Ross and his colleagues exposed some students to a message that was designed to convince them of the desirability of frequent toothbrushing.[17] Shortly afterwards, in a supposedly different experiment, these students recalled brushing their teeth more often during the preceeding two weeks than did other students who had not heard the message. Noting the similarity of such findings to happenings in George Orwell's *1984*—where it was "necessary to remember that events happened in the desired manner"—social psychologist Anthony Greenwald surmises that we all have "totalitarian egos" that continually revise our past in order to preserve our positive self-evaluations.[18]

Stream #5: Falling into Self-Justification

If an undesirable action cannot be forgotten, misremembered, or undone, then often it is justified. If social psychological research has established anything, it is that our past actions influence our current attitudes.[19] Every time we act, we amplify the idea lying behind what we have done, especially when we feel some responsibility for having committed the act. In experiments, people who harm someone—by delivering electric shocks, for example—tend later to express disdain for their victim. Such self-justification is all the more dangerous when manifest in group settings: Iran justified its taking of hostages as a just response to morally reprehensible American policies in Iran; the United States saw the moral lunacy on the other side. So everyone felt righteous, and a standoff occurred.

Stream #6: Believing in One's Personal Infallibility

Researchers who study human thinking have often observed that people overestimate the accuracy of their beliefs and judgments. So consistently does this happen that one prominent researcher has referred to this human tendency as "cognitive conceit." Here are two examples of such.

The I-knew-it-all-along phenomenon. As Baruch Fischhoff and others have demonstrated, we often do not expect something to happen until it does, at which point we overestimate our ability to have predicted it.[20] People told the outcome of an experimental or historical situation are less surprised at the outcome than people told only about the situation and its possible outcomes.

If the I-knew-it-all-along phenomenon is pervasive, you may be feeling now that you "knew it all along." Almost any result of a psychological experiment can seem like common sense—after you know the result. The phenomenon can be crudely demonstrated by giving half of a group some purported psychological finding and the other half the opposite result. For example:

Social psychologists have found that whether choosing friends or falling in love, we are most attracted to people whose traits are different from our own. There seems to be wisdom in the old saying that "opposites attract."

Social psychologists have found that whether choosing friends or falling in love, we are most attracted to people whose traits are similar to our own. There seems to be wisdom in the old saying that "birds of a feather flock together."

It is my experience that when fifty people are given one of the above "findings," another fifty are given the opposite "finding," and all are asked to "explain" the result and then indicate whether it is "surprising" or "not surprising," virtually all one hundred people will claim that the result they were given is "not surprising."

The overconfidence phenomenon. The intellectual conceit evident in our judgments of our past knowledge (the I-knew-it-all-along phenomenon) extends to estimates of our current knowledge. Daniel Kahneman and Amos Tversky have given people factual questions, asking them to fill in the blanks (for example, "I feel 98 percent certain that the number of cars imported into the United States in 1980 was more than _____ but less than _____ "), and found that people fail to recognize their own vulnerability to error.[21] For with regards to such questions, nearly 30 percent of the time the true answer is outside the range about which those questioned feel 98 percent confident. This overconfidence phenomenon has become an accepted fact among researchers. If people say the chances are 70 percent that their answer to a factual question is right, the odds are almost 50-50 that they will be wrong. Even if people feel 100 percent sure, they still err about 15 percent of the time.

Stream #7: Maintaining Unrealistic Optimism

Margaret Matlin and David Stang have amassed evidence pointing to a powerful "Pollyanna principle"—that people more readily perceive, remember, and communicate pleasant than unpleasant information.[22] Positive thinking predominates over negative thinking. In recent research with Rutgers University students, Neil Weinstein has further discerned a tendency toward "unrealistic optimism about future life events."[23] Most students perceived themselves as far more likely than their classmates to experience positive events (such as getting a good job, drawing a good salary, and owning a home) and as far less likely to experience negative events (such as getting divorced, having cancer, and being fired). Likewise, most college students believe they will easily outlive their actuarially predicted age of death[24] (which calls to mind Freud's joke about the man who told his wife, "If one of us should die, I think I would go live in Paris").

Stream #8: Overestimating How Desirably One Would Act

Researchers have discovered that, under certain conditions, most people will act in rather inconsiderate, compliant, or even cruel ways. When other similar people are told in detail about these conditions and asked to predict how *they* would act, nearly all insist that their own behavior would be far more virtuous. Similarly, when researcher Steven Sherman called residents of Bloomington, Indiana, and asked them to volunteer three hours to an American Cancer Society drive, only 4 percent agreed to do so.[25] But when a comparable group of other residents were called and asked to predict how they would react to such a request, almost half predicted they would help.

So, to summarize the argument thus far: It is true that high self-esteem and positive thinking are adaptive and desirable. But unless we close our eyes to a whole river of evidence, it also seems true that the most common *error* in people's self-images is not unrealistically low self-esteem, but rather a self-serving bias—not an inferiority complex, but, if you will, a superiority complex. In any satisfactory theory of self-esteem, these two "truths" must somehow coexist.

OBJECTIONS TO THE SELF-SERVING BIAS

Many readers have no doubt found this portrayal of the pervasiveness of pride either depressing or somehow contrary to what they have experienced and observed. Let us imagine some of their objections.

(1) *I hear lots of people being self-disparaging, and I'm sometimes hampered by inferiority feelings myself.* Let us see why this might be. First, those of us who exhibit the self-serving bias—and that's most of us—may nevertheless feel inferior to certain specific individuals, especially when we compare ourselves to someone who is a step or two higher on the ladder of success, attractiveness, or whatever. Thus we may *believe* ourselves to be relatively superior yet *feel* discouraged—because we fall short of certain others or fail to reach our own goals fully.

Second, not everyone has a self-serving bias. Some people *do* suffer from unreasonably low self-esteem. For example, several recent studies have found that while most people shuck off responsibility for their failures on a laboratory task, or perceive themselves as having been more in control than they were, depressed people are more accurate in their self-appraisal.[26] Sadder but wiser, they seem to be. There is also evidence that while most people see themselves more favorably than other people see them (thus providing yet another demonstration of the "normal" self-serving bias), depressed people see themselves *as* other people see them.[27] This prompts the unsettling thought that Pascal may have been right: "I lay it down as a fact that, if all men knew what others say of them, there would not be four friends in the world." And that truly is a depressing thought.[28]

Third, self-disparagement can be a self-serving tactic. As the French sage La Rochefoucauld detected, "Humility is often but a . . . trick whereby pride abases itself only to exalt itself later."[29] For example, most of us have learned that putting ourselves down is a useful technique for eliciting "strokes" from others. We know that a remark such as "I wish I weren't so ugly" will at least elicit a "Come now, I know a couple of people who are uglier than you." Researchers have also observed that people will aggrandize their opponents and disparage, or even handicap, themselves to convey an image of modesty and to protect themselves. This tactic provides both an excuse for failure and extra credit for success.[30] The coach who publicly extols the upcoming opponent's awesome strength renders a loss understandable, while a win becomes a praiseworthy achievement. Thus, self-disparagement can be subtly self-serving.

(2) *Perhaps all this "pride" is just an upbeat public display; underneath it, people may be suffering with miserable self-images.* Actually, when people must declare their feelings publicly, they present a more *modest* self-portrayal than when they are allowed to respond anonymously.[31] Other evidence also points to the conclusion that most people really do *see* themselves favorably and do not simply describe themselves that way to researchers. Self-serving bias is exhibited by children before they learn to inhibit their real feelings.[32] And if, as many researchers believe, the self-serving bias is rooted partly in how our minds process information—I more easily recall the times I've bent over and picked up the laundry than the times I've overlooked it—then it will be an actual self-perception, more a self-deception than a lie. Consider, finally, the diversity of evidence that converges upon the self-serving bias. Were it merely a favorability bias in questionnaire ratings, then we might find some way to explain the finding away.

(3) *Is not the self-serving bias adaptive?* It likely is, for the same reasons that high self-esteem and positive thinking are adaptive. (Indeed, the three concepts are difficult to distinguish, although I would like to believe that we can be self-accepting and self-affirming without the self-delusions of the

self-serving bias.*) For example, it has been argued that the bias has survival value—that cheaters, for example, will give a more convincing display of honesty if they believe in their honesty. Belief in our superiority can also motivate us to achieve, and can sustain our sense of hope in difficult times.

However, the self-serving bias is not always adaptive. Pride does, as Proverbs reminds us, often go before a fall. A series of experiments by Barry Schlenker at the University of Florida shows how self-serving perceptions can poison a group.[33] In nine different experiments, Schlenker had people work together on some task. He then gave them false information that suggested that their group had done either well or poorly. In every one of these studies, the members of successful groups claimed more responsibility for the group's performance than did members of groups who supposedly failed at the task. Likewise, most presented themselves as contributing more than the others in their group when the group did well; few said they contributed less.

Such self-deception can be detrimental to a group. It can lead its members to expect greater-than-average rewards when their organization does well and less-than-average blame when it does not. If most individuals in a group believe they are underpaid and underappreciated, relative to their better-than-average contributions, disharmony and envy will likely rear their ugly heads. College presidents will readily recognize the phenomenon. If, as one survey revealed, 94 percent of college faculty think themselves better than their average colleague, then when merit salary raises are announced and half receive an average raise or less, many will feel an injustice has been done them. Note that the complaints do not necessarily signify that any actual injustice has been done. Even if, unknown to the professors, God himself had determined the raises according to his most perfect justice, discontent would likely still exist.

Biased self-assessments can also distort managerial judgment. Corporation presidents widely predict more growth for their own firms than for their competition.[34] Similarly, production managers often overpredict their performance.[35] As Claremont University investigator Laurie Larwood has observed, such overoptimism can produce disastrous consequences. If those

---

*One possible distinction is that self-esteem concerns one's overall feelings about oneself, while the self-serving bias generally concerns one's reaction to specific events (such as success/failure). However, those who explain their successes and failures with self-serving bias tend also to score high on tests of self-esteem. Moreover, people who score high on tests of self-esteem tend also to score high on tests of "defensiveness."

who deal in the stock market or in real estate perceive their business intuition to be superior to that of their competitors, they may be in for some severe disappointments.

(4) *Does not the Bible portray us more positively, as reflecting God's image?* The Bible offers a balanced picture of human nature—as the epitome of God's creation, made in his own image, and yet also as sinful, as attached to false securities. Two complementary truths. This chapter affirms the sometimes understated second truth. "This then is the religious meaning of sin," writes Langdon Gilkey:

> Sin may be defined as . . . an overriding loyalty or concern for the self, its existence and its prestige, or for the existence and prestige of a group. From this deeper sin, that is, from this inordinate love of the self and its own, stem the moral evils of indifference, injustice, prejudice, and cruelty to one's neighbor, and the other destructive patterns of actions that we call "sins."[36]

In the biblical account, pride is self-deceit, ignorance of the truth about ourselves. In John's gospel, the religious leaders are portrayed as blind, self-righteous teachers who typify our unwillingness to come to the light, lest our hypocrisy be seen. The experimental evidence that human reason is adaptable to self-interest is thus entirely congenial to the Christian contention that becoming aware of our sin is like trying to see our own eyeballs. There are self-serving, self-justifying biases in the way we perceive our actions, observes the social psychologist. "No one can see his own errors," notes the Psalmist.[37] Thus the Pharisee could thank God "that I am not like other men" (or at least better than the average sinner). St. Paul must have had such self-righteousness in mind when he admonished the Philippians to "in humility count others better than yourselves."[38] Pride alienates us from God and leads us to disdain one another. It fuels conflict among individuals and nations, each of which sees itself as more moral and deserving than others. The Nazi atrocities were rooted not in self-conscious feelings of inferiority, but in Aryan pride. And so, for centuries, pride has been considered the fundamental sin, the deadliest of the seven deadly sins.

(5) *These researchers seem like killjoys. Where is there an encouraging word?* Are not the greater killjoys those who would lead us to believe that, because we're number one, we can accomplish anything? Which means that if we don't—if we are unhappily married, poor, underemployed, or have rebellious children—we have but ourselves to blame. Shame. If only

we had tried harder, been more disciplined, less stupid. This was the experience of Boston Red Sox star Carl Yastrzemski:

The game used to eat me up. If I had a bad day it would just destroy me inside. If I went 0-for-4, I'd get so messed up, it would still affect me mentally the next day. If I went 4-for-4 I was so "up," it carried me over too. Everything was "me." What did *I* do, was all that mattered.

I don't know how far into my career it was—maybe 10 years—when I finally learned the secret. The thing that drives you nuts in this game is not giving credit to the other guy. Now when I go 0-for-4 I remind myself that the pitcher had performed well, I give him the credit instead of tearing myself apart.[39]

To know and accept ourselves—foibles and all, without pretensions—is not gloomy, but liberating. As William James noted, "To give up one's pretensions is as blessed a relief as to get them gratified." Our first step towards the experience of genuine self-affirmation is thus to come to terms with our not-godness—with our vanity and illusions. Jesus' Sermon on the Mount hints at the paradoxical ways by which comfort, satisfaction, mercy, peace, happiness, and visions of God are discovered: "Happy are those who know they are spiritually poor; the Kingdom of heaven belongs to them!"[40]

"Christian religion," said C. S. Lewis, "is, in the long run, a thing of unspeakable comfort. But it does not begin in comfort; it begins in [dismay], and it is no use at all trying to go on to that comfort without first going through that dismay."[41] In coming to realize that self-interest and illusion taint our thoughts and actions, we take the first step toward wholeness. The new insights gained from psychological research into vanity and illusion therefore have profoundly Christian implications, for they drive us back to the biblical view of our creatureliness and spiritual poverty, the very view that, in our pride, we are so prone to deny.

Christians furthermore believe that God's grace is the key to human liberation—liberation from the need to define our self-worth solely in terms of achievements, or prestige, or physical and material well-being. Thus, while I can never be worthy or wise enough, I can, with Martin Luther, "throw myself upon God's grace." This is what St. Paul did, and in the surrender of his pretensions, he proclaimed victory: "I no longer have a righteousness of my own, the kind that is gained by obeying the Law. I now have the righteousness that is given through faith in Christ, the righteousness that comes from God and is based on faith."[42] The Lord of the universe loves me, just as I am.

This "forgiveness of sins," as the Bible calls it, means that when ex-

hausted in our quest to be virtuous, we can come bask in the warmth of
God's love. There is tremendous relief in confessing our vanity—in being
known and accepted as we are. Having confessed the worst sin—playing
God—and having been forgiven, we gain release, a feeling of being given
what we were struggling to get: security and acceptance.[43] The feelings one
has in this encounter with God are like those we enjoy in a relationship with
someone who, even after knowing our inmost thoughts, accepts us unconditionally. This is the delicious experience we enjoy in a good marriage or an
intimate friendship, where we no longer feel the need to justify and explain
ourselves or to be on guard, where we are free to be spontaneous without
fear of losing the other's esteem. Such was the experience of the Psalmist:
"Lord, I have given up my pride and turned away from my arrogance.
. . . I am content and at peace.[44]

(6) *What, then, is true humility?* First, we must recognize that the true
end of humility is *not* self-contempt (which still leaves people concerned
with themselves). To paraphrase C. S. Lewis, humility does not consist in
handsome people trying to believe they are ugly, and clever people trying
to believe they are fools. When Muhammad Ali announced that he was
the greatest, there was a sense in which his pronouncement did not violate
the spirit of humility. False modesty can actually lead to an ironic pride in
one's better-than-average humility. As a pastor of one modest church re-
marked to me, "We are a humble people—and we're proud of it!" (Perhaps
some readers have by now similarly congratulated themselves on being
unusually free of the inflated self-perception this chapter is describing.)

True humility is more like self-forgetfulness than false modesty. It leaves
people free to esteem their special talents and, with the same honesty, to
esteem their neighbor's. Both the neighbor's talents and one's own are
recognized as gifts and, like one's height, are not fit subjects for either
inordinate pride or self-deprecation.

Obviously, true humility is a state not easily attained. "There is," said
C. S. Lewis, "no fault which we are more unconscious of in ourselves.
. . . If anyone would like to acquire humility, I can, I think, tell him the
first step. The first step is to realize that one is proud. And a biggish step,
too." The way to take this first step, continued Lewis, is to glimpse the
greatness of God and see oneself in light of this. "He and you are two things
of such a kind that if you really get into any kind of touch with Him you
will, in fact, be humble, feeling the infinite relief of having for once got
rid of [the pretensions which have] made you restless and unhappy all your
life."[45]

NOTES

1. Stanford Lyman, *The Seven Deadly Sins: Society and Evil* (New York: St. Martin's Press, 1978), p. 135.

2. Joel Brockner and A. J. Blethyn Hulton, "How to Reverse the Vicious Cycle of Low Self-Esteem: The Importance of Attentional Focus," *Journal of Experimental Social Psychology* 6 (1978): 564–578; Thomas Ashby Wills, "Downward Comparison Principles in Social Psychology," *Psychological Bulletin* 90 (1981): 245–271.

3. For reviews of the locus-of-control literature, see E. Jerry Phares, *Locus of Control in Personality* (Morristown, N.J.: General Learning Press, 1976); A. P. MacDonald, "Internal-External Locus of Control," in J. P. Robinson and R. P. Shaver, *Measures of Social Psychological Attitudes* (Ann Arbor, Mich.: Institute for Social Research, 1973), pp. 169–243; Daniel Bar-Tal and Yaakov Bar-Zohar, "The Relationship Between Perception of Locus of Control and Academic Achievement," *Contemporary Educational Psychology* 2 (1977): 181–199; and Timothy M. Gilmor, "Locus of Control as a Mediator of Adaptive Behaviour in Children and Adolescents," *Canadian Psychological Review* 19 (1978): 1–26.

4. Carl R. Rogers, "Reinhold Niebuhr's *The Self and the Dramas of History:* A Criticism," *Pastoral Psychology* 9 (1958): 15–17.

5. Miron Zuckerman, "Attribution of Success and Failure Revisited, or: The Motivational Bias is Alive and Well in Attribution Theory," *Journal of Personality* 47 (1979): 245–287.

6. Richard R. Lau and Dan Russell, "Attributions in the Sports Pages," *Journal of Personality and Social Psychology* 39 (1980): 29–38; Christopher Peterson, "Attribution in the Sports Pages: An Archival Investigation of the Covariation Hypothesis," *Social Psychology Quarterly* 43 (1980): 136–141.

7. Robert M. Arkin and Geoffrey M. Maruyama, "Attribution, Affect, and College Exam Performance," *Journal of Educational Psychology* 71 (1979): 85–93; William M. Bernstein, Walter G. Stephan, and Mark H. Davis, "Explaining Attributions for Achievement: A Path Analytic Approach," *Journal of Personality and Social Psychology* 10 (1979): 1810–1821; Timothy M. Gilmor and David W. Reid, "Locus of Control and Causal Attribution for Positive and Negative Outcomes on University Examinations," *Journal of Research in Personality* 13 (1979): 154–160; Anthony Greenwald, "The Totalitarian Ego: Fabrication and Revision of Personal History," *American Psychologist* 35 (1980): 603–618; Walter G. Stephan, William M. Bernstein, Cookie Stephan, and Mark H. Davis, "Attributions for Achievement: Egotism vs. Expectancy Confirmation," *Social Psychology Quarterly* 42 (1979): 5–17; Eliot R. Smith and Barbara Bolling Manard, "Causal Attributions and Medical School Admissions," *Personality and Social Psychology Bulletin* 6 (1980): 644–650.

8. Michael Ross and Fiore Sicoly, "Egocentric Biases in Availability and Attribution," *Journal of Personality and Social Psychology* 37 (1979): 322–336.

9. R. Baumhart, *An Honest Profit* (New York: Holt, Rinehart & Winston, 1968); Steven N. Brenner and Earl A. Molander, "Is the Ethics of Business Changing?" *Harvard Business Review* (January-February, 1977): 57–71.

10. James M. Fields and Howard Schuman, "Public Beliefs about the Beliefs of the Public," *Public Opinion Quarterly* 40 (1976): 427–448; K. J. Lenihan, "Perceived Climates as a Barrier to Housing Desegregation," unpublished manuscript, Bureau of Applied Social Research, Columbia University, 1965; Hubert J. O'Gorman and Stephen L. Garry, "Pluralistic Ignorance—A Replication and Extension," *Public Opinion Quarterly* 40 (1976): 449–458.

11. For a review of these studies, see Ruth C. Wylie, *The Self-Concept: Revised Edition* (Lincoln: University of Nebraska Press, 1979), vol. 2, pp. 675–678.

12. Jean Paul Codol, "On the So-Called 'Superior Conformity of the Self' Behavior: Twenty Experimental Investigations," *European Journal of Social Psychology* 5 (1976): 457–501.

13. 1976–1977 data from the College Board's *Student Descriptive Questionnaire.*

14. B. R. Forer, "The Fallacy of Personal Validation: A Classroom Demonstration of Gullibility," *Journal of Abnormal and Social Psychology* 44 (1949): 118–123; C. R. Snyder, "Why Horoscopes Are True: The Effects of Specificity on Acceptance of Astrological Interpretations," *Journal of Clinical Psychology* 30 (1974): 577–580.

15. C. R. Snyder, Randee Jae Shenkel, and Carol R. Lowery, "Acceptance of Personality Interpretations: The 'Barnum Effect' and Beyond," *Journal of Consulting and Clinical Psychology* 45 (1977): 104–114.

16. For a review of other evidence supporting this point, see Barry R. Schlenker, "Egocentric Perceptions in Cooperative Groups: Conceptualization and Research Review," Final Grant Report to the Organizational Effectiveness Research Programs, Office of Naval Research, Arlington, Virginia 22217 (November 1, 1976).

17. Michael Ross, Cathy McFarland, and Garth J. O. Fletcher, "The Effect of Attitude on the Recall of Personal Histories," *Journal of Personality and Social Psychology* 40 (1981): 627–634.

18. Greenwald, "The Totalitarian Ego."

19. See chapter five of David G. Myers, *The Human Puzzle: Psychological Research and Christian Belief* (San Francisco: Harper & Row, 1978).

20. See, for example, Paul Slovic and Baruch Fischhoff, "On the Psychology of Experimental Surprises," *Journal of Experimental Psychology: Human Perception and Performance* 3 (1977): 544–551.

21. Daniel Kahneman and Amos Tversky, "Intuitive Prediction: Biases and Corrective Procedures," *Management Science,* in press.

22. Margaret W. Matlin and David J. Stang, *The Pollyanna Principle: Selectivity in Language, Memory, and Thought* (Cambridge, Mass.: Schenkman, 1978).

23. Neil D. Weinstein, "Unrealistic Optimism About Future Life Events," *Journal of Personality and Social Psychology* 39 (1980): 806–820.

24. C. R. Snyder, "The 'Illusion' of Uniqueness," *Journal of Humanistic Psychology* 18 (1978): 33–41.

25. Steven Sherman, "On the Self-Erasing Nature of Errors of Prediction," *Journal of Personality and Social Psychology* 39 (1980): 211–221.

26. Nicholas A. Kuiper, "Depression and Causal Attributions for Success and Failure," *Journal of Personality and Social Psychology* 36 (1978): 236–246; Lauren B. Alloy and Lyn V. Abramson, "Judgment of Contingency in Depressed and Nondepressed Students: Sadder but Wiser?" *Journal of Experimental Psychology: General* 108 (1979): 441–485; Lauren B. Alloy and Lyn Y. Abramson, "The Cognitive Component of Human Helplessness and Depression: A Critical Analysis," *Human Helplessness: Theory and Applications,* eds. J. Garber and M. E. P. Seligman (New York: Academic Press, 1980); Lyn Y. Abramson, Lauren B. Alloy, and Robert Rosoff, "Depression and the Generation of Complex Hypotheses in the Judgment of Contingency," *Behavior Research and Therapy* 19 (1981): 35–45; Lauren B. Alloy, Lyn Y. Abramson, and Donald Viscusi, "Induced Mood and the Illusion of Control," *Journal of Personality and Social Psychology,* in press.

27. Peter M. Lewinsohn, Walter Mischel, William Chapline, and Russell Barton, "Social Competence and Depression: The Role of Illusory Self-Perceptions," *Journal of Abnormal Psychology* 89 (1980): 203–212. (The depressed people in this study were also less socially com-

petent, which may also have contributed to their depression.) Many other research studies confirm that, although most people see themselves the way they *think* others see them, this is often not the way others actually see them (S. Sidney Shrauger and Thomas J. Schoeneman, "Symbolic Interactionist View of Self-Concept: Through the Looking Glass Darkly," *Psychological Bulletin* 86 (1979): 549–573.

28. Pascal, *Pensees*, Sec. ii, No. 101.
29. La Rochefoucauld, *Maxims*, 262.
30. Robert Gould, Paul J. Brounstein, and Harold Sigall, "Attributing Ability to an Opponent: Public Aggrandizement and Private Denigration," *Sociometry* 40 (1977): 254–261. See also, Michael H. Bond, "Winning Either Way: The Effect of Anticipating a Competitive Interaction on Person Perception," *Personality and Social Psychology Bulletin* 5 (1979): 316–319; Edward E. Jones and Steven Berglas, "Control of Attributions about the Self Through Self-Handicapping Strategies: The Appeal of Alcohol and the Role of Under-achievement," *Personality and Social Psychology Bulletin* 4 (1978): 200–206; Steven Berglas and Edward E. Jones, "Drug Choice as a Self-Handicapping Strategy in Response to Noncontingent Success," *Journal of Personality and Social Psychology* 36 (1978): 405–417.
31. Robert M. Arkin, Alan Appelman, and Jerry M. Burger, "Social Anxiety, Self-Presentation, and the Self-Serving Bias in Causal Attribution," *Journal of Personality and Social Psychology* 38 (1980): 23–35; Schlenker, "Egocentric Perceptions in Cooperative Groups."
32. William M. Bernstein, "The Private-Public Attribution Distinction: Theoretical Implications for Egotism," paper presented at the American Psychological Association Convention, 1979; Gifford Weary, "Self-Serving Attributional Biases and Concern Over Public Defen-

sibility of Causal Judgments," paper presented at the Midwestern Psychological Association convention, 1980.
33. Schlenker, "Egocentric Perceptions in Cooperative Groups." (For examples of Schlenker's experiments, see B. R. Schlenker and R. S. Miller, "Group Cohesiveness as a Determinant of Egocentric Perceptions in Cooperative Groups," *Human Relations* 30 (1977): 1039–1055; and "Egocentrism in Groups: Self-Serving Biases or Logical Information Processing?" *Journal of Personality and Social Psychology* 35 (1977): 755–764.
34. Laurie Larwood and W. Whittaker, "Managerial Myopia: Self-Serving Biases in Organizational Planning," *Journal of Applied Psychology* 62 (1977): 194–198.
35. J. B. Kidd and J. R. Morgan, "A Predictive Informations System for Management," *Operational Research Quarterly* 20 (1969): 149–170.
36. Langdon Gilkey, *Shantung Compound* (New York: Harper & Row, 1966), p. 233.
37. Psalms 19:12.
38. Philippians 2:3.
39. Carl Yastrzemski, quoted in *The Toronto Globe and Mail*, March 24, 1979, S5, cited by Michael Ross, "Self-Centered Biases in Attributions of Responsibility: Antecedents and Consequences," *Social Cognition: The Ontario Symposium*, eds. E. T. Higgins, C. P. Herman, and M. P. Zanna (Hillsdale, N.J.: Lawrence Erlbaum, in press).
40. Matthew 5:3.
41. C. S. Lewis, *Mere Christianity* (New York: Macmillan, 1960), p. 25.
42. Philippians 3:9.
43. Keith Miller, *The Becomers* (Waco, Tex.: Word Books, 1973), p. 134.
44. Psalm 131:1–2a, *Good News Bible*.
45. Lewis, *Mere Christianity*, p. 99.

BIOGRAPHICAL SKETCH

DAVID G. MYERS is professor of psychology at Hope College in Michigan. He earned his B.A. in chemistry from Whitworth College, and his M.A. and Ph.D. in psychology from the University of Iowa. His research articles have appeared in periodicals ranging from *Science* and *American Scientist* to *Psychological Bulletin* and *Journal of Personality and Social Psychology,* and he is the author of *The Human Puzzle: Psychological Research and Christian Belief.* He has also written for the lay public in magazines such as *Saturday Review, Psychology Today, Today's Education, Science Digest,* and *Christianity Today.* This chapter was adapted from two of his recent books, *The Inflated Self: Human Illusions and the Biblical Call to Hope* and a social psychology text to be published in 1982.

Self-Esteem Tests:
Assumptions and Values

JOHN D. GARTNER

WHILE Christian thinkers have written extensively on the concept of self-esteem, the field of self-esteem testing has remained almost entirely secular. Virtually all of the more than 200 measures of self-esteem reflect subtle, antibiblical, value assumptions that, from a Christian perspective, severely limit their usefulness and bias their results.[1] The purpose of this chapter is to identify and evaluate those assumptions, and to propose the construction of a Christian test of self-esteem.

A glance at the current research comparing the self-esteem of religious Christians to that of nonbelievers is confusing at best. Of the studies I surveyed, four found Christians lower in self-esteem,[2] eight found no difference between the groups,[3] and six found Christians higher.[4] Few patterns can be seen in these conflicting findings, in terms of either populations sampled or tests used.[5] This suggests that Christians vary quite a bit in how they think of themselves. It may also be that self-esteem, especially Christian self-esteem, is more complex and multifaceted than current measures are able to detect. I suggest that, in addition to being biased against biblical values, current tests of self-esteem simply do not provide the information Christian professionals would want about their research samples, congregations, or therapeutic clients.

Limiting ourselves to the most popular form of self-esteem test, the self-report questionnaire, I have isolated six types of questions that represent different components of self-esteem and make up the majority of items on existing tests. Each of these types have their own unique, antibiblical value bias and a corresponding potential to be reshaped in accordance with biblical values.

SELF-EVALUATION

"Self-evaluation," an important component of almost all self-esteem measures, is a subject's rating of his or her traits and abilities on a numerical scale—that is, a quantitative estimate of how good one believes one is. Many secular self-esteem test writers assume that honest, positive self-evaluation strongly correlates with mental health, so that the more we think of ourselves, the better adjusted we are.[6] This assumption underlies two types of self-evaluation: moral (such as, "I am satisfied with my moral behavior")[7] and nonmoral (Such as, "I pick up new sports and games easily").[8]

Moral Self-Evaluation

Any type of self-evaluation involves comparing oneself to some ideal[9] or reference group.[10] Here Christian subjects run into trouble, for their fundamental standard for moral self-evaluation is supposed to be absolute perfection, Christ himself.[11] They should score dramatically lower on any moral self-evaluation question, and thus such items are implicitly biased against them.

The Self-Ideal Discrepancy Test, a type of measure first popularized by Carl Rogers in the 1950s,[12] makes this bias an explicit part of its logic. Subjects sort a series of cards or fill out a self-esteem questionnaire twice, first describing their "real selves" and then their "ideal selves."

The scores are interpreted in a very interesting way: the more the "real" resembles the "ideal" self, the higher the self-esteem. Evidence validating the self-ideal technique is mixed, plagued by a number of unique methodological problems,[13] but more importantly for our discussion is how this test clearly discriminates against any subject who emulates a high moral standard. The higher one's ideal self is, the greater a discrepancy there is likely to be between one's real and ideal self. Predictably, one study comparing priests to nonreligious professionals on one self-ideal test found them "lower" in self-esteem.[14]

This bias reflects a human-centered value system which assumes that people's values should conform to their natural abilities. In contrast, Christian values affirm that one must seek to conform one's self to and be judged by God's immutable standards.[15] In short, God's morals are the measure of humanity, not humanity the measure of morals for the Christian.

It would be falsely idealistic to believe that Christians compare their moral stature only to Christ and never to others. While three studies have found Christians lower in moral self-evaluation than nonbelievers,[16] three have found them higher.[17] It is likely that some of the subjects in the "Christian" samples were not Christians at all by biblical standards, and it is equally probable that some felt that the experimenter wanted them to compare themselves to others, since many people complete such tests in this way.[18] Finally, there is a good chance that some Christians do not faithfully maintain a biblical standard when evaluating their moral behavior. Nevertheless, it should be emphasized that this does not in the slightest obscure the fact that most existing measures are themselves antibiblical.

A biblical test, on the other hand, assumes that all mankind is profoundly sinful,[19] and that a healthy understanding of ourselves involves recognizing this.[20] Where secular tests award points for people rating themselves highly on a moral scale, a biblical test would award points for people acknowledging deep moral flaws in themselves. A high moral self-evaluation on the biblical test would be interpreted as pathological narcissism or pride, which, of course, is a part of the fallen, human condition. As the Bible tells us, human beings want to deny their moral turpitude, "everyman's way appears right in his own eyes" (Prov. 21:2). Secular self-esteem tests demonstrate their participation in this universal human denial by assuming that "being right in one's own eyes" is not a sign of sin, but of mental health.

I do not mean by this that there is nothing good about people. All human beings are made in the image of God,[21] and the redeemed possess his Spirit as well.[22] As we shall see in section three, to acknowledge genuine moral strength in oneself is a crucial aspect of self-worth. It does mean that all human beings are far from the goal of perfect holiness, and that this fact must come to light in a *quantitative* evaluation of their moral caliber. In short, there is goodness in each person, but it must be regarded as small in comparison to Christ's.

Interestingly, one of the biggest problems for self-report, self-esteem tests is distinguishing between honest, positive self-evaluation and "defensive" self-evaluation,[23] which is motivated by a desire to make oneself look good to oneself and/or others. In fact, almost all of these tests correlate meaningfully with tests designed to measure a person's motivation to appear socially desirable,[24] which suggests that a significant portion of the variance on self-esteem tests might be accounted for by people's defensive self-esteem. Surprisingly, only a few tests, such as the Tennessee Self-Concept Scale[25] and one recently developed by O'Brien and Epstein,[26] include "lie scales" designed to detect patently unrealistic positive self-

SELF-ESTEEM TESTS   67662   101

evaluations (such as, "I always practice what I preach").[27] However, even if such a scale were included in all tests, it would not solve the problem. Alexander found that subjects reporting high self-esteem, many of whom avoided falling for the lie items, are most likely to be diagnosed as lying by means of a polygraph when giving a positive self-evaluation.[28] All of this serves to support the Christian contention that a sizable portion of a person's self-satisfaction is simply self-deception.

Self-esteem testers could reply that, with some exceptions,[29] research has shown that high self-esteem is an indication of mental health.[30] However, most of the studies lump moral self-evaluation along with other self-esteem questions, making it impossible to know the specific effect of moral self-evaluation on mental health. In addition, many of the tests used to measure mental health are also based on antibiblical values.[31] Finally, if a connection were found between positive moral self-evaluation and mental health, it should be most pronounced in unbelievers. The natural person's sense of worth and well-being is inextricably linked to moral self-evaluation. Such people must deceive themselves into believing that they are morally adequate to feel good about themselves. Christians, on the other hand, because they are unconditionally loved and forgiven,[32] can freely recognize their sinfulness[33] and yet still feel accepted, happy, and worthwhile.[34] Some Christians, of course, do unfortunately suffer from feelings of unrelieved guilt and condemnation. One of the purposes of this proposed test would be to detect such individuals and subgroups by their ability to recognize personal sin on a moral humility scale, in combination with low scores on the other self-esteem scales discussed later in this chapter.

Nonmoral Self-Evaluation

Unlike moral self-evaluation, it is legitimate, from a biblical perspective, to use both human and divine standards when evaluating one's nonmoral traits and skills. Acknowledging that our strength and abilities are dwarfed by God's is an essential part of humility.[35] A Christian measure of self-concept might measure this appropriate sense of awe. However, inasmuch as I Corinthians 12 calls us to recognize our diverse gifts and abilities, it is also appropriate to compare ourselves to others, if for no other reason than to choose our ministry and vocation, for presumably, there is some connection between the abilities God has given us and his plan for our lives. It would be "false modesty" for Terry Bradshaw to say he is "average" at football or for Billy Graham to claim he is just "okay" at evangelism. Christians should be able to evaluate their abilities honestly, like anyone

Lincoln Christian College

else, and questions on a Christian test of self-esteem in this area should be similar to those on a secular test.

There should, however, be a key difference in the importance this evaluation plays for Christian and non-Christian subjects. In the world's view, people's ultimate worth is intrinsically linked to their abilities. The world's treatment of the poor, the defective, and the unborn attest to that. Ideally, a Christian's sense of self-worth should be completely independent of his or her ability, for all abilities come from God as gifts, and reflect no more glory on the possessor than the color of a sweater that individual received for Christmas.[36]

This suggests two sorts of questions, relevant to both moral and non-moral self-evaluation, that might be included in a Christian measure of self-esteem. First, to what extent do subjects feel that their self-worth is contingent on their self-evaluation? I have suggested that believers will be less likely to feel that it is. These questions would allow us to test such hypotheses empirically, as well as discover individuals who place unhealthy emphasis on self-evaluation. Secondly, given that they exhibit some degree of positive self-evaluation, do subjects see their positive traits as having their source in God? If they do, they evidence a type of self-evaluation that is psychologically and spiritually different than that found in unbelievers, for it is "God-centered," containing the humble recognition that their good qualities come from Another.

For all types of questions, there is the danger that subjects will answer defensively in accordance with how they would like to appear, rather than how they most deeply believe themselves to be. This is an unavoidable hazard of the self-report technique for Christian and secular tests alike. Some Christians might even "fake humble" in the same way that some unbelievers fake self-satisfaction. A "defensiveness scale," detecting impossibly unrealistic self-evaluations of both positive and negative types should be included. There is a second danger that Christians will answer questions in accordance to their doctrinal beliefs, which may have little relationship to their experience. One approach to this problem would be to include some questions on all scales which direct subjects to give answers based on their experience only.

SELF-ACCEPTANCE

The term *self-acceptance* has been used almost interchangably with *self-esteem* by some test writers.[37] Technically, it has a specific meaning. People recognize that they fall short of their ideal standards, but still accept themselves and their failings. Wylie defines this situation as "respecting oneself and one's admitted faults."[38] Or, as Rosenberg puts it, "the term implies that the individual knows who he is, is aware of his virtues and deficiencies, and accepts what he sees without regret."[39]

At first glance, this might sound like a refreshingly Christian concept. As Christ forgave the woman caught in the act of adultery,[40] he accepts all who come to him "just as they are." Yet, Christ does not "respect" our moral shortcomings, nor "accept them without regret." Secular self-esteem writers assume that you cannot accept yourself if you condemn any of your flaws. For example, the index of adjustment and values of Shostrom's Personal Orientation Inventory measures self-acceptance by asking subjects to indicate after each item of self-evaluation, "How much do you like being as you are in this respect?"[41] On the self-acceptance scale of the Personal Orientation Inventory, subjects must endorse one of the following sentences, "People should repent of their wrongdoings" (incorrect) *vs.* "People should not always repent of their wrongdoings" (correct).[42] In both cases, rejecting an aspect of one's behavior is seen as rejecting the self. In contrast, Christian doctrine has always been that we should "hate the sin, but love the sinner." Christ did not accept adultery when he accepted the adulterous woman; he told her to "go and sin no more" (John 8:11b). Neither can we accept our moral flaws. In fact, we must fight against feeling too comfortable with them. A Christian test of self-esteem should measure one's ability to accept oneself *in spite of* moral flaws. Some nonmoral limitations, such as, "there are some things I will never be good at," should be accepted, and questions might be devised to measure this.

A second aspect of self-acceptance is its source. Christians' self-acceptance should be based on the experience of God's atonement, forgiveness, and love through Christ.[43] As with self-evaluation, this represents a qualitatively different type of self-acceptance than nonbelievers'. "God-centered self-acceptance," like "God-centered self-evaluation," is humble because it recognizes that one's ability to be at peace with oneself comes from Another. Questions concerning the source of self-acceptance should be included in a Christian test of self-esteem.

SELF-WORTH

I define self-worth as a person's appreciation of his or her own good qualities. Unlike self-evaluation, it involves no quantitative judgment of how well those qualities measure against an ideal. Comparing my skill at baseball with Reggie Jackson's is self-evaluation; enjoying my own time up at bat is the feeling of self-worth.

Fortunately, there are a number of tests that incorporate this concept, most notably Rosenberg's Self-Esteem Scale (such as, "I feel that I am a person of worth, at least on an equal plane with others"),[44] the Janis-Field Feelings of Inadequacy Scale (such as, "Do you ever think that you are a worthless individual?"),[45] and Phillips-Berger Self-Acceptance Scales (such as, "I don't question my worth as a person, even if others do").[46]

The reader should be advised, however, that all of these tests both exclude God-centered items, and mix self-worth questions indiscriminately with self-evaluation questions, which, as I have said, reflects the erroneous link that unsaved persons as a whole make between these two distinct aspects of self-esteem.

The Christian self-concept is free of this fallacy and presents instead a paradox. Though I am a depraved sinner (low moral self-evaluation), God esteems me significant, valuable,[47] and rejoices over a moral act as small as my giving a cup of water to a thirsty traveler[48] (high self-worth). Though my abilities are miniscule (low nonmoral self-evaluation) in comparison to His, and perhaps even in comparison to other men's, He is greatly pleased to see me exercise them toward any good goal[49] (high self-worth). The key to the remarkable paradox lies in one word: love. "He [God] really loves the hairless bipeds,"[50] fumes C. S. Lewis's senior devil, Screwtape. His love finds, indeed creates, tremendous value in people who, by "objective" standards, would seem to possess little.[51] Like a human father, He rejoices in his children's first gurgles and baby steps as if they were masterpieces, not because they are, but because they are made by His children. Thus, a Christian test of self-esteem should score self-evaluation items separately from items measuring self-worth and the other components of self-esteem.

Additionally, a Christian test of self-esteem should include items that distinguish between feelings of self-worth based on the experience of God's love and those that are not. In a recent study, Ellison and Economos have included items of this sort, "assessing the extent to which a person's self-esteem is based on God's evaluation of him."[52]

RELATIONSHIPS

Many self-esteem tests include items assessing the quality of one's personal relationships, because these relationships exert such a powerful influence on one's view of oneself. My only objection to these items is that none assesses the quality of the person's relationship with God, which centuries of religious experience and convincing psychological research[53] have shown dynamically affects self-esteem. A Christian test of self-esteem should include items such as those found on Paloutzian and Ellison's Spiritual Well-Being Scale (for example, "I have a personally meaningful relationship with God," and "I don't find much satisfaction in private prayer with God").[54]

HAPPINESS

A number of tests include a small number of items measuring simply how happy the subject claims to be. Again, the only objection is that no questions concern God as a possible source of happiness. The Spiritual Well-Being Scale can serve as a model for questions of this type as well (for example, "My relationship with God contributes to my sense of well-being," and "My relationship with God helps me not to feel lonely").[55]

ASSERTIVENESS

Assertiveness is defined by Anderson as "the ability or predisposition to express preferences, opinions and feelings by words or actions; the emphasis is on any act which serves to maintain one's rights in a socially desirable manner."[56] Assertiveness questions can be found in a number of self-report questionnaires, including the Coopersmith Self-Esteem Inventory (such as, "If I have something to say I usually say it")[57] and the Berger-Phillips Self-Acceptance Scales (such as, "I change my opinion or the way I do things to please someone else").[58]

Christian psychologists, such as Bufford[59] and Irwin,[60] have suggested that the secular concept of assertiveness is in conflict with biblical values. According to renowned psychologist Joseph Wolpe, one of the creators of the assertiveness concept, assertiveness is "the golden mean. . . . The individual places himself first but takes others into account."[61] It seems clear that this self-oriented philosophy is in conflict with Christ's call to selflessness: "Love one another as I have loved you" (John 13:34). Bufford offers an alternative principle for a Christian model of assertiveness, which inverts the secular definition in much the same way Christian love inverts natural self-love: "The individual places other first, but also considers himself."[62] If a Christian test of self-esteem were to measure assertiveness, only this definition, or one like it, would be acceptable.

CONCLUSIONS

In summary, antibiblical value assumptions render current secular tests of self-esteem grossly biased and, from a Christian perspective, inaccurate in the understanding of humanity and mental health that they reflect. I would caution any researcher, especially a Christian one, to consider carefully before using them.

This paper presents a rough outline for biblical alternative. Most importantly, it proposes a moral humility scale, a clear distinction between self-evaluation and self-worth, as well as the inclusion of God-centered items. People who score high on humility but low on the other aspects of self-esteem most likely suffer from feelings of inferiority, self-hate, and unrelieved guilt. Individuals who score low on humility but high on other self-esteem scales are probably defensively self-righteous, or have low or relativistic moral standards. People who score high on moral and/or non-moral self-evaluation but low on self-esteem are most likely insecure overachievers with a compulsive strain in their personality. Finally, mature healthy believers are those who score high on humility, self-acceptance, self-worth, happiness, and Christian assertiveness scales, as well as reporting positive relationships with others. In addition, they will experience, as well as believe, that their self-esteem comes from a personal relationship with Christ.

It is my belief that Christians must carefully examine the assumptions behind not merely these, but all personality tests, and in most cases design new ones consonant with their own values and beliefs. Goldsmith[63] has suggested that biases in secular personality tests can in many cases be reversed by using statistical techniques, such as the analysis of covariance, to correct for the differences in the scores of Christian and secular groups. While such work is extremely valuable, I do not believe it eliminates the need for the construction of Christian personality tests. As this paper has shown in the case of self-esteem, secular personality tests often fail to provide information a Christian professional would consider important (such as, God-centered items), confound critically different variables (such as, self-evaluation and self-worth), and apply a different value to the information they do elicit (such as, moral self-evaluation).

A Christian test should tell us what we want to know about the psychological and spiritual health of the people we are testing, by asking the right questions and evaluating the answers in accordance with the principles found in God's Word.

NOTES

1. For an excellent summary of the purely methodological problems that plague this field, see Ruth Wylie, *The Self-Concept: A Review of Methodological Considerations and Measuring Instruments* (Lincoln: University of Nebraska Press, 1974), vol. 1; and Rick Crandall, "The Measurement of Self-Esteem and Related Constructs," *Measures of Social Psychological Attitude,* ed. John P. Robinson and Phillip R. Shaver, rev. ed. (Ann Arbor, Mich.; Institute for Social Research, 1974), pp. 45–167.

2. Emery Cowen, "The Negative Self-Concept as a Personality Measure," *Journal of Consulting Psychology* 18 (1954): 138–142; Larry Eberlein, James Park, and Wayne Maitheson, "Self-Ideal Congruence in Five Occupational Groups," *Alberta Journal of Educational Research* 17 (1971): 95–103; Thomas Janas, "Catholic Identification and Personal Identity," doctoral dissertation, University of Tennessee, 1974; Jerry S. Schein, "A Study in Self Concept Ratings of Christian Church (Disciple of Christ) Ministers Serving Congregations of 240 or More," doctoral dissertation, University of Utah, 1975.

3. Bernard R. Shirley, "A Comparison of the Effect of Short Term Secular and Religious Counseling on the Self-Concept and Values of College Students," doctoral dissertation, University of South Dakota, 1972; Lilliam R. P. Holcomb, "Role Concepts and Self-Esteem in Church Women with Implications for Pastoral Counseling," doctoral dissertation, University of Syracuse, 1974; Edward F. Coughlin, "Religious and Lay Graduate Students in Training for Helping Roles in N. Y. State: A Study in Self-concept and Attitudes Toward Feminism and Sexuality," doctoral dissertation, Catholic University of America, 1976; Mark Heintzelman and Lawrence T. Fehr, "The Relationship Between Religious Orthodoxy and Three Personality Variables," *Psycho-logical Reports* 38 (1976): 756–758; Charles Buehler, Andrew Weigart, and Thomas Darwin, "Antecedents of Adolescent Self-Evaluation: A Cross National Application of a Model," *Journal of Comparative Family Studies* 8 (1977): 29–45; Lawrence Fehr and Mark Heintzelman, "Personality and Attitude Correlates of Religiosity: A Source of Controversy," *Journal of Psychology* 95 (1977): 63–66; Duane M. Zuckerman, "Self-Concept, Family Background, and Personal Traits Which Predict the Life Goals and Sex Role Attitudes of Technical College and University Women," doctoral dissertation, Ohio State University, 1977; Craig W. Ellison and Tom Economos, "Religious Experience and Quality of Life," paper presented at the annual meeting of the Christian Association for Psychological Studies, San Diego, April, 1981.

4. Orlo J. Strunk, "The Relationship Between Self-Reports and Adolescent Religiosity," *Psychological Reports* 4 (1958): 683–686; Robert E. Sutton, "A Comparison of the Expressed Self-Concepts of Students in a Seventh Day Adventist College to Students in a Public Supported University," doctoral dissertation, University of Idaho, 1975; Elliot R. Worthington, "Post-Service Adjustment and Vietnam Era Veterans," *Military Medicine* 142 (1977): 865–866; Paul Lingren, "Personality and Self-Concept Variables in Adolescent Religious Conversion Experiences," doctoral dissertation, Rosemead Graduate School of Professional Psychology, 1978; Eloise M. Archibald, "Religiosity, The Experience of Discrimination and Self-Esteem in Black Americans," doctoral dissertation, New York University, 1979; Christopher Smith, Andrew Weigart, and Thomas Darwin, "Self-Esteem and Religiosity: An Analysis of Catholic Adolescents from Five Cultures," *Journal for the Scientific Study of Religion* 18 (1979): 51–60.

5. The only exception that I can see is that religious participation increases self-esteem scores in groups who have experienced unusual stress or discrimination such as blacks and Vietnam vets. See Worthington, "Post-Service Adjustment and Vietnam Era Veterans"; Archibald, "Religiosity."

6. Robert Alexander, "Self-Esteem, Defensiveness and Psychophysiological Reactions During Self-Disclosure," paper presented at the annual meeting of the American Psychological Association, Montreal, August, 1980.

7. William H. Fitts, Tennessee Self-Concept Scale (Nashville, Tenn.: Counselor Recordings and Tests, 1964), p. 3.

8. D. Jackson, quoted in Crandall, "The Measurement of Self-Esteem," p. 98.

9. Stanley Coopersmith, The Antecedents of Self Esteem (Princeton, N.J.: Princeton University Press, 1965).

10. Wylie, The Self-Concept.

11. Leviticus 11:44; Matthew 11:29; 1 John 3:2.

12. Carl R. Rogers and Rosiland F. Dymond, eds., Psychotherapy and Personality Change (Chicago: University of Chicago Press, 1954).

13. J. Block and H. Thomas, "Is Satisfaction with Self a Measure of Adjustment?" Journal of Abnormal Social Psychology 15 (1951): 254–259; D. L. Varble and A. W. Landfield, "Validity of the Self-Ideal Discrepancy as a Criterion Measure for Success in Psychotherapy," Journal of Counseling Psychology 16 (1969): 150–156; Crandall, "The Measurement of Self-Esteem"; Wylie, The Self-Concept.

14. Eberlein et al., "Self-Ideal Congruence."

15. Psalm 119; Matthew 5:17–20.

16. Lawrence A. Fehr and Leighton E. Stamps, "The Mosher Guilt Scales: A Construct Validity Extension," Journal of Personality Assessment 43 (1979): 257–260; Raymond Paloutzian and Craig Ellison, "Religious Commitment, Loneliness and Quality of Life," CAPS Bulletin 5, no. 3 (1979): 3–4; W. Mack Goldsmith and Billy D. Sanborn, "The 'Guilty Personality' May be Religious:

The Relationship of the Mosher Guilt Scales and EPPS, with Value Orientation Controlled" (in preparation).

17. Archibald, "Religiosity"; Lingren, "Personality and Self-Concept Variables"; and Sutton, "Comparison of Expressed Self-Concepts."

18. Wylie, The Self-Concept.

19. Isaiah 64:6; Romans 3:22–23.

20. 1 John 1:8–10.

21. Genesis 1:26.

22. Romans 8:9.

23. Crandall, "The Measurement of Self-Esteem"; Wylie, The Self-Concept.

24. Crandall, "The Measurement of Self-Esteem"; Wylie, The Self-Concept.

25. Fitts, Tennessee Self-Concept Scale.

26. Edward J. O'Brien, "The Self-Report Inventory: Development and Validation of a Multidimensional Measure of the Self-Concept and Sources of Self-Esteem," doctoral dissertation, University of Massachusetts, 1980.

27. O'Brien, "The Self-Report Inventory," p. 246.

28. Alexander, "Self-Esteem, Defensiveness and Psychophysiological Reactions."

29. Block and Thomas, "Is Satisfaction with Self a Measure of Adjustment?"; Varble and Landfield, "Validity of the Self-Ideal Discrepancy."

30. C. Wahl, "Some Antecedent Factors in Family Histories of 109 Alcoholics," Quarterly Journal for Studies on Alcohol 17 (1956): 643–654; Coopersmith, The Antecedents of Self-Esteem; E. Aronson and D. Mettee, "Dishonest Behavior as a Function of Differential Levels of Induced Self-Esteem," Journal of Personality and Social Psychology 1 (1965): 156–171; M. Brehm and W. Back, "Self-Image and Attitudes Toward Drugs," Journal of Personality 36 (1968): 299–314; William Fitts et al., The Self Concept and Self-Actualization (Nashville, Tenn.: Counselor Recordings and Tests, 1971); Ruth Wylie, The Self Concept: Theory and Research on Selected Topics (Lincoln: University of Nebraska Press, 1979), vol. 2.

31. Mack W. Goldsmith and Dick Harig,

"Glossalalia and Internal-External Locus of Control: A Replication," paper presented at the annual meeting of the Western Association of Christians for Psychological Studies, Malibu, Calif., June, 1978; John Gartner, "Anti-Biblical Value Assumptions in Psychological Testing: The Personal Orientation Inventory," paper presented at the annual meeting of the Christian Association for Psychological Studies, San Diego, Calif., April, 1981; Robert Hogan and David Schroeder, "Seven Biases in Psychology," *Psychology Today*, July, 1981; Paul C. Vitz, "Kohlberg's Scale of Moral Development," *The New Oxford Review* (in press).

32. Romans 5:6–11.

33. 1 John 2:1–2.

34. John 6:37; John 15:11; Matthew 10:29–31.

35. Psalm 8:3–4; Job 38–41.

36. 1 Corinthians 4:7.

37. Ruth Wylie, *The Self-Concept: A Review of Methodological Consideration and Measuring Instruments* (Lincoln: University of Nebraska Press, 1974), vol. 1.

38. Wylie, *The Self-Concept*, p. 127.

39. Morris Rosenberg, *Society and the Adolescent Self Image* (Princeton, N.J.: Princeton University Press, 1965), p. 31.

40. John 8:1–11.

41. Everett L. Shostrom, *The Personal Orientation Inventory* (San Diego, Calif.: Educational and Industrial Testing Service, 1963), p. 5.

42. Robert Bills, Edgar Vance, and Orison McLean, "An Index of Adjustment and Values," *Journal of Consulting Psychology* 23 (1959): 362.

43. Romans 8:30–34.

44. Rosenberg, *Society and the Adolescent Self Image*, p. 18.

45. Irving L. Janis and Peter B. Field, "The Janis Field Personality Questionnaire," *Personality and Persuasability*, eds. Carl Hovland and Irving Janis (New Haven, Conn.: Yale University Press), p. 300.

46. E. Berger, quoted in Crandall, "The Measurement of Self-Esteem," p. 109.

47. Romans 8:15–16.

48. Matthew 25:35–40.

49. Philippians 4:8.

50. C. S. Lewis, *The Screwtape Letters* (New York: Macmillan, 1959), p. 65.

51. 2 Corinthians 3:5.

52. Ellison and Economos, "Religious Experience and Quality of Life," p. 7.

53. Peter Benson and Bernard Spilka, "God-Image as a Function of Self-Esteem and Locus of Control," *Journal for the Scientific Study of Religion* 11 (1973): 297–310; David A. Flakall, "The Effects of Theological Views of Self Acceptance on High and Low Self-Esteem Christians," doctoral dissertation, Fuller Theological Seminary Graduate School of Psychology, 1974; Myron R. Chartier and Larry A. Goehner, "A Study of the Relationship Between Parent-Adolescent Communication, Self-Esteem and God Image," *Journal of Psychology and Theology* 4 (1976): 227–232; Edwin H. Hearon, "Self-Image and God-Image in Male Alcoholics," doctoral dissertation, University of South Carolina, 1976; Buehler, Weigart, and Darwin, "Antecedents of Adolescent Self-Evaluation"; William G. Bixler, "Self-Concept, God-Concept Concurrency as a Function of Differential Needs for Esteem and Consistency," doctoral dissertation, Fuller Theological Seminary Graduate School of Psychology, 1979; Rick Campise, Craig W. Ellison, and Rita Kinsman, "Spiritual Well Being: Some Exploratory Relationships," paper presented at the annual meeting of the American Psychological Association, New York, September, 1979; Ellison and Economos, "Religious Experience and Quality of Life."

54. Raymond F. Paloutzian and Craig W. Ellison, "Loneliness, Spiritual Well-Being and the Quality of Life," in Letitia Anne Peplau and Daniel Perlman, *Loneliness: A Sourcebook of Current Theory, Research and Therapy* (New York: John Wiley and Sons, 1982), p. 232.

55. Ibid.

56. David E. Anderson, quoted in Timothy Irwin, "A Theological Study of Assertion and Assertiveness Training," *CAPS Bulletin* 4, no. 4 (1978): 8–14.
57. Coopersmith, *The Antecedents of Self Esteem*, p. 266.
58. E. Phillips, quoted in Crandall, "The Measurement of Self-Esteem," p. 111.
59. Roger K. Bufford, "Assertiveness: Recognizing the Limits," *CAPS Bulletin* 7, no. 1 (1981): 1–3.
60. Irwin, "Theological Study of Assertion."
61. Wolpe quoted in Bufford, "Assertiveness," p. 2.
62. Bufford, "Assertiveness," p. 2.
63. Mack W. Goldsmith, personal communication.

BIOGRAPHICAL SKETCH

JOHN GARTNER is a doctoral student in clinical psychology at the University of Massachusetts, Amherst. He received his B.A. *(magna cum laude)* from Princeton University and has co-authored publications in *Brain and Language* and *Neuropsychologia*.

Self-Regulation and Self-Esteem

PAUL W. CLEMENT

PEOPLE have unique potential. Each person is capable of carrying out two essential roles simultaneously. The same individual can be teacher and student, experimenter and subject, counselor and client, or therapist and patient. Each pair of roles has a corresponding set of role-related behaviors. Teachers teach and students study. Experimenters experiment and subjects behave. Counselors counsel and clients talk. Therapists treat and patients act troubled. Once each set of role-related behaviors is identified, the same person may engage in both kinds of performance. The first kind may be called *regulating actions* and the second, *regulated actions*. When one person is the source of both the regulating and regulated actions, the basic requirements for self-regulation exist.

For the most part, we regulate ourselves by the same mechanisms we use to influence the behavior of others. Understanding the principles of the psychology of behavior change in others is highly relevant for changing oneself. Before changing oneself, however, the individual must decide what personal behaviors to change and what behaviors to maintain. Self-evaluation facilitates such decisions. Self-evaluation leads to establishing the goals of self-regulation efforts and determining how effective those efforts turn out.

SELF-EVALUATION AND SELF-ESTEEM

Self-evaluation and self-esteem are closely related concepts, as is illustrated by the following definition:

By self-esteem we refer to the evaluation which the individual makes and customarily maintains with regard to himself: it expresses an attitude of approval or disapproval, and indicates the extent to which the individual believes himself to be capable, significant, successful, and worthy. In short, self-esteem is a personal judgment of worthiness that is expressed in the attitudes the individual holds toward himself. It is a subjective experience which the individual conveys to others by verbal reports and other overt expressive behavior.[1]

No one ever sees or hears another person's self-esteem; rather, self-esteem is *inferred* from what the person does and says. Such inferences come after the fact—that is, after we have seen what the person does and heard what the person says. In light of the nonpublic nature of self-esteem, self-esteem cannot be the direct focus of any counseling or psychotherapy that is administered by another person. In contrast, self-administered treatments can be aimed directly at self-esteem.

Since self-esteem is a global concept covering general trends in self-evaluation, attempts to change oneself must deal with more specific goals. Examples of such goals can be found in a list of indicators of high self-esteem: (1) giving and receiving affection, (2) resisting social pressures to conform, (3) identifying threatening stimuli, (4) solving problems creatively, (5) playing an active role in social groups, (6) identifying one's own capabilities and distinctiveness, (7) expressing one's own views frequently and effectively, and (8) moving directly and realistically toward personal goals.[2] Some indicators of low self-esteem are: (1) seeking professional psychological help, (2) using anxious talk, (3) expressing self-doubts, (4) avoiding closeness in personal relations, (5) manifesting a large discrepancy between personal objectives and present performance, (6) reporting guilt, shame, depression, and unworthiness, (7) avoiding normal activities and situations, and (8) evaluating oneself as unimportant, unsuccessful, and unworthy.[3]

Once personal goals are identified, a fundamental choice occurs regarding what dimension(s) to use in self-evaluating success. The most basic alternative is to use qualitative or quantitative criteria. Words that often express qualitative criteria are *good/bad, right/wrong, useful/useless, valuable/worthless, beautiful/ugly,* and *satisfying/terrible.* Corresponding expressions of quantitative criteria are *faster/slower, sooner/later, higher/lower, louder/quieter, longer/shorter,* and *heavier/lighter.*

Qualitative criteria may prove helpful in selecting one's goals, but they provide a defective basis for evaluating progress toward those goals. In contrast, the individual can self-evaluate personal progress best by using quantitative criteria. Using quantitative criteria seems to facilitate a number of helpful processes: (1) keeps the person focused on the central goal,

(2) identifies cumulative movement toward the goal, (3) points out success rather than failure, (4) evaluates actions and their effects rather than the actor, and (5) promotes self-acceptance rather than self-rejection.

The advantages of quantitative self-evaluation are part of a large set of benefits available from self-administered psychological interventions.[4] Such self-control strategies blossomed in the 1970s, and they have been used to master a wide range of problems, such as academic achievement, anxiety, assertiveness, career planning, creativity, depression, dieting, epileptic seizures, fears, headaches, high blood pressure, insomnia, obsessions, pain, physical aggression, sexual deviations, smoking, stuttering, substance abuse, and tics.

ADVANTAGES OF SELF-ADMINISTERED THERAPY

The research data suggest that the individual can learn to self-administer any psychological treatment that may be administered by a professional counselor or therapist. Furthermore, self-regulation has many advantages over interventions conducted by another person. Self-control procedures can: (1) change behavior in the real world, (2) promote self-understanding and self-mastery, (3) take advantage of the client's control of personal reinforcers, (4) save money for the client, (5) minimize the time the professional counselor spends on each case, (6) keep the client informed of the therapeutic process, (7) take advantage of self-modeling mechanisms, (8) develop personal competencies and confidence to deal with future problems, (9) provide more treatment per week, (10) reduce resistance to personal change, and (11) alter the person's perception of self-efficacy. As defined by Bandura, *self-efficacy* seems to provide a more clinically useful concept than self-esteem:

Psychological procedures . . . alter expectations of personal efficacy. Within this analysis, efficacy and outcome expectations are distinguished . . . . An outcome expectancy is defined here as a person's estimate that a given behavior will lead to certain outcomes. An efficacy expectation is the conviction that one can successfully execute the behavior required to produce the outcomes. Outcome and efficacy expectations are differentiated because individuals can come to believe that a particular course of action will produce certain outcomes, but question whether they can perform those actions.[5]

Self-regulation experiences demonstrate that the individual can perform these key actions.

SELF-REGULATION PROCEDURES

Early Self-Evaluation

The person who would like to change self-esteem, self-efficacy, or personal behavior may find starting off with providing answers to the following questions to be helpful: What do I do or say that gets me into trouble, that makes me or others unhappy, or that scares or angers others? What thoughts do I have that seem to produce fear, anxiety, anger, depression, or other negative feelings? What things don't I do or say often enough? What thoughts might I think that would lead me to become more happy, peaceful, and content, and less fearful, anxious, angry, or depressed? What are my good points? What do I like about myself as a person? What do other people seem to like about me? What do I expect to accomplish as a result of changing my own behavior? In what ways and how much must I change in order to be satisfied? What are the one, two, or three behaviors that I *most* want to change? What might be the most effective, efficient, powerful, practical, and realistic methods to produce such changes?

These questions are framed primarily in terms of what the person does or does not *do*. Answers to these questions suggest *actions* that the individual may take to achieve desired outcomes. The behavioral parts of these outcomes were identified in the opening paragraph as *regulated actions*. Self-management procedures consist of *regulating actions* that one controls oneself. A careful examination of Bandura's definition of *self-efficacy* given above suggests that self-control of regulating actions is the essence of self-efficacy. Since self-efficacy is an action-oriented synonym for self-esteem, there appears to be a positive relationship between effective self-regulation and high self-esteem.

In contrast, when one person counsels or treats another, self-efficacy is not necessarily promoted. Also, treatment approaches that emphasize reflection and self-exploration run the risk of promoting a passive set. Self-evaluations expressed in terms of the verb *to be* are symptomatic of such a passive set. For example, statements such as "I am worthless, I am a born loser, I am inadequate," do not suggest any course of action. They implicitly communicate helplessness. Helplessness implies low self-efficacy, but low self-efficacy is usually synonymous with low self-esteem. Self-regulation procedures are an antidote for helplessness.

There are four broad categories of methods for changing one's own behavior: (1) setting events, (2) cues, (3) primary behaviors, and (4) consequences. Within each category, there are several classes of operations. Any given self-regulation program will usually consist of several such operations. These operations are the self-regulating actions that change the target behavior(s).

Setting Events

Setting events are interventions that change the general state of the person. They change thresholds for various forms of stimulation by making the individual more or less responsive or they alter some dimension of acting or responding. There are at least eight classes of setting events. Each is briefly described below.

Administration of a deprivation schedule.   An individual may increase the power of a particular reinforcer by systematically avoiding that event for specified periods and circumstances. Doing so will tend to make the reinforcer more attractive, thereby providing one means of increased self-control. For example, one man complained that he did not enjoy sexual intercourse with his wife as much as he did earlier in their marriage. On the other hand, he volunteered that he masturbated about four times a week. His therapist suggested that he stop masturbating and have sexual intercourse with his wife as the sole source of direct sexual gratification. The husband implemented the suggestion, and his marital relationship improved. Correspondingly, as he increased giving and receiving affection with his wife, his self-esteem rose.

Administration of a satiation schedule.   In order to decrease the power of a reinforcer, one can consume large amounts of the reinforcer in a short period of time. Janet, a twelve-year-old girl who complained of being overweight, expressed the desire to reduce. She was a compulsive candy-eater. She decided that one of the first steps in her weight reduction program should be to weaken the attractiveness of candy; therefore, she bought three pounds of chocolate and ate all of them in one sitting. By the last bite, she was quite sick of chocolate and stated that she felt in a much better position to control her eating. This rise in self-confidence seemed to have grown out of her creatively solving a personal problem.

Administration of drugs.   Human beings have a long history of self-administering drugs. The whole field of psychopharmacology has developed because of the impact certain drugs have on psychological functioning. Drugs may be used as part of a self-control program; however, taking drugs may lower rather than elevate a person's perception of self-control or self-efficacy.[6] Using drugs may increase self-doubts about mastery over one's world, thereby further lowering self-esteem.

Application of physical restraints.   As is true with drugs, the use of physical restraints has a long history in controlling human behavior. Although application of restraints is usually done by another, self-administration of restraints may also occur. Bert, a nineteen-year-old college sophomore, returned home from a fight with his girlfriend. She had just told him that their relationship was over. He was acutely depressed and began having suicidal thoughts. These thoughts scared him; so he took his little brother's handcuffs, opened them, left the key in the hallway, entered his bedroom, handcuffed himself to the bed, and waited for someone to come home. Bizarre as the story may sound, Bert felt he had successfully controlled himself. He had identified a special threat to himself and taken effective action to protect himself from his own destructive impulses. His accurate self-diagnosis and effective intervention raised his sense of self-efficacy.

Providing or identifying choices.   A powerful means of evaluating one's mood is to provide oneself with choices or alternative goals. Not surprisingly, most systems of counseling and psychotherapy place an emphasis on helping people decide what they want. However, most of these systems do not point out that the process of identifying choices does not just give personal guidance as to where to move—it changes our basic sense of well-being. Choice is a corner stone of perceived control.[7] Identifying personal alternatives for action is a cornerstone of self-esteem.

Application of pleasant stimulation.   When positive reinforcers are delivered *without* a contingent relationship to the target behavior, their delivery should be identified as a setting event, rather than as a consequence. Also, every occurrence of positive reinforcement serves both to strengthen the reinforced behavior and at least slightly to change the state of the person. Pleasure-seeking is a major human pastime. What may often not be clear is that providing oneself with reasonable amounts of pleasure is one of the basic ways of self-regulation. When the individual fails to provide a minimum level of pleasure, depression occurs. Arranging one's life to provide a regular flow of pleasant experiences is good preventive medicine against anxiety, depression, and a negative self-evaluation.

Application of aversive stimulation.   When unpleasant events occur without a contingent relationship to the target behavior, their delivery should be identified as a setting event. Also, aversive consequences have an impact in changing the general state of the recipient as well as affecting the consequated behavior. As indicated earlier, persons who appear to have low self-esteem have difficulty in clearly identifying threatening stimuli.[8] Such discriminations are a prerequisite to presenting or removing aversive stimulation. Self-regulating the amount of aversive stimulation received is another means of increasing self-control.

Providing a relationship. Making and maintaining contact with other human beings is essential to normal functioning. Not only are human relationships necessary for psychological well-being, they are also important to bodily functioning and physical health.[9] Developing and maintaining friendships, working on a marriage, and spending time with family and loved ones are basic ingredients for self-management. A key element in such relationships is being aware of one's "rooting section." Knowing that there are people who are following how one is doing seems to improve the individual's performance in a fashion similar to the improved play shown by sports teams when they compete on their home fields. The ultimate such relationship is the one that is formed with God. Perceiving that he is always present and knowing that Jesus himself prays for each of us does have transforming power. This power comes through an event controlled by the individual: acceptance of the Gift that God has provided. Acceptance of a relationship with another person is intimately related to self-acceptance. Self-acceptance is an important facet of self-esteem.

Whereas the eight preceding classes of setting events have the greatest power for making broad changes in an individual, the remaining categories and classes have increasingly narrower impacts on limited numbers of behaviors. They are the remaining alternatives for self-regulation.

Cues

Cues provide information *before* the individual acts. Often the cue signals what consequence is likely to occur if a particular action takes place. Such cues are sometimes called *signals* or *discriminative stimuli.* Other cues elicit reactions or reflexes rather than providing information about subsequent reinforcers. Such cues are sometimes identified as *prods* or *unconditioned stimuli.* Both basic types of cues may be managed by the individual as ways to increase self-mastery.

Choosing a target behavior is an important first step in a self-regulation program. *Defining the target behavior* clearly, and preferably in empirical terms, is a second and closely related step. Both of these operations serve as cues, pointing out the direction in which the person wants to move. Having decided what to do, most persons still need an *immediate cue* to tell them when to start, stop, or continue the course of action they have selected. Appointment books, lists of tasks to be performed today, and clocks are among the more common cuing devices that people use to regulate their own behavior. Such mechanisms of self-direction allow the individual to resist social pressures to conform. Being able to resist social pressures to conform is a characteristic of the person with high self-esteem. *Setting a goal* for the target behavior is also important. Goals may be directional (set to increase or decrease the behavior) or absolute (set to reach a particular level of performance). In order to be useful, they should be realistic, reachable, and prioritized. Effective goal-setting lies at the heart of the self-managed life-style. If the person plans to provide consequences for moving toward or reaching the goal, he or she should *set the performance standards* for doing so. Deciding the performance standards before actually initiating the self-regulation program will increase the intervention package's impact. Because memory is imperfect and good resolutions are quickly forgotten, the self-manager will be wise to prepare a *written performance contract* containing all elements of the plan for change. If rewards or punishments will be included, they also should be identified before starting the program. Selecting back-up reinforcers before implementing the total plan is another way to increase the impact on one's own behavior. The greater the impact on one's own behavior, the greater the sense of self-efficacy.

Probably the most complex types of cues are social models. Most of what people learn that is distinctively human is acquired by observing others.[10] But observational learning is not limited to watching others; we can also learn from ourselves. Watching ourselves in a mirror, on a movie screen, or on a television monitor, listening to ourselves on a tape recorder, or reading our own descriptions, directions, or statements are means of *providing models* to ourselves. In general, exposing ourselves to models who demonstrate how to cope with the kinds of problems that we are trying to solve is a powerful way to modify ourselves. Traditional forms of "talking therapies" have not suggested the power available in observational learning for achieving higher levels of self-efficacy, but using one's own behavior as a model for new learning has much potential. Self-modeling helps the person to identify his or her own capabilities and distinctiveness, and this latter identification process is another characteristic of high self-esteem.

Primary Behaviors

Primary behaviors are the third broad category of regulating actions, but they have a fundamental difference from all other regulating actions in that one can only use these operations on oneself. They cannot be done to another person; therefore, they only have meaning within the context of self-control.[11] There are three classes of primary behaviors: *engaging in a desired behavior, engaging in an action that competes with an undesired behavior,* and *directly withholding a behavior.*

Although psychotherapists have tended to overlook the role of primary behaviors in changing human behavior, other experts have suggested their value. For example, Guthrie gave the following advice many decades ago:

> The general rule for all habit-breaking: find the associative cues responsible for the start of the habit . . . and to these cues or conditioners practice some less undesirable response.[12]

This approach identifies the individual as the holder of a great deal of power for changing his or her own behavior at will. Recognition of primary behaviors as a means for regulating oneself is also a key element of self-efficacy. A final category of sources of self-regulation appears below.

Consequences

A person can change his or her own actions by altering what immediately follows these actions. *Observing the designated action, providing feedback,* or *observing behavior by-products* are methods of increasing self-control. Making a written or other *permanent record* of the behavior or its by-products is a closely related procedure. By transforming such records into a *graph* the individual can gain a clear picture of progress. This progress can then be *compared with the person's goal* as well as *with the self-set standards for consequating* the target behavior. Then the individual may apply a specific consequence by applying or removing a positive or negative reinforcer. Positive reinforcers are what most people would identify as rewarding events, and negative reinforcers are punishing events. Provided that realistic, reachable goals have been set initially, the person who uses the above procedures of self-evaluation and self-reinforcement will tend to move directly toward their personal goals. They will minimize the gap between personal objectives and present performance; therefore, they are more likely to evaluate themselves as successful. Such an approach to self-evaluation bypasses feelings of shame, depression, and unworthiness. The self-management of consequences promotes high self-esteem.

SUMMARY

Human beings have the capacity to regulate their own behavior systematically. Persons with low self-esteem do not seem to perceive the potential power they have to control their own behavior, but the concept of *self-esteem* does not help prepare people to take charge of their own lives. *Self-evaluation* is a more helpful means of achieving higher levels of self-control and self-mastery, but it is not as comprehensive as the concept of *self-regulation*. *Self-regulation* strategies promote a perception of *self-efficacy*. They are probably more potent for increasing a sense of personal mastery than are therapeutic interventions provided by others. Of the four broad categories of self-regulation procedures, *setting events* are the most potent but the least focused on any particular behavior. *Cues* have a less potent impact, but they are still relatively powerful and have the advantage of being focused so that a limited range of behavior can be influenced. Less efficient than cues but still a good way of changing one's own actions are *primary behaviors* (that is, direct practice). Finally, the least efficient, but still helpful, methods of self-control involve the management of *consequences* for one's own behavior. Persons who get identified as having high self-esteem probably have learned to use many of these approaches to regulate their own actions. Persons who get identified as having low self-esteem need to acquire the self-management technology that is available to them. Teaching persons to regulate their own behavior is a powerful approach for raising their self-esteem.

NOTES

1. Stanley Coopersmith, *The Antecedents of Self-Esteem* (San Francisco: W. H. Freeman, 1967), pp. 4–5.
2. *Ibid.*
3. *Ibid.*
4. David L. Watson and Roland G. Tharp, *Self-directed Behavior: Self-Modification for Personal Adjustment* (Belmont, Calif.: Brooks/Cole Publishing Co., 1972); Marvin R. Goldfried and Michael Merbaum, eds., *Behavior Change through Self-Control* (New York: Holt, Rinehart & Winston, 1973); Carol Foster, *Developing Self-Control* (Kalamazoo, Mich.: Behaviordelia, 1974); Michael J. Mahoney and Carl E. Thoresen, *Self-Control: Power to the Person* (Monterey, Calif.: Brooks/Cole Publishing Co., 1974); Carl E. Thoresen and Michael J. Mahoney, *Behavioral Self-Control* (New York: Holt, Rinehart & Winston, 1974); Robert L. Williams and James D. Long, *Toward a Self-Managed Life-Style* (Boston: Houghton Mifflin Co., 1975); Dwight L. Goodwin and Thomas J. Coates, *Helping Students Help Themselves: How You Can Put Behavior Analysis into Action in Your Classroom* (Englewood Cliffs, N.J.: Prentice-Hall, 1976); David R. Wheeler, *Control Yourself* (Chicago: Nelson-Hall, 1976).
5. Albert Bandura, *Social Learning Theory* (Englewood Cliffs, N.J.: Prentice-Hall, 1977), p. 79.
6. Alan O. Ross, *Psychological Disorders of Children: A Behavioral Approach to Theory, Research, and Therapy,* 2nd ed. (New York: McGraw-Hill Book Co., 1980), pp. 248–249.
7. Lawrence C. Perlmuter and Richard A. Monty, eds., *Choice and Perceived Control* (Hillsdale, N.J.: Lawrence Erlbaum Associates, 1979).

8. Coopersmith, *The Antecedents of Self-Esteem*, pp. 45–71.
9. James J. Lynch, *The Broken Heart: The Medical Consequences of Loneliness* (New York: Basic Books, 1977).
10. Albert Bandura, ed., *Psychological Modeling: Conflicting Theories* (Chicago: Aldine–Atherton, 1971).
11. Paul W. Clement, *A System for Describing Therapeutic Interventions* (Pasadena, Calif.: Fuller Theological Seminary, 1980; ERIC Document Reproduction Service No. ED 192 195).
12. Edwin R. Guthrie, *The Psychology of Human Conflict: The Clash of Motives within the Individual* (Boston: Beacon Press, 1963; originally published by Harper & Brothers, 1938), p. 75.

BIOGRAPHICAL SKETCH

PAUL W. CLEMENT is professor of psychology and director of the Psychological Center, Graduate School of Psychology, Fuller Theological Seminary. He received his Ph.D. in clinical psychology from the University of Utah and is a fellow in the Division of Clinical Psychology of the American Board of Professional Psychology. His research on self-regulation has been published in *Behavioral Counseling Quarterly, Biofeedback and Self-regulation, Child Behavior Therapy, Journal of Applied Behavior Analysis, Journal of School Health,* and *Psychological Reports.* He has published forty articles in eighteen journals, authored nine original chapters in books, made two movies (one of these on self-management in children), co-edited one book and co-authored another, made a twelve-hour tape series on child psychotherapy (published by the Behavioral Science Tape Library), and presented over fifty papers at professional and scientific conventions. Since 1971, his clinical research has focused on self-regulation in child psychotherapy. He is a diplomate in clinical psychology (American Board of Professional Psychology), a fellow of the American Psychological Association, and a member of the editorial boards of *Professional Psychology* and *The Bulletin.*

PART II

Applied Issues

Self-Esteem: Practical Applications

RELATIONSHIPS in the home have a powerful influence on self-esteem. Those who are the most intimate and psychologically significant to us shape and affect self-perception. This is especially true of the impact that parents have on their children.

PARENTING

It is in the context of the parent-child relationship that social feedback central to self-esteem normally begins.

Results of several studies support the commonly held assertion that acceptance of children by their parents, as measured by parental warmth either in early childhood or more reflectively later on, is positively correlated with high self-esteem.[1] Acceptance is communicated by parents in a variety of ways. For the young infant, it involves gentleness in handling, time spent holding the child, time elapsed in meeting expressed needs, appropriateness of the attempts to meet needs, expressions of delight and the amount of spontaneous, non-need-oriented interaction, such as in play. For the older child, it involves gentleness of responses to transgression and in discipline, time spent encouraging and responding to the child's ideas and positive behavior, and use of praise and other language indicating delight and acceptance.[2] Language becomes a powerful tool in the shaping of children's self-image as they apply their new language to themselves as they experience it being applied by the most significant people in their world. The impact of parental feedback is especially critical during early childhood because parents are viewed as omniscient during most of the formative years of the self-concept.

Several studies support the notion that self-esteem is at least partly due to identification with the parent, usually the mother.[3] The results could also be explained in terms of differences in the way that mothers relate to and reinforce their children. Regardless, the evidence is consistent that high self-esteem mothers tend to have high self-esteem children and vice versa.

Parents with low self-esteem are likely to stimulate similar negative self-worth in their children by: (1) pushing their children so hard to make up for their own inadequacies that the children feel inferior because they cannot meet parental standards; (2) providing a negative model for the children to identify with; and (3) being overly sensitive to the children's shortcomings because they might reflect the parents' inadequacies as parents and as people.

The more parents genuinely and healthily love themselves, the more they will have the confidence to establish positive goals for raising their children. They will also be able to relax and accept their children and to give love freely. These psychological findings are, of course, consistent with the scriptural mandates to love your neighbor as yourself (Luke 10:27), and to love your wife as yourself (Eph. 5:28). Feeling positive about oneself frees one to fully appreciate and affirm others. This includes children.

There is also evidence that those who are higher in sex-role identification are higher in self-esteem,[4] as are those who mature earlier in adolescence, and that the sources of self-esteem as mediated through socialization agents are different for boys and girls.[5] Among white middle-class student males it appears that self-esteem may be based more on what is accomplished and external sources of evaluation, while for females social self-esteem may not only be more stable but also less related to approval needs in an academic achievement situation and more centered in social adequacy.[6] These differences, of course, may be traced back to differences in the way that parents may set standards and give positive feedback for boys and girls. It is too early to tell what kind of effect current attempts at unification of socialization for the sexes during childhood will have upon the bases of self-esteem, though the stress on moving females more into male roles may lead to women becoming more achievement- or power-oriented.

Stanford psychologist Robert Sears found that high self-esteem was significantly related for both sexes with academic achievement, small family size, early birth position in the family, and high warmth on the part of both parents. For boys, high self-esteem was associated with low father-dominance in the marital relationship.

Stanley Coopersmith, author of a highly regarded book, *Antecedents of Self-Esteem,* found that high self-esteem was related to close relationships between parents and boys, as indicated by parental interest in the boys' welfare, concern about companions, availability for discussion of problems and joint activities. Parents of high self-esteem boys were also less permissive. They set high standards of behavior and were consistently firm in enforcement, though they were less punitive in style. They tended to use rewards and nonphysical punishment for discipline. In addition, family governance for high self-esteem boys was more democratic, with parents encouraging input from the boys and allowing dissent and persuasion within the context of well-defined guidelines for privilege and responsibility. Finally, a significantly greater proportion of boys came from families marked by divorce or separation.

Both Sears and Coopersmith found that those with high self-esteem had higher goals and were more successful in achieving them. The parents of the boys in the Coopersmith study placed greater value on achievement than on adjustment or accommodation to other persons. This reflects the sex-based differences indicated in the Hollander study and is also consistent with Sears' finding that low self-esteem was associated with femininity, which, in turn, is not associated with achievement as a base of self-esteem. The fact that a nonachievement base is associated with lower self-esteem is undoubtedly a reflection of societal values, as well as possibly due to the greater difficulty in discriminating evaluation that is not contingent upon specific responses. At least one study partially contradicts these findings and concludes that praise of the person, rather than praise of task performance, is generally positively related to self-esteem.[7] This is consistent with another study which suggests that privileged adolescents of parents intensively engaged in academic work have *lower* self-esteem.[8]

Nevertheless, it certainly seems true that competence and confidence are closely interrelated, each fostering the other.[9] In our society, the greatest reinforcements come for competence in task achievements, at least for boys, though at least minimal levels of interpersonal competence must also be demonstrated for positive feedback.

MARITAL RELATIONSHIPS

The intimacy of marriage provides continuous opportunities for the construction and destruction of self-esteem. Generally, it is within marriage that adults are most emotionally vulnerable. The evaluation of a spouse, especially with regard to personality and character qualities, carries considerable impact. This is because of the human desire for affirmation and unconditional love that has been focused on the partner. Marital intimacy, the glue of the relationship, requires risk-taking or the sharing of foibles, faults, fears, and fantasies. How such intentional or unintentional revelation is received by one's partner will either strengthen both one's self-worth and the relationship or contribute to their demise. It is certainly possible to view the breakup of marriages as a function of the breakdown in self-esteem due to criticism and conflict. Strong marriages are built on mutual affirmation. Affirmation is simply the practice of focusing on the positive qualities of another, believing in that person, helping them to develop because of the faith being expressed in them, and choosing to ignore faults as having any significant meaning for the assessment of character or stability of the relationship. In a word, affirmation is love. 1 Corinthians 13 clearly expresses the kind of love that builds self-worth and, in turn, strengthens the relationship:

Love is patient, love is kind. It does not envy, it does not boast, it is not proud. It is not rude, it is not self-seeking, it is not easily angered, it keeps no record of wrongs. Love does not delight in evil, but rejoices with the truth. It always protects, always trusts, always hopes, always perseveres. (vv. 4–7, NIV)

The inverse of such love is rejection.

Acceptance and affirmation allow intimacy to blossom. Criticism and rejection destroy. Couples communicate rejection in several common ways: infidelity, perfectionism, not showing interest in their partner's life, and anger.[10] Within marriage, it is extremely important to accentuate the positives explicitly by regularly complimenting each other, doing enjoyable things together, and avoiding blaming.[11] Forgiveness is vital in marriage because it communicates acceptance and love *in spite of* faults each partner has and the hurts each may cause. Forgiveness frees the relationship from the destructive cycle of justification and counterattack that simply escalates mutual (emotional) destruction.

Marriage partners may also communicate rejection often unintentionally, in the way they make decisions and handle conflicts. Marital conflicts often originate or are expressed when couples have to make decisions. The decisions may be as simple as where to put the new couch or as complex as how to cope with a handicapped baby or care for a widowed parent. The intensity and length of conflicts may not be directly related to the complexity of the decision. Couples can get into serious disagreements over the simplest matters—should the heat be turned down at night or the window opened, what color should the house be painted, or who should wash the car or mow the lawn. Decisions need to be made daily. And there's no umpire to call balls and strikes. Partners often come to a decision with different values, needs, perceptions, and goals. These differences can become the basis for deeper intimacy and togetherness or lead to intense power struggles in which one or both partners feel put down and hurt. The biggest difficulties in most marital decision-making are usually the willingness to really hear out the partner's views, failure to adopt a problem-solving approach to the decision, a tendency to get off the issue and onto supposed hidden motives or blindnesses of the partner, and unwillingness to compromise. If decisions and conflicts are approached constructively, they provide opportunities for partners to express and clarify real feelings, to learn more about each other's values and goals, and to build each other's self-worth. If, however, these decisions and conflicts are battlegrounds (which they easily become if such a pattern develops early in marriage), we will find ourselves like armed enemies in splendid, horrible emotional isolation and loneliness. Usually, it is the way the decisions and conflicts are conducted that gives feelings of rejection: stony silence or uncontrolled screaming do not readily convey a willingness to reason lovingly; insisting on always having one's own way makes a partner feel worthless; being unwilling to listen to one's partner denies the partner's importance and very existence in the relationship. The list could go on almost indefinitely, but I am sure the point is well made. Decisions and conflicts are opportunities for the growth or death of intimacy. They provide a garden of belonging or a gravel pit of emptiness.

Singles have traditionally struggled with feelings of inferiority because of societally induced perceptions. Until recently at least, to be single was to be a social failure. Those who didn't get married were somehow lacking in certain essential qualities. Fortunately, attitudes toward singleness are changing. To be single, in general, is not as much of a stigma as it once was. As societal norms change, the rejection message is bound to diminish and singles will not look down on themselves quite so quickly and automatically. Singleness will begin to be seen as a choice and therefore an expression of character strength.

CHRISTIANITY AND THE CHURCH

In order for a person to experience emotional and social well-being, he or she must have a belief system with related practices that promote positive self-esteem. For many, religious belief and experience have significant impact upon self-evaluation. Such beliefs and behaviors may be central to the construction of a person's ideal self and provide salient criteria for self-evaluation.

Rosenberg has examined the concept of self-esteem extensively and has found that there is a higher level of self-esteem among Jews, while Catholics and Protestants have very similar levels.[12] However, Rosenberg did not take into account differences in religious beliefs and practices within these broad religious systems that might affect self-esteem.

Other writers have suggested that belonging to a religious community promotes self-esteem,[13] and that the removal of one's sins and working out God's image created in humanity has a positive effect.[14] The nature of these relationships is primarily theoretical, though a recent major survey of teenagers conducted by the Assemblies of God suggested that regular church attendance, spiritual conversion, and close spiritual ties with parents are associated with high self-esteem.[15]

Other research indicates that self-esteem is highly associated with spiritual well-being,[16] and especially with the existential well-being subscale of Paloutzian and Ellison's Spiritual Well-Being Scale.[17] A recent study by Ellison and Economos[18] has further clarified relationships between self-esteem, spiritual well-being, and religious beliefs and practices. Although their findings are primarily correlational and must be regarded as tentative, they found that quality of life, as measured by self-esteem and spiritual well-being, was consistently related to those doctrinal, liturgical, devotional, and organizational beliefs and practices that emphasize God's affirmation and acceptance of the individual, personal communion with God that is perceived as positive, and the feeling of being part of a caring community. The value of more refined measures of religious orientation than those typically employed in psychology and sociology of religion was confirmed. Though there was no difference between "born-again" and "ethical" Christians with regard to self-esteem, specific beliefs and practices did distinguish self-esteem levels. Contrary to a frequently stated assumption, they did not find that born-again Christians had more negative self-esteem than ethical Christians. Furthermore, for Protestant evangelical Christians, it was found that self-esteem was positively associated with the average number of devotional periods per week and the average amount of time spent in devotions each day. Ellison and Economos suggest the need for even more refined kinds of analysis, such as intrinsic-extrinsic religiosity[19] or the centrality of one's Christian faith, or further delineation of Protestant born-agains into "fundamentalist" or "evangelical" categories. The implications of this study seem fairly clear: those religious beliefs and practices that promote a sense of affirmation and communication both with God and the Christian community are associated with positive self-esteem.

THE SOCIETY

Many of the key values promoted by the socialization process have significant implications for self-esteem. To the extent that such values are internalized, they become vital to construction of ideal-self images and to internal evaluation. They are also applied as evaluation criteria by other persons. To the extent that a person exemplifies valued characteristics, self-esteem is strengthened. To the extent that there is perceived discrepancy, self-worth will be negated.

COMMUNITY AND CULTURE

Perhaps the most powerful influence shaping the valued characteristics of Americans is the media. Through the presentation of various "heroes" and the selection and reinforcement of certain behavior, standards, and characteristics, television in particular feeds into and actually defines the "ideals" that become part of our ideal self. Most children watch television for two to three hours per day, and 78 percent of America's families use the television as a babysitter.[20]

There has, of course, been extensive debate as to whether television conditions responses and creates socially undesirable responses, or allows for the cathartic release of emotions and aids the society's adjustment. Beginning with early studies of vicarious imitation[21] and considering more recent conclusions, the results seem reasonably conclusive: television acts as a model and shaper of responses.

What kinds of models or ideals are being presented? Liebert *et al.* indicate that the single most characteristic value presented by television is violence.[22] It has been estimated that the average American child between the ages of five and fifteen sees the violent destruction of more than 13,000 persons on television. Despite some promises made by major broadcasters, things seem to be about the same, with the addition of increasingly explicit sex and the presentation of both romance and broken families as the norms (ideals?) for life. Liebert found that the most powerful group on television was the white American male, usually middle-class, unmarried, and involved in violence as an aggressor. Women are increasingly portrayed with a kind of feminine machismo: slick, single, aggressive, and power-hungry. Other misconceptions and consequently distorted values involve racial and ethnic groups, occupational roles, normal family life, and the routine of living.

In summary, contemporary American television tends to offer a distorted view of real life and to place value, by virtue of characteristics portrayed and rewarded on the screen, on power and success, with manipulation of others the way to the goal. Stable and mature love in the context of friendships, marriages, and family life are grossly underrepresented, and therefore undervalued. To the extent that television shapes our values and consequently our self-images, it leads us away from the biblical basis of self-esteem and into a misleading search for esteem that can be only unstable and negative in results.

A second major influence upon self-esteem is that represented by the intertwining of education and capitalism. It should be understood that capitalism, or, perhaps more correctly, greed for money, also is a major determinant of what is shown on television. Advertisers spend over $30 billion a year to persuade viewers that their lives will be happier, sexier, and more peaceful if they will just buy the latest miracle product. Commercials are not known for encouraging integrity. Rather, such half-truths and exaggerations have been found to promote cynicism and distrust toward adult trustworthiness on the part of pre-adolescents. After a while, even kids begin to wonder about toothpaste with sex appeal, colognes that promise instant love, and laundry detergent that gets wash whiter than white. By the time they have turned eighteen and watched between 400,000 and 650,000 commercials, they will either be hooked on the things-make-happiness message or tend to see life and people through distrusting eyes.

One of the major symbols of achievement in our society is *acquisition*. As a guiding value, acquisition focuses us on things as the way to happiness. Having the newest, biggest, best, or most becomes a kind of psychological security blanket for many. Clothes, houses, cars, property, and cash are the way to acceptance. If we have them, we are worth getting to know. The problem is that this also means people are related to in terms of what they own rather than in terms of who they are. We become very careful to display those goods that tell others they would benefit from relating to us. Acquisition also gives us a measure of control. Those who do not have what we have either do not seek our friendship or can be summarily dismissed. People are treated as commodities, nuisances, and threats. We can look down upon, reject, and dehumanize those who have less as "no-good," "lazy," or "worthless." Although this approach may partially restore our sense of self-esteem, it also launches us into an ocean with no shoreline. Manufacturers will always make sure there are new items to be bought— new inventions, new revisions. They make us feel inadequate, unattractive, and less than complete without their soap, mouthwash, toothpaste, and hair spray.

It is easy to start focusing on protection of our acquisitions. The more we have, the more others want what we have; and this can lead to a sense of defensiveness about people, a feeling that all people want is to get out of us what they can. Perhaps the most dramatic, but not the only, illustration of the effects of acquisition on loneliness is billionaire Howard Hughes. Hughes spent most of the truly wealthy years of his life as a recluse, isolated from true friendship. He had everything that our society claims is necessary for happiness. He died financially rich, but emotionally poor and lonely.

A side effect of centering on acquisition has been the quantification of value. What is really important can be measured. The more there is of something, the more valuable it is. Numbers count, individuals do not. Bigger is better.

Third, the American educational system strongly rewards the characteristic of achievement, as demonstrated in the 1950s by McClelland and his colleagues. Human value comes to be measured in terms of how much one produces. We subtly come to judge ourselves comparatively in terms of salary levels. Simple decisions as to who should be treated first in the hospital, for example, come down to perceived value as judged by evident material success or economic class. The result, of course, is that those who, for one reason or another, cannot achieve adequately are surrounded with negative feedback and come to view themselves negatively. The problem is not only that an unstable basis for self-esteem is created through the emphasis on achievement, but that modern industrial production techniques (factory or office) make it difficult for a sense of achievement even to be experienced. Work is fragmented, routinized, and separated from the end creation or is aimed at such artificial ends that it becomes meaningless and also unable to confer a sense of accomplishment. Some find themselves so identified that they face continuous obstacles in gaining the tools necessary to achieve or to reach economically valued positions, such as in the case of rejected minorities (the aged, poor, racial minorities, and physically handicapped, for example). Unemployment rates among blacks in central cities are typically three to four times higher than for comparable white groups, among those looking for work.

The devaluing begins way back in the educational process, when such individuals begin to fail because they do not meet the middle-class standards of achievement. In one classic study of teacher expectations, it was shown that teacher expectations strongly and subtly influence the performance of children.[23] Children that teachers expected greater intellectual gains from showed significant gains and were described as having a better chance of being successful and happy in later life. The children were randomly assigned to the experimental groups so that intellectual promise at the outset was merely in the mind of the teacher. Furthermore, children whom the teachers perceived as "slow track" were not only rated negatively, but were rated even less favorably if they showed unexpected gains. It is exactly these kinds of expectations that tend to be expressed toward lower-class and minority children, thus beginning a vicious negative cycle in which, for many, death becomes the only relief.

In addition to achievement, both the media and our educational system highly value physical beauty and powers. Dobson points out the pernicious effects of this valuing upon the self-esteem of countless people.[24] Research evidence exists which indicates that the mesomorphic or athletic body type is rated most favorably and that heavy children report less positive self-concepts than their more athletic peers.[25] Finally, the media in particular tends to foster an attitude of disdain and rejection toward those who are physically or functionally different, such as the physically handicapped or mentally retarded. At least these persons are met with anxiety by those unsure how to relate, and at best they are actively scorned and rejected with consequent effects upon their self-esteem.

A fifth major value that affects most Americans today is *actualization*. Thousands of people are spending millions of dollars in the quest for self-fulfillment. People are incessantly searching for peace and happiness. Due to the pervasive influence of secular psychology, which has replaced God for many, and Eastern mystical religions, people have turned inward. Psychologists have replaced pastors for many people who do not really have serious emotional problems, but are unhappy with who they are and are expecting more out of themselves and life. One is struck by the observation that many who would have been considered "put together" fifty years ago are involved in deep, inner exploration that all too often seems to bring anxiety and confusion instead of actualization. In many cases, the quest for self-actualization results in the abandonment of spouses and families, who restrict the free-flying quest of the searchers with down-to-earth responsibilities. Instead of fulfillment, the search for self and happiness has brought separation, sadness, and loneliness for many. One cannot help wonder if the intensity of the search in modern culture is simply an attempt to fill the inner emptiness that has come with the removal of God from many lives. Is the search for self really a search for God?

Daniel Yankelovich has found that over 70 percent of Americans "spend a great deal of time thinking about themselves and their inner lives. . . . We have become a society of individual seekers of self-fulfillment who want to modify life in every one its 1950s dimensions—family, career, leisure—the meaning of success, relationships with other people, and relations with oneself."[26] Yankelovich suggests that most people are employing defective strategies in their search for self-fulfillment. Trying to expand their lives by focusing on their own needs results only in broken relationships, the loss of the very intimacy that provides affirmation, and the closing off of the self, rather than fulfillment.

Even within the Christian community, we are more likely to hear sermons on self-fulfillment than on being God's servants, on happiness rather than on hell, on salvation as relief from distresses rather than as redemption from sin. Historically, a Christian's self-fulfillment has been seen as a by-product of commitment to the purpose of following God's leading wholeheartedly. That seems to be changing in today's church.

While the development of positive, healthy self-concepts is vital, self-centeredness and self-fixation must be discouraged.

NOTES

1. For example, P. W. Luck, "Social Determinants of Self-Esteem," *Dissertation Abstracts International* 30 (1969) 2-A: 810; R. R. Sears, "Relation of Early Socialization Experiences to Self-Concepts and Gender Role in Middle Childhood," *Child Development* 41 (1970) 2: 267–289; S. Coopersmith, *The Antecedents of Self-Esteem* (San Francisco: W. H. Freeman, 1967).

2. It is important here to introduce the notion of noncontingent reinforcement, or reinforcement that is given simply for who the child is and not in relation to some set of behaviors. Praise might be regarded as contingent, or performance-oriented reinforcement, while delight and acceptance refer to noncontingent. R. M. Baron, A. R. Bass, and P. M. Vietze, "Type and Frequency of Praise as Determinants of Favorability of Self-Image, An Experiment in a Field Set-

ting," *Journal of Personality* 39 (1971) 4: 493–511, found that praise of the person is generally more effective in enhancing self-concept than praise of task performance.

3. D. M. Pederson and G. H. Stanford, "Personality Correlates of Children's Self-Esteem and Parental Identification," *Psychological Reports* (1969): 41–42; T. S. Tocco and C. M. Bridges, Jr., "Mother-Child Self-Concept Transmission in Florida Model Follow Through Participants," paper delivered at American Educational Research Meeting, New York, February, 1971.

4. D. M. Connell and J. E. Johnson, "Relationship between Sex Role Identification and Self Esteem in Early Adolescents," *Developmental Psychology* 3 (1970): 268.

5. J. Hollander, "Sex Differences in Sources of Social Self-Esteem," *Journal*

of Consulting and Clinical Psychology 38 (1972) 3: 343–347.

6. E. Douvan and J. Adelson, *The Adolescent Experience* (New York: Wiley and Sons, 1966).

7. R. M. Baron, A. R. Bass, and P. M. Vietze, "Type and Frequency of Praise as Determinants of Favorability of Self-Image."

8. M. Rosenberg, *Society and the Adolescent Self-Image* (Princeton, N.J.: Princeton University Press, 1965).

9. R. White, "Motivation Reconsidered: The Concept of Competence," *Psychological Review* 66 (1959): 297–334.

10. Craig W. Ellison, *Loneliness: The Search for Intimacy* (New York: Christian Herald Books, 1980), pp. 101–104.

11. Ibid., pp. 188–190.

12. M. Rosenberg, *Conceiving the Self* (New York: Basic Books, 1979).

13. M. Wagner, *Put It All Together* (Grand Rapids, Mich.: Zondervan, 1975).

14. B. Narramore, *You're Someone Special* (Grand Rapids, Mich.: Zondervan, 1978).

15. "High Self-Esteem Shown in Pentecostal Youth Survey," *Los Angeles Times*, June 11, 1977.

16. R. L. Campise, C. W. Ellison, and R. Kinsman, "Spiritual Well-Being: Some Exploratory Relationships," paper presented at APA Convention, September, 1979.

17. R. F. Paloutzian and C. W. Ellison, "Loneliness, Spiritual Well-Being, and the Quality of Life," *Loneliness: A Sourcebook of Current Theory, Research, and Therapy*, eds. D. Perlman and L. A. Peplau (New York: Wiley Interscience, in press).

18. C. W. Ellison and T. Economos, "Religious Orientation and Quality of Life," paper presented at the annual meeting of the Christian Association for Psychological Studies, San Diego, Calif., April, 1981.

19. G. W. Allport and J. H. Ross, "Personal Religious Orientation and Prejudice," *Journal of Personality and Social Psychology* 5 (1967): 432–443.

20. R. M. Liebert, Joyce N. Sprafkin, and Emily S. Davidson, *The Early Window: Effects of Television on Children and Youth* (New York: Pergamon Press, 1982).

21. A. Bandura and S. Ross, "Transmission of Aggression through Imitation of Aggressive Models," *Journal of Abnormal and Social Psychology* 63 (1961): 575–582.

22. Liebert, Sprafkin, and Davidson, *The Early Window*.

23. R. Rosenthal and L. F. Jacobson, "Teacher Expectations for the Disadvantaged," *Scientific American* 218 (April 1968) 14: 19–23.

24. J. Dobson, *Hide or Seek* (Old Tappan, N.J.: Fleming H. Revell Co., 1974).

25. P. A. Johnson and J. R. Stafford, "Stereotypic Affective Properties of Personal Names and Somatotypes in Children," *Developmental Psychology* 5 (1971): 176; D. W. Felker, "Relationship Between Self-Concept, Body Build, and Perception of Father's Interest in Sports in Boys," *Research Quarterly* 39 (1968): 513–517.

26. Daniel Yankelovich, *New Rules: Searching for Self-fulfillment in a World Turned Upside Down* (New York: Random, 1981).

SECTION I:
MARRIAGE AND FAMILY

Introduction

I T I S within the family that self-esteem normally originates and is shaped along positive or negative lines. Although the identities of significant others change throughout our lives, basic feelings of self-worth are grounded in what those who are emotionally closest feel about us.

Mary Stewart Van Leeuwen warns against the naive acceptance of psychological theory and research findings in light of underlying assumptions that may result in partial or inaccurate conclusions regarding sex-role development. She then provides an in-depth overview of biological, psychoanalytic, behavioristic, social-learning, and cognitive-developmental perspectives on sex-role identity. Stewart proposes the need to consider, sensitively and gingerly, the respective contributions and interplay that theology and psychology make to our understanding of sex-related functioning. Finally, she recommends avoiding polarization and treating persons primarily as individuals rather than as members of either sex.

According to Joyce Hulgus, marriage is critically influenced by the self-perceptions and self-feelings each partner brings into the relationship on the basis of childhood and adolescent experience. One's self-acceptance affects perceptions of dating and marital partners as well as the nature of the marital interaction itself. Self-accepting partners are more accepting of each other, tend to have similar needs (which is likely to increase mutual understanding), and are less likely to develop conflicted and neurotic interaction patterns.

Self-Esteem and Sex-Role Development

MARY STEWART VAN LEEUWEN

IN PREVIOUS chapters of this volume, various contributors have attempted to grind and place a biblically based lens before the subject of self-esteem.[1] It is now my task to direct that lens toward psychological theory and research on self-esteem as it relates to sex-role development. My strategy for organizing this increasingly vast literature will be a roughly developmental one. Hence, we will begin with a brief consideration of prenatal, biological influences, proceed to several theories on how children acquire a stable sex-linked self-concept, and weave throughout these some consideration of the hurdles presented by adolescence and adulthood. The chapter will also include some attempts to link these themes to the concerns of the individual and the corporate church community. Before we proceed, however, some methodological *caveats* are in order. As the Christian reader considers the following overview of psychological theory and research on sex-role development and self-esteem, he or she should remember not to accord the social scientific endeavor a power or absolute character that it does not warrant. The working assumptions of the North American social sciences are largely *materialistic, functionalistic, reductionistic,* and *probabalistic.*[2] When we say that they are *materialistic,* we mean that they have no methodology (beyond that of handling and classifying observables) for dealing with such nonmaterial phenomena as revealed truth, inherent meaning, or ultimate purpose. Consequently, we cannot expect them to do our homework for us in terms of how, if at all, any of their particular findings apply to our situation as Christians. To say that the social sciences are *functionalistic* is to pinpoint their preference for seeing all human behavior in terms of cause-and-effect relationships—and often oversimplified ones at that. Hence they can say little about the existence and importance of noncausal entities such as choice and accountability. When we describe social science methodology as *reductionistic,* we mean that, in addition to viewing human phenomena in cause-and-effect terms, they tend to prefer *simple,* as opposed to complex or interactive explanations. Thus one easily gets the impression (not altogether unjustified) that psychoanalysis reduces human psychology to "nothing but" the bodily passions, cognitive psychology sees "nothing but" the unfolding rational processes, and behaviorism sees "nothing but" outward motor activity.[3] In one sense, it is inevitable and even desirable that this kind of reductionism occur in scholarship and research: after all, if one is going to look at anything closely and painstakingly, one must inevitably examine it in isolation from almost everything else. But the accompanying risk is that, having compartmentalized human behavior into separate emotional, cognitive, behavioral, and other components, one never "puts Humpty-Dumpty back together again," as a being who feels, thinks, perceives, chooses, worships, and acts as one integrated person. In addition, in the constant quest for measurables, multifaceted phenomena (such as self-esteem, or sex-role self-concept) are often reduced to the number of "agree" or "disagree" responses to a list of questions or statements, or to a count of simple, contrived laboratory behaviors. Finally, to say that the social science endeavor is *probabilistic* is another way of saying that it has scant use for individual differences. Instead, in the quest for universal laws of behavior, the individual person's performance disappears into a statistical generalization, or, if atypical, is considered just so much annoying "error variance," rather than a unique and fascinating entity worth pursuing further. With such limitations now in mind, let no reader feel either personally paralyzed or prematurely omniscient after reading the findings and theories reviewed in this chapter. Psychological research on self-esteem and sex-role development is but one roughly sketched piece in the vast human puzzle which we continue, when all is said and done, to view through a glass darkly.

BIOLOGICAL INFLUENCES ON SEX-ROLE DEVELOPMENT

It was once fashionable, in the wake of Darwin's immense influence on science and popular worldview, to assume that the observation and manipulation of animal behavior could provide a simple key to unlock the mysteries of sexual functioning in humans. We are somewhat less naive now, knowing that the diversity and complexity of sex-related behavior in both humans and animals is too great to permit facile generalizations either way. Nevertheless, the "language of biology" still provides one useful approach to the question of sex and identity, provided that we do not let it lead us into the reductionistic error mentioned above.[4] It seems accurate to say that biological factors do at least provide behavioral *tendencies* that are subsequently inflated or, oppositely, rerouted by socialization and developing personal preferences. But even these merely biological tendencies are much more complex than previously assumed. Between the conception of a normal, genetic male or female and the birth of either, many developmental hurdles must be overcome. The genetic message ("XX" for females, "XY" for males) must sensitively orchestrate hormonal and morphological development in a way that makes the internal sexual apparatus congruent with external appearance, and both compatible with the glandular physiology that will later produce the matching secondary sex-characteristics in adolescence. Thus, even on the purely biological level, sexual identity is not a simplistic dichotomy. Rather, it would be more accurate to speak of "chromosomal sex," "gonadal sex," "hormonal sex," "internal organic sex," and "morphological" (or external genital) sex—all of which, through this complex process of prenatal orchestration, usually develop in matching fashion to produce a normal male or female infant whose sex upon delivery is correctly assigned.

But there are cases where one or more of these five aspects of biological sexuality go awry during prenatal development, with the result that a genetic male may appear, externally, to be a female at birth, and vice versa, resulting in a misassignment of sexual identity and subsequent rearing as a member of the opposite sex.[5] When such mistakes are finally uncovered (often at puberty, when the secondary characteristics of the child's true, genetic sex begin to manifest themselves), an obviously pertinent question is this: How do children so affected feel about their own identities? Do they welcome the prospect of a belated return to a gender-identity congruent with their "true" chromosomal sex? The bulk of the clinical evidence seems to support the power of nurture over nature in human beings: regardless of the source of the original abnormality (be it chromosomal, gonadal, internal-accessory, or morphological), such children almost always prefer to maintain the gender-identity into which they have been socialized, and indeed, are willing to undergo whatever surgical and/or hormonal procedures are necessary to assure the compatibility of external appearance with self-perceived psychosexual identity. The one possible exception may be related to *hormonal* sex, where a prenatal superabundance of male hormones in those mistakenly reared as girls, or of female hormones in those mistakenly reared as boys, seems to result in children dissatisfied with both their gender-assignment and sex-role socialization, and who welcome puberty and its revelation of their true, genetic sex, towards which they had always leaned in terms of self-concept and activity preference. In addition, there are numerous cases of girls, correctly sex-assigned and reared, who were nevertheless exposed *in utero* to abnormally high amounts of androgens. Almost without exception, such girls grow up with much more typically boyish interests (preference for more vigorous sports and outdoor play and for more utilitarian clothing; indifference towards dolls and young infants), even though they show no evidence of either homosexual or transsexual leanings.[6]

While it is risky to generalize from abnormal to normal human development, we seem left with the tentative conclusion that biology creates broad, behavioral tendencies in each sex which are normally confirmed and further exacerbated by postnatal socialization. In those cases where nature and nurture conflict, the impact of nurture is usually—but not inevitably— paramount. We cannot discard the broad, shaping influence of male or female hormones on subsequent preferences and activity-tendencies. Yet, having said this, it is also well to remember that even in biologically normal persons, *both* male (androgenic) and female (estrogenic) hormones are present, with only their *ratios* distinguishing one sex from the other, and even these ratio-differences are not absolute, but variable within a normal range. Thus, to the extent that hormonal influences *do* shape male or female behavioral tendencies, they do not do so in a simple, either/or fashion. Rather, it is entirely likely that there will be a significant minority of quite normal males whose behavioral preferences are less aggressive and competitive than the male stereotype (due *in part* to their particular mix of androgenic and estrogenic hormones), and a correspondingly significant minority of females whose behavioral preferences are more assertive and achieving than the female stereotype. That we have, in the past, subjected children of both sexes to the demands of the stereotypes, instead of being sufficiently sensitive to individual differences, has been one reason for the low self-esteem with which the "sensitive" male or "tomboy" female have had to cope.[7]

Freud and the Development of Gender Identity

Within the history and current practice of psychology, four different schools of thought have offered theories and supporting research as to the way postnatal acquisition of sex-role identity takes place. These include *psychoanalytic, behavioristic, social-learning theory,* and *cognitive-develop-*

mental approaches. However, because the cognitive-developmental literature on sex-role development is still rather scant, we will concentrate our
attention on the first three, referring the interested reader on to the appropriate literature on the fourth.[8]

Basic psychoanalytic theory, beginning with Freud, emphasizes the irrational, largely unconscious constellation of emotional relationships between
parents and young children as the most significant determinant of sexual
identity.[9] According to this approach, infants of both sexes begin with an
oral, erotic attachment to their mothers by way of the essential, gratifying
nursing relationship. Later, as they pass from a preoccupation with oral,
then anal, pleasure to a consciousness of their own and others' genitals, boys
conclude that girls once had, but at some point lost, their penises, and that
they may suffer a similar fate. Since this awareness and articulation of
physical sex differences parallels a stage (around ages three to four) when
children tend to feel particularly attracted to the opposite-sexed parent (the
so-called Oedipus complex), the little boy concludes that his father's resentment over the son's desire for the mother may become the precipitating
cause for such a disciplinary castration. Hedging his bets, he concludes that
if he cannot replace his father in his mother's affections, he may as well
join him. This is the process Freud labeled "identification with the aggressor," which he considered to be the major impetus towards the healthy
development of masculine self-concept. Having concluded that he cannot
marry mother (since she belongs to the possessive and all-powerful father),
the boy decides that the next best solution is to become like father, so that
at maturity he can, if not marry his own mother, at least have "a girl just
like the girl that married dear old dad." In addition, according to Freud,
the continuing, unconscious anxiety about castration serves as a constant
impetus towards socially desirable achievement and internalized moral sentiments, as role-modeled by the father who is society's representative.

Thus, while predicated on an uneasy anxiety, Freud's male children
(unless they fail to resolve the Oedipus complex) eventually arrive at a
stable, satisfying, and productive male identity that includes internalized
social norms and a strong desire to achieve. Little girls, according to Freud,
are not so fortunate. They are assumed to envy the boy's more visible
genital equipment, to conclude that at some time they had similar organs
but lost them, and to transfer their early affection for the mother to the
father, since they discover that mothers lack the coveted organ and fathers
have it. Like their brothers, little girls discover that they cannot break up
the parental marriage bond and, being unable to afford their mothers'

disapproval, reluctantly decide to role-model themselves after her instead. Although the dynamics of sex-role identity formation are thus the same for both sexes (passion for the opposite-sexed parent reluctantly replaced by identification with the same-sexed parent), Freud claimed there was also a difference. The girl does not have the admittedly dubious advantage of castration-anxiety as a motivating force to overcome the Oedipus complex and become a well-socialized, achieving adult. She remains somewhat ambivalently attached to the father, is far less capable in adulthood of achievement and detached moral judgment, and remains far more dependent. Hence, in Freud's analysis, although the boy's male self-concept is indeed hard-won (he speaks of the Oedipus complex as being "literally smashed to pieces by the shock of threatened castration"),[10] the end result is a stable, presumably satisfying, male identity. Females, on the other hand, seem unable to win either way: their envy of the male's physical superiority [sic] is presumed to be quite understandable—yet if they try to emulate males in any way, this is taken to be a sign of pathological rejection of one's femininity. It is difficult to see the emergence of healthy self-esteem in women socialized under such a rhetoric.

Yet, it is no exaggeration to say that almost all the rhetoric of child-rearing in the decades prior to the mid-sixties can be classed as "footnotes to Freud." Concern for the traumas of toilet-training, proper and stereotypic sex-role development, and the presumed importance of unconscious, emotional forces over rational and behavioral factors all characterized the popular child-rearing trends (not to mention the training of pediatricians and psychiatrists)[11] of that period. Nor should we, as Christians, be too quick to reject in its entirety Freud's "language of passion" as it applies to sex-role development. I suspect that one of the reasons Freud was never accepted into the rational-humanist university circles of his day was precisely because of his emphasis on the *force of the irrational* in human development and behavior. Such reminders do not sit easily with the academic grandchildren of the Enlightenment, who often seem to vacillate between seeing themselves as totally rational and self-determined, or totally shaped by mechanistic, impersonal, amoral forces.[12] Yet in the Christian worldview, the nonrational, passionate forces at the heart of human beings are central themes, and include both good and evil impulses that must both be taken seriously. The ambivalent passions of young children towards parents of both sexes, while not as all-determining as Freud claimed, are matters of common record, and require sensitivity in terms of discerning what to tolerate and what to discourage in the interest of attaining a balanced Christian maturity that includes a comfortable sense of sexual worth.

At the same time, while Freud was probably right, in general terms to stress the importance of parent-child emotional dynamics, some details of his scheme need correction. In the case of both boys and girls, his theorized dynamics of socialization are too conservative. They make no allowance for the fact that succeeding generations *do* differ from their predecessors, at least in some respects, rather than blindly copying them by the mechanics of identification postulated by Freud. Unless Christians are prepared to say that parent-child identification patterns should not have changed an iota since the Apostolic age (every such change being labeled as pathological, including any difference *we* have from *our* parents!), then even the general mechanics of Freud's theory (not to mention his tendency towards sexual reductionism) are too limiting. Furthermore, in the case of girls, while Freud claimed that literal penis-envy, and its subsequent relinquishment, were the key to universal female psychology, there is good cross-cultural evidence to suggest that what Freud saw as mere anatomical jealousy is an understandable reaction by women to their lack of status and dignity in many male-dominated societies. This is a situation that Christians have long tried to reverse in their missionary endeavors.[13] Indeed, using Freud's own techniques for dream analysis, one exhaustive cross-cultural study has shown that dream reports filled with overt or symbolic penis-envy are most frequent in cultures where women's status is lowest, and least frequent where their social position is highest.[14] Thus, it seems that penis-envy is symbolic, not literal, and represents not envy of the male organ, but of male status and mobility. Where the status of the two sexes is more equal (and this does *not* necessarily mean that women and men do exactly the same things—merely that whatever the division of labor, the activity, and the voices of both sexes have equal value),[15] the envy is much reduced.

BEHAVIORIST, SOCIO-BIOLOGICAL, AND INTERACTIONIST VIEWS

The reader may have discerned that while much of Freud's theory of sex-role development has a plausible ring, it is convoluted and difficult to test. Perhaps because of these features, as well as Freud's exaggerated emphasis on unobservable, unconscious processes, the more parsimonious and testable views of the school known as *behaviorism* have eclipsed the Freudian view of child-rearing and development in the past two decades. In its purest form, behaviorism ignores (and sometimes even denies) the existence and power of the very internal processes and developmental dynamics to which Freud attached such significance. Instead, it focuses its consideration of all behaviors—including those related to sex-roles—on the conditioning process said to result from the differential application of rewards and punishments.[16] In its most doctrinaire form, behaviorism claims that behaviors are strengthened or weakened entirely as a result of their environmental consequences: behaviors that are consistently rewarded become more habitual, while those that are not rewarded, or are actually punished, fade away or are "extinguished."[17]

It is of interest to our present topic that behaviorism's position of extreme environmental determinism regarding sex-linked and other behaviors is beginning to be challenged. B. F. Skinner (the acknowledged living patriarch of behaviorism) insisted that virtually all stereotypic male or female behaviors are socially acquired, and that under a different system of carefully planned and executed reinforcers, such behaviors could easily be changed. Indeed, he even fantasized a utopia where this took place.[18] On the other hand, sociobiologists, such as Harvard's Edward O. Wilson, have begun to claim that such sex-stereotypic behaviors as female coyness, domesticity, and monogamy, or male dominance, restlessness, and promiscuity are biologically embedded tendencies hearkening back to our animal and higher-primate past, when such behaviors maximized the chance of genetic diversity (and hence stronger, more adaptable species) through assortative mating. Consequently, such thinkers warn, sex-specific behavior may not be as malleable as today's feminists and other exponents of androgyny would like to believe.[19]

It is extremely important for Christian readers not to be seduced by a simplistic temptation presented by this "nature/nurture" controversy I have just outlined, concluding that if the "nature" side wins, science can be invoked in support of a more absolutist hermeneutic regarding sex-roles, whereas if the "nurture" side wins, science can be paraded in support of a competing, more historically relativist interpretation of Scripture. We must not forget that *both* positions (and indeed, even a combination of the two) reduce human behavior to materialist mechanics, leaving no real place for rational reflection, choice, or accountability, and certainly none for an infinite-personal God to whom even secular scientists are accountable. Nevertheless, to the extent that both nature and nurture *influence* (if not totally determine) us, it is possible that their relative strengths do have some bearing on the development of sex-role-related self-esteem. For if it is true that men by nature "lean towards" certain types of activities, while women lean towards others, the long-term result of enforced homogenization may simply be that members of both sexes will feel uncomfortable and out of place. Conversely, if sex-role socialization is as arbitrary as most behaviorists and feminists argue, then it is under a more traditional system of dichotomized sex-roles that members of both sexes will chafe.

Of course, it is possible to adopt a position somewhere between the extremes of nature and nurture. Those psychologists (including myself) who favor such an "interactionist" approach to sex-role identity formation stress that biology can neither be ignored nor held to constitute the entire destiny of either sex.[20] The position has the advantage of being able to account for certain trends that are probably too complex to be explained by either a simple nature or nurture stance. For example, it is a well-documented fact that at the primary school level, boys are much more likely than girls to suffer from a variety of developmental and learning disabilities, including stuttering and reading problems,[21] and to receive much more disciplinary correction.[22] While these differences may, in part, be accounted for by biologically ingrained tendencies (since both the language advantage of girls and the greater aggressiveness of boys appear quite early and remain fairly consistent),[23] their relationship to self-esteem may be best understood in combination with the differential socialization of each sex. One pair of psychologists suggests that boys' biologically rooted tendencies to greater aggressiveness and impulsivity combine very poorly with a system of primary schooling (largely female-dominated) that stresses conformity and routine skill acquisition.[24] The result, they suggest, is an early disadvantage, followed by a longer-term advantage over females in terms of self-esteem. More specifically, because boys get so much less reinforcement than girls for their natural tendencies, they are bound to have more *early* problems, in both the educational and socio-emotional spheres. Yet the very unreliability of adult approval, it is suggested, forces boys to look elsewhere (to their extracurricular achievements, to their peers, and within themselves) for a stable self-concept, and in the long run, this is to their advantage as adults.[25] On the other hand, the more characteristic coping styles of little girls, which involve greater verbal facility and orientation towards other people, are rewarded in early life, presumably giving them an advantage in terms of socio-emotional self-esteem. (At least, they appear far less frequently than boys in clinical settings in the preadolescent years.)

The crunch for girls comes at adolescence, just when the independence, aggressiveness, and individual-achievement tendencies of boys begin to have more social payoff than previously. At this point, there is a double reason for girls not to change: in the first place, they generally have a long history of being rewarded for a nonassertive, conforming style; in the second place, the onset of puberty, with its heralding of adult sexuality and questions of marriageability, tends to make both the youths and their parents more concerned to stress differences, rather than similarities, between the sexes. As a result, most young women (even now) remain more oriented towards interpersonal than intellectual or professional achievements, and the minority who do venture into traditionally male enclaves do so very ambivalently, sensing that to achieve as a person may result in being considered a failure as a woman.[26] On the other hand, those who adopt more traditionally feminine roles do not, in general, feel any better about themselves for doing so. There is a fairly large body of literature documenting the greater social value placed by both sexes on most traditionally masculine (as opposed to feminine) characteristics and activities. Yet, when women describe themselves, both as they really are and as they perceive the feminine ideal to be, they incorporate all of the negatively perceived traits ascribed to their own sex (such as dependence, irrationality, concern about appearance, lack of ambition and self-confidence)—traits that most clinicians consider to be unhealthy when used to describe an adult of *unspecified* sex.[27] This negative self-image tends to persist throughout adulthood, including marriage, motherhood, and beyond, with accompanying indications of less-than-optimal mental health.[28] Indeed, there is another substantial body of literature documenting the regularity with which men attribute their accomplishments to personal, positive traits, such as ability and hard work, whereas women with objectively similar accomplishments tend to credit nonpersonal, external factors such as "luck," or "the ease of the task."[29] Women also express a greater lack of confidence than men in their *anticipated* performance on tasks.[30]

This is not to say that adult *male* self-esteem is always more easily won than that of women. For although it is true that fewer traditionally female than male traits are considered socially desirable,[31] men in general still seem to suffer when they *lack* such "feminine" qualities as tact, gentleness, social ease, or orderliness. Indeed, there is evidence to suggest that although a one-sided masculine personality profile makes for high self-esteem in *adolescent* males, a more "mixed" (masculine-plus-feminine) self-concept is associated with higher self-esteem in *adult* men, particularly in complex, urban settings where individualism and aggressiveness must be tempered with a capacity to interact smoothly with others in large organizations and crowded residential areas.[32] In addition, when the definition of "achievement" or "competence" is not restricted to the individual performance of a work task, but redefined as what might be termed *social* competence (ease of interaction with others, attractiveness to others), it is women, not men, who score the highest in self-confidence.[33] Further, it has even been suggested that men's greater self-confidence in the face of individualized work-tasks is not to be taken at face value, but may merely reflect females' greater willingness to admit their own limitations to others, and men's greater defensiveness about doing so.[34] If this is even partially the case, it may explain why the tremendous output of the women's movement (in terms of organizations, literature, self-help groups, and so forth) has not been paralleled by a similar avalanche of materials pertinent to *men's* liberation. Until you are willing to admit there is a problem, you are unlikely to generate much momentum for change.[35] A second reason for this "men's liberation lag" may be that women's greater ease and self-confidence in affiliative situations may be better suited to the development of a grass-roots movement, where tasks and goals are more diffusely and interpersonally defined than most men are comfortable with. A third reason may be found in the fact that although (as we have seen) both sexes have "typical" traits that are considered positive by both sexes, the list of *male*-positive traits is much longer than the *female* one. Thus, it may be considered understandable (even by those who oppose it) for women to want to be liberated from the confines of a mostly negative self-image and be free to incorporate into it some of the more valued, stereotypically male traits. But the social payoff for *men* to become more cross-sex-typed may seem considerably less, inasmuch as, in doing so, they would be perceived as wanting to identify not with the winners, but with the losers, of the sex-role status race. Yet, for Christian males, should not the very example of Christ himself, who "though He was rich, yet for our sakes became poor," make it easier to risk diluting the strength of the socially valued male profile?[36] Or (to look at the question another way) is the very temptation of that worldly powerful profile one of the reasons why men seem to be converted to Christianity in vastly fewer numbers than women?

Social Learning Theory

Before closing our consideration of self-esteem and sex-role development, we will briefly consider one other approach to this question—namely, that of the social learning theorists. Although social learning theory is perhaps best characterized as a kind of qualified behaviorism, it also maintains that the pure behaviorist focus on environmental reinforcers and resultant, observable behaviors is far too limited as a way of analyzing specifically *human* behavior. For *consciousness,* however unobservable in the strict empiricist sense of the word, is one of the distinguishing characteristics of human beings, and any analysis of human development that ignores this reality is bound to be one-sided, if not actually distorted. Thus, while social learning theorists share with behaviorists the conviction that maternal approval becomes an effective reinforcer to young children through its association with maternal nurturance, they maintain that such simple response-reinforcement connections cannot account for the sophistication of older children's learning.[37] For as developing children become more and more observant of their adult dispensers of rewards and punishments, a new and more complex form of learning, involving *imitation* and *modeling* of these adults, becomes available. This is seen as a "higher" form of learning because it entails the acquisition of larger, more diffuse response patterns (including attitudes and emotions), rather than just the isolated, visible behavior fragments on which behaviorism tends to focus. Moreover, such learning-through-imitation can occur even when the child does not immediately reproduce the learned behavior, and even when the child is not rewarded for producing it at a later time. Indeed, according to social learning theory, the behaviors acquired by the child may depend less on how an adult reinforces the child's behavior (verbally or otherwise) than on how the adult *himself* is observed to behave. The child, merely by observing an adult model, may *infer* reinforcement consequences. Moreover, the child need not perform the behavior at the time it is observed, because he or she is capable of retaining it symbolically, in words or concepts, and of employing these as-yet-unrehearsed behaviors at a time when they are appropriate or likely to be rewarded.

According to social learning theory, sex-role self-concept, like any other set of behaviors and attitudes, develops through direct reinforcement for sex-appropriate behavior (as defined by the parents and community), combined with an increasing tendency on the child's part to imitate and identify with adults who are nurturant, affectionate, competent, and successful. Since it is an established finding of social learning research that children are more apt to imitate models who are similar to themselves, this gives the same-sex parents (and, by generalization, other same-sex adults) an edge over the opposite-sex parent in terms of power as a role-model[38] —provided (and this is a crucial qualifier) that there is not a great discrepancy between the parents in terms of their perceived nurturance, competence, and success.

A couple of rather significant implications stem from this last statement and deserve further comment. The first is that, contrary to one type of traditional wisdom (including the conventional wisdom of some Christians), a healthy, masculine self-concept in boys is *not* normally guaranteed by a father-image that is powerful and competent *if at the same time the father lacks affectionate and nurturing qualities toward the son.* Conversely, a healthy feminine self-concept in girls will not necessarily result from a mother-image that is nurturing and affectionate *if at the same time the mother is perceived to lack power and personal competence.* [39] Thus, according to social learning theory, the rigid dichotomizing of parental roles along the lines of a powerful-but-remote father and a nurturant-but-basically-powerless mother, far from assuring children's healthy sex-role development, may actually hinder it and produce an ambivalent desire to identify with the opposite-sexed parent who models some of the essential, identification-producing qualities lacking in the other.

A second, equally significant implication is this: provided that both parents are equally attractive models in terms of their perceived nurturance, competence, and success, the mere sexual similarity of each to the same-sex children is usually sufficient to assure healthy and satisfying sex-role development. Another way of phrasing this is to say that a boy will grow up wanting, and happy, to "be a male" whether his father is a "typical" male (such as a lawyer or a steelworker) or an atypical one (such as a hairdresser or a daycare worker) provided that the father is perceived as *both* nurturant and powerful. Conversely, girls are likely to grow up with a satisfactory, and satisfied, female identification whether their mothers are engaged primarily in work typical or atypical of most women, provided that they too are perceived as both nurturant and in possession of reasonable control over the course of their own lives. It needs to be added, of course, that parents are (fortunately) not the only adults chosen as role models by growing children, and that the limitations (whether deliberate or naive) of the home setting are often offset by the availability of other adult models—a fact that both Christians and non-Christians turn to positive advantage when they deliberately cultivate a strong community life that includes tolerance for many different life-styles within an underlying context of a shared set of basic values.

There is obviously much in the social-learning approach with which the thoughtful Christian can easily identify. However, it too has certain limitations of which we should be aware. The first is that despite its departure from the simplistic conditioning model of behaviorism, and despite its concessions to the existence of conscious thought-processes, social learning theory still has a highly mechanistic view of sex-role and other types of learning, with only scant recognition of the dynamics of individual choice and responsibility, and no recognition at all of concepts such as calling, redemption, or the existence of moral absolutes. Indeed, there is a highly relativistic quality to the entire approach, suggesting that, given the right combination of reinforcers and role models, one can (at least, in theory) turn out any kind of human being one wants, and that since patterns of reinforcement and role-modeling differ across time and cultures, there is no way of saying that one is better than another.

The second limitation of social learning theory revolves around its characteristic way of gathering support for its hypotheses. For although each of its above-mentioned theoretical aspects has strong support in empirical research, that research has leaned almost exclusively towards contrived laboratory experiments. (An exception is the material in the immediately preceding paragraph but one, which is also strongly anchored in observations of natural home settings.) Now, when behaviors and attitudes are demonstrably manipulable in closed laboratory settings, this merely tells us that they *can* be influenced in a certain way—not that they typically *are* under less restrictive and more everyday conditions. (By analogy, a prisoner-of-war camp is a closed setting with a very deliberate manipulation of reinforcers and role models, yet few people would say that the behavior so extracted from its inmates is prototypical of them.) Another way of expressing this limitation is to say that social learning theory, like its behaviorist cousin, has concentrated on the exclusively *changeable* aspects of children's sex-role behavior, to the exclusion of any possibly *stable* traits—including whatever sex-linked (and other) tendencies may arise from innate predisposition. This may, in fact, be too simple. For example, social learning theory requires that parents and other significant persons constantly reinforce children for engaging in sex-appropriate behavior and for imitating same-sex adults. Yet when the entire corpus of research (both laboratory *and* naturalistic) is reviewed, it appears that most parents (at least middle-class ones) do not do this; if anything, they actively *discourage* certain "sex-typical" behaviors, such as noisy, aggressive play in boys and passivity in girls.[40] This suggests the possibility of innate tendencies in each sex which have to be, not conditioned, but (to a degree) *counterconditioned* in the interests of attaining that moderate degree of "cross-sex typing" that is associated with healthy self-esteem in adults of both sexes. It also suggests that parents generally have some intuitive awareness that this is a good thing to do, and therefore act accordingly.

SOME CONCLUDING REMARKS

I have attempted to review the topic of self-esteem and sex-role development from the major theoretical and research perspectives current in my own discipline of psychology. While I have interspersed certain caveats and criticisms throughout this process, there remain some concluding suggestions as to how Christians should use the materials and methods represented here. To begin with, from a biblical standpoint, we are realizing more and more that human beings are seen as responding to God in their totality—not as minds truncated from behavior or emotions, nor even as minds at one time, behavior at another, and emotions at still another. Consequently, it is dangerous to become a "true believer" in any one of these approaches, since each is in some way reductionistic and oversimplified. Nor can we Christianize the entire endeavor by adopting an eclectic mix of all of them at once—because even such a mixture remains insensitive to certain cosmic realities with which we must contend. I suspect, for instance, that the very character of the Fall, in which one sex is portrayed as persuading the other to a joint disobedience and the other sex is subsequently shown trying to deny responsibility for his part in it, has left us with a legacy of tension in relations between the sexes for which secular scientific research cannot account, and which psychological techniques, however elaborate, cannot totally overcome. An additional legacy of weakness in our sex-related functioning is implicit in the curse resulting from this human disobedience, when (it seems to me) women's ambivalence about themselves, and men's tendency to be overbearing and excessively task-oriented become forces to be reckoned with (Gen. 3:16–19).

Because these tensions and tendencies are part of the cosmic, human condition—and not mere freaks of biological evolution or cultural conditioning—they can be neither fully explained nor fully overcome by an appeal to social-scientific analysis. Rather, we must resort to the language of creation, fall, and redemption, and try to understand the scope of both our sexual brokenness *and* the possibilities for its restoration and sanctification in Christ, given the reality of our existence in the era of "the already, but not yet." Does this mean that we pass the buck back to the theologians and biblical scholars, ignoring the corpus of social scientific research and theorizing? To the extent that social science cannot, in its pure form, cope with questions of ontology, morality, and eschatology, I am sometimes tempted to answer "yes." But to the extent that science represents one attempt to describe and account for reality in lawful terms according to well-policed procedures, it can be of some help in our deliberations. For one thing, the accumulated psychological research reminds us that sex-role development takes place, and goes awry, on various levels, and that while (for instance) an appeal to biology may be appropriate in one case, an analysis in terms of psychodynamics, or reinforcement history, may be most appropriate in another. The wealth of research presented here may, in other words, enrich the ways in which we understand the *outworking* of our cosmic condition as males and females. It may, in addition, help to keep us from being judgmental; for although there are grounds for decrying the mechanistic amorality of a purely scientific analysis of behavior, it does have the virtue of reminding us that, however morally accountable we remain, we are in fact strongly influenced by a host of emotional, biological, and social forces that interact differently in different people. Consequently, (as Paul reminded his readers in Galatians 6), we are each subject to a variety of temptations and have differing burdens that we bear. Restoration should thus always be in a spirit of gentleness, knowing that we are as weak as any others.

Further, social science, honestly and painstakingly done, continues to shed light not only on the underlying similarities, but also the differences among people. Without pushing this to a conclusion of total relativism (in either moral or sexual realms), it ought to help us deal with persons as individuals more than as categories. For although I have argued that there may, indeed, be innate tendencies that, in a very general way, differentiate the sexes, it is well to remember that the amount of variability *within* each sex far outstrips any average differences that exist *between* them. There may occasionally be historical circumstances whose urgency demands that we sort people by crude categories rather than taking the time to consider individual differences. But I do not think that this is normative. We are called by God as individuals with "varieties of gifts, but the same Spirit," and throughout biblical history, we constantly see God calling individuals to tasks that transcend the apparent limitations of age, sex, education, and wealth. To do otherwise ourselves is to risk very real damage to a person's self-image, which is vitally bound up with this sense of individual vocation from God.

Finally, in suggesting that we treat persons more as individuals than as members of a given sex, I do not think that we are inviting the triumph of a unisexual society. We have already seen that polarized sex-role socialization, far from assuring healthy sex-role development, may actually jeopardize it, producing persons who may *act* as stereotypical men or women, but are far from being at peace in doing so. In addition, there is enough of biology in our sexuality that, even though it does not constitute our destiny, it continues to exert its pull. With all of this in mind, perhaps we can proceed in greater confidence with the tasks that confront our generation of Christians.

NOTES

1. See, for example, the chapters by Hoekema and Ellison.

2. For a more detailed discussion of the limitations of North American social scientific (and particularly psychological) methodology, see Amadeo Giorgi, *Psychology as a Human Science* (New York: Harper & Row, 1970), and Mary Stewart Van Leeuwen, *The Sorcerer's Apprentice: North American Psychology in Transition* (Downers Grove, Ill.: InterVarsity Press, in preparation).

3. A more extensive critique of reductionism (or "nothing buttery") from a Christian perspective can be found in two books by Donald MacKay: *The Clockwork Image* (London: Intervarsity Press, 1974), and *Science, Chance, and Providence* (Oxford University Press, 1978).

4. For a good, brief introduction to the biological aspects of sex-role identity, see B. G. Rosenberg and Brian Sutton-Smith, *Sex and Identity* (New York: Holt, Rinehart, and Winston, 1972), particularly chapter 3. For a more extensive treatment from a medical perspective, see John Money and Anke A. Ehrhardt, *Man and Woman, Boy and Girl* (Baltimore: Johns Hopkins University Press, 1972).

5. Money and Ehrhardt, *Man and Woman*, especially chapter 7.

6. H. J. Baker and R. J. Stoller, "Biological Force Postulated as Having Role in Gender Identity," *Roche Reports: Frontiers of Hospital Psychiatry* 4 (1967): 3. Also, Money and Ehrhardt, *Man and Woman*, chapter 10.

7. There are also some interesting *intellectual* advantages of moderate cross-sex typing in both sexes. In this regard, see Eleanor E. Maccoby, *The Development of Sex Differences* (Stanford University Press, 1966), chapter 2. See also E. E. Maccoby and C. N. Jacklin, *The Psychology of Sex Differences* (Stanford University Press, 1974).

8. Lawrence Kohlberg, "A Cognitive-Developmental Analysis of Children's Sex-Role Concepts and Attitudes, in Maccoby, *Development of Sex Differences*, pp. 82–173. Also, L. Kohlberg and D. Z. Ullian, "Stages in the Development of Psychosexual Concepts and Attitudes," in R. C. Friedman et al., *Sex Differences in Behaviour* (New York: John Wiley, 1974).

9. A good summary of Freud's approach can be found in Rosenberg and Sutton-Smith, *Sex and Identity*, chapter 4. Primary sources include S. Freud, *New Introductory Lectures in Psychoanalysis* (New York: W. W. Norton, 1933); S. Freud, "Some Psychological Consequences of the Anatomical Distinction between the Sexes," *Collected Papers*, trans. J. Rivière (London: Hogarth Press, 1948), vol. 5.; and S. Freud, *An Outline*

of Psycho-analysis (New York: W. W. Norton, 1949).

10. Freud, "Some Psychological Consequences," p. 196.

11. Benjamin Spock and Bruno Bettelheim are among the child-rearing specialists whose training and writings have been distinctly psychoanalytic in character.

12. For a more detailed analysis of intellectual tensions resulting from the era of the Enlightenment, see H. Dooyeweerd, A New Critique of Theoretical Thought (Philadelphia: Presbyterian and Reformed Publishing Co., 1953); or, for a summary of Dooyeweerd's thinking, see L. Kalsbeek, Contours of a Christian Philosophy (Toronto, Canada: Wedge Publishing Co., 1975).

13. Some historical background to this concern can be found in Ian C. Bradley, The Call to Seriousness: The Evangelical Impact on the Victorians (New York: MacMillan, 1976).

14. See Sharon Nathan, "The Sexes: Power Envy," Psychology Today 15, no. 6 (1981) pp. 29, 80. (The original report appears in Psychiatry 44, no. 1).

15. A more detailed cross-cultural consideration of sex roles, as related to cognitive style and self-esteem, can be found in Mary Stewart Van Leeuwen, "A Cross-Cultural Examination of Psychological Differentiation in Males and Females," International Journal of Psychology 13 (1978) 2:87–122.

16. For a representative survey of behaviorism, see Howard Rachlin, Introduction to Modern Behaviourism (San Francisco: W. H. Freeman, 1976); B. F. Skinner, About Behaviorism (New York: Random House Vintage Books, 1976); and Alan E. Kazdin, Behavior Modification in Applied Settings, rev. ed. (Homewood, Ill.: Dorsey Press, 1980).

17. A development of this critique can be found in Mary Stewart Van Leeuwen, "The Behaviourist Bandwagon and the Body of Christ," parts I, II, and III, Journal of the American Scientific Affiliation 31 (1979): 3–8; 31:88–91; 31:129–138.

18. B. F. Skinner, Walden II (New York: MacMillan, 1948, 1976).

19. Edward O. Wilson, On Human Nature (Harvard University Press, 1978).

20. The "interactionist" approach is well represented in Judith M. Bardwick, Psychology of Women: A Study of Biocultural Conflicts (New York: Harper & Row, 1971); J. M. Bardwick and E. Douvan, "Ambivalence: the Socialization of Women," in V. Gornick, and B. K. Moran, eds., Woman in Sexist Society (New York: Basic Books, 1971), chap. 9. and J. M. Bardwick et al., Feminine Personality and Conflict (Belmont, Calif.: Brooks/Cole, 1970).

21. Maccoby and Jacklin, Psychology of Sex Differences, chapter 3, pp. 119 ff.

22. Ibid., chapter 9, pp. 131 ff.

23. Ibid., chapter 3, pp. 75 ff.

24. Bardwick and Douvan, "Ambivalence."

25. Ibid.

26. Matina S. Horner, "Femininity and Successful Achievement: A Basic Inconsistency," in Bardwick et al., Feminine Personality and Conflict, pp. 45–64. Also, Matina A. Horner, "Towards an Understanding of Achievement-Related Conflicts in Women," Journal of Social Issues 28 (1972) 2: 157–175.

27. The pertinent research in this area is well summarized in Inge K. Broverman et al., "Sex-role Stereotypes: A Current Appraisal," Journal of Social Issues 28 (1972) 2:59–78; and also in Janet T. Spence and Robert L. Helmreich, Masculinity and Femininity: Their Psychological Dimensions, Correlates, and Antecedents (Austin: University of Texas Press, 1978).

28. Jessie Bernard, "The Paradox of the Happy Marriage," and Pauline B. Bart, "Depression in Middle-Aged Women," both in Gornick and Moran, Woman in Sexist Society.

29. A good summary of attribution theory and research, as it pertains to the sexes, can be found in Kay Deaux, The Behaviour of Women and Men (Belmont, Calif.: Brooks/Cole, 1976).

30. Maccoby and Jacklin, Psychology of Sex

Differences, chapter 4, pp. 154 ff.
31. Broverman et al., "Sex-role Stereo-types."
32. This research is summarized, with references, in Paul H. Mussen, John J. Conger, and Jerome Kagan, *Child Development and Personality*, 4th ed. (New York: Harper & Row, 1974), chapter 13.
33. Maccoby and Jacklin, *Psychology of Sex Differences*, chapter 4, pp. 160 ff.
34. Ibid., chapter 4.
35. Some noteworthy exceptions include Joseph H. Pleck and Jack Sawyer, eds., *Men and Masculinity* (Englewood Cliffs, N. J.: Prentice-Hall, 1974); Deborah S. David and Robert Brannon, *The Forty-Nine Percent Majority: The Male Sex Role* (Reading, Mass.: Addison-Wesley, 1976); and Mirra Komarovsky, *Dilemmas of Masculinity: A Study of College Youth* (New York: W. W. Norton, 1976).
36. Not surprisingly, it is from the historic "peace churches" that we get some of the most perceptive development of this

possibility. See, for example, Perry Yoder and Elizabeth Yoder, *New Men, New Roles: A Study Guide for Christian People in Social Change* (Newton, Kansas: Faith and Life Press, 1977).
37. For a general consideration of social learning theory, see Albert Bandura, *Social Learning Theory* (Englewood Cliffs, N. J.: Prentice-Hall, 1977). For its application to sex-role development, see Walter Mischel, "A Social Learning View of Sex Differences in Behavior," in Maccoby, *Development of Sex Differences*, chapter 5.
38. Bandura, *Social Learning Theory;* Mussen, Conger, and Kagan, *Child Development*, chapter 9.
39. J. Kagan, "Acquisition and Significance of Sex-typing and Sex-role Identity," *Review of Child Development Research*, eds. M. L. Hoffman and L. W. Hoffman (New York: Russel Sage Foundation, 1964), vol. 1.
40. Maccoby and Jacklin, *Psychology of Sex Differences*, chapter 8.

BIOGRAPHICAL SKETCH

MARY STEWART VAN LEEUWEN received her B.A. from Queens University (Ontario) and her M.A. and Ph.D. from Northwestern University. She is currently associate professor of psychology at York University, Toronto, Ontario, and a visiting professor and fellow at the Calvin Center for Christian Scholarship, Calvin College, in Grand Rapids, Michigan. She co-authored *Intergroup Relations* and has written a book entitled *The Sorcerer's Apprentice: North American Psychology in Transition*. Her articles have been published mainly in *International Journal of Psychology, Journal of the American Scientific Affiliation*, and *Christian Scholars' Review*.

Marriage and Self-Esteem

JOYCE HULGUS

MARRIAGE as an interpersonal relationship is a highly significant dimension in the lives of roughly 90 percent of the American population. It is predicted, according to "the Family Letter" published by the National Alliance for Family Life in January, 1982, that with the current "back-to-the-family" trend, by 1990 there will be 17 million more households. Most of these, it is forecast, will be husband-wife households. Countless people are, and will be, attempting to keep this state called marriage intact.

Recently, one such couple was sitting in the office of a marriage counselor. The couple was experiencing withdrawal pains from each other. As the therapist explored the roots of this couple's experience, he heard the husband express for the first time his feelings about an incident he had experienced twelve years earlier during their engagement. At the end of a prayer service, the pastor had invited the congregation to form a fellowship circle. In doing so, this man's fiancee ended up holding hands with another young man. This brief experience had remained sharply focused in this husband's mind. He could not forget it. "She must have felt better about that man than me. I felt stupid." It was obvious this husband did not mean he thought he was ignorant. Rather, it became clear he meant he felt inadequate, undesirable, valueless. Though this young woman had married him and though they had been married for twelve years, these feelings persisted and had so adversely affected the marital relationship that the couple were contemplating dissolving it.

ANTECEDENTS TO SELF-ESTEEM

These two people, like all other persons who consider marriage, had come to it as novices. Neither of them had ever been this age before, ever sworn before God and humanity to be committed to this unique person before, ever lived each of the forthcoming unique experiences before. To this monumental task, they brought with them only that which had preceded each of them, the perspectives each of them had about themselves, others, and God.

When looking at self-other perspectives, one must rewind the tape of life back to its beginning, for the earliest antecedents are humanly (not divinely) *un*chosen. They are "inborn" for all of us—aptitudes, race, sex, intellectual capacities, biophysiological heritage, temperament. This is the equipment with which newborns meet, and begin to differentiate from, and adjust to their environment. This is no small nor telescopic task. To young children, their whole world is larger (quickly imagine Lily Tomlin portraying Edith Ann in the rocker many sizes too large for her), more mobile, more knowledgeable, more experienced than they. They "look up," in more ways than one, to significant persons who send a steady stream of signals and messages to them about how life is to be lived. And as each child in turn responds from moment to moment with his or her own thoughts, feelings, and actions, he or she begins to learn through a long process of trial and error, which of his or her own thoughts, feelings, and actions are acceptable or unacceptable to the significant persons and which ones fit into the value system being transmitted.

In effect the child is learning how to match up his moment-to-moment thoughts, feelings, and actions with the demands, desires, requests, instructions, and directions of the PFLs [perceptions for life] and patterns of Significant Persons in his world.

In response to how his moment-to-moment thoughts, feelings, and actions "test out" (i.e., how well or poorly they measure up to the demands of Significant Persons and to his understanding of his experiences and his world), the child gradually develops tentative patterns of thinking, feeling and acting. Now his moment-to-moment interactions with Significant Persons and his world help to test out not only his individual thoughts, feelings, and actions but also his tentative patterns of thinking, feeling and acting.

As this continual trial-and-error testing out occurs again and again, the child is slowly forming a concept of the self. This SELF-CONCEPT consists of his SELF-IMAGE (how he "sees" and "thinks" about himself) and his SELF-ESTEEM (how he "feels" about himself). As he develops his self-concept, he is learning to "serve two masters" —Significant Persons and himself.[1]

In adding one year to another and another, children, who become adolescents who become adults, learn which perceptions of life to keep, or reject, or change. They learn what patterns of thinking, feeling, and behaving tend to help them feel most comfortable in reference to the expectations of significant others, to their self-concepts, and to reality as they have learned to perceive it.

In essence, we bring to every relationship, to every commitment, a self-concept or self-esteem "set." No other relationship is so critically affected by this "set" as marriage. No one "sees" us as we are—vulnerable, defended, successful, failing, elated, depressed, hostile, jubilant—as our spouse. As an individual "I" struggle with how "I" handle the component parts of life. And the greater the gap between how I think I should be (ideal self) and how I actually function, the greater the internal tension and, concomitantly, the greater my sensitivity to others' responses. Dr. James Dobson says that at least 90 percent of our self-concept is built from what we think others think about us.[2] Mead suggests that self-esteem is largely derived from the reflected appraisal of others, and that individuals constantly carry within themselves the reflecting mirror of their social groups.[3] Even more thought-provoking is Coopersmith's conclusion about the permanency of one's self-appraisal.[4] He sees it as relatively stable and enduring: "This appraisal can presumably be affected by specific incidents and environmental changes but apparently it reverts to its customary level when conditions resume their 'normal' and typical course." Aronson and Lecky both indicate that persons are generally unwilling, due to the need for psychological consistency, to accept evidence that they are better or worse than they have concluded, and usually resolve any dissonance between the evidence and their judgment in favor of their customary self-evaluation.[5]

On the basis of the fact that change in perception moves so slowly, it is not shocking that Pineo,[6] Blood and Wolfe,[7] and numerous others found that a certain disappointment with marriage is the inevitable lot of most persons the longer they are married, although more recent findings indicate there might be a curvilinear effect with respect to long-term marriages.

Almost no one, Christian or non-Christian, disagrees with the impact of one's self-esteem on "everything," including an accurate assessment of self, of others, and, no less, of God.[8] Thoughtful reflection on one's own experience confirms that as well. As the rain falls on both the just and the unjust, so the laws of learning affect us all, not by default, but by God's design.

MENTAL HEALTH AND MARITAL SATISFACTION

The issue of mental health, including self-concept, and marriage has increasingly been the focus of researchers interested in marital satisfaction.

Murstein began his series of studies in this area by looking at the relationship of mental health to marital choice and courtship progress.[9] He found that couples similar in mental health (on the basis of some MMPI scales) chose each other as "steadies" or fiances. The results were significantly associated with courtship progress for the male, who most often is the one who actively initiates the dating relationship. Later Murstein published the results of his study of the discrepancy between the self and the ideal self, and the choice of a marital partner.[10] As to whether a man would choose someone similar or opposite to himself, Murstein thought it logical to assume that if he were highly satisfied with himself, as determined by a high self-ideal-self correlation, then it would follow that he would attempt to marry someone whom he perceived as highly similar to himself. If he were quite dissatisfied with himself (low self-ideal-self correlation), he would still want to marry someone whom he perceived as close to both his ideal self and ideal mate. This would seem to support the theory that "opposites attract."[11] The results of his study supported his hypotheses. He found that girlfriends of the high self-acceptance men showed significantly higher self-ideal-self correlations than did the girlfriends of low self-acceptance men, and the boyfriends of high self-acceptance women also showed a higher positive correlation than the boyfriends of low self-acceptance women. Murstein also found that high self-accepting men perceived themselves to be more similar to their girlfriends than did low self-accepting men, and high women likewise exceeded low women. The same trend occurred when the data regarding the similarity between ideal spouse and current dating partner were analyzed. High self-accepting men showed a greater correlation between spouse desired and their perception of their partner than low men, and similar results were found for high and low self-accepting women. With further analysis of fifteen various need scores from the revised Edwards Personal Preference test, it was found that men who were high in self-acceptance were higher on order and sought spouses higher on order than did the low self-accepting males. Women high on self-acceptance were found to be higher on order as well as endurance. Interestingly, they were lower on exhibition, heterosexuality, and aggression. This suggests that self-acceptance in women may be associated with more traditional nonaggressive roles. It is this author's opinion that it is only the self-accepting woman who can actually be both the excellent wife of Proverbs 31, and the submissive wife of Ephesians 4 (otherwise, women who are "wives" would feel the full impact of being "least among the brethren"—lesser than males, as some would imply, because she came from man and is called the helper, and less than singles since she is the one commanded biblically to be "submissive" to her husband). It is interesting to note that when Fineberg and Lowman[12] looked at marital interactions that were coded by a system based on the Leary[13] circumplex, the results indicated that adjusted spouses communicated more affection and submission than did maladjusted couples. And, moreover, most of the variance in submission was accounted for by the wife. In their discussion of these findings, Fineberg and Lowman commented that "the adjusted wives may seem to better fit the traditional role of the submissive woman and the maladjusted wives, the common stereotype of the castrating shrew."[14] Future research needs to investigate further the relationship of submission and self-esteem. It also needs to be careful to avoid the circular thinking that concludes that adjustment for women equals acceptance of the submissive role and then selects research participants on the basis of this adjustment. Research in this area seems especially needful as more and more consideration is given to the concept of androgeny (the blending of behaviors and characteristics that have traditionally been thought of as masculine and feminine). The androgynous person is purported to be both independent and tender, both aggressive and gentle, both assertive and yielding, both masculine and feminine, depending on the situational appropriateness of these various behaviors.

Goodman looked at self-acceptance in relationship to interspousal needs.[15] He found that the newlywed couples who had high self-esteem, as measured by the Bills Index of Adjustment and Values, tended to manifest positive correlations for interspousal needs such as dominance, nurturance, and succor. Those couples with low self-esteem were complementary in the need areas of dominance, dominance and deference, nurturance, and nurturance and succorance. Although Goodman had to assume that his couples had actually chosen each other on the basis of self-esteem, there is seemingly a thread in the evidence which would suggest that "opposites attract" when self-acceptance is lacking, but that the more self-accepting person does not need to derive a completion of self from external sources—namely, a mate—to the extent that an individual will who is lower in self-acceptance.

In his discussion of his results, Goodman made another comment that warrants consideration. He noted that although there was the tendency for persons in high self-acceptance couples to have similar needs, these individuals showed more flexibility in their choice of a mate and "probably also in person choice in general."[16] It seems apparent that some individuals may limit the breadth of interpersonal relationships and, therefore, marital potential because of low self-acceptance. Or, in the low self-accepting person's search for completion of the self, he or she may find his or her marriage to be a complementary neurotic relationship in which there is reciprocity of need satisfaction, but in an inconsistent and self-defeating manner. Shostrom and Kavanaugh seem to address the same issue in *Between Man and Woman*, where they elaborate on six pairs (marital) that consist of individuals whom they see as being in an "immature stage of growth."[17] They say these men and women—mother and son, daddy and doll, bitch and nice guy, master and servant girl, hawks, and doves—lean on each other for survival, or avoid each other out of fear, or compete with each other out of personal inadequacy. In contrast to these, he suggests that the persons who do not exaggerate one part of their personality while repressing another are the more mature "rhythmic" persons who express "strength" or "weakness" and "anger" (or control) or "love" with balance. Shostrom and Kavanaugh indicate that the rhythmic couple "have sought to end their loneliness and personal pain, their guilt and anxiety, their sadness and insecurity, by asking another to do what each must do for himself or herself."[18] They go on to say that "in the rhythmic relationship there are ideally no denials or exaggerations of the polarities. Each person has his own identity or core, and thus is able to express strength or weakness, anger or love. Each is free to relate as he or she really is. There are no frozen roles."[19]

In the process of expanding his theory, Murstein, along with Beck, looked at the relationship between person perception, marriage adjustment, and social desirability.[20] And in looking at the relationship of these dimensions, they found, as Murstein had found previously, that self-acceptance was significantly correlated with marital adjustment. A parallel finding became evident when Barnett and Nietzel looked at the relationship of instrumental (meals and shopping, children, finances, personal appearance, etc.) and affectional behaviors and self-esteem to marital satisfaction in distressed and nondistressed couples.[21] Their most important finding was the degree to which self-esteem correlated with overall rated marital satisfaction. Self-esteem differentiated well the distressed and nondistressed couples, and was especially significant with relationship to wives' self-esteem. Wives' self esteem correlated significantly with the frequency of activities performed with their mates, with family members, with husband and other adults, and with the distribution of time spent during the weekend on rewarding and nonrewarding tasks. Significant correlations also were found between self-esteem and sexual activity level. Nondistressed couples engaged in sexual intercourse significantly more frequently than did distressed couples.

On the basis of his research, Schumm would say that the process of mate selection accounts for the observed similarity in self-esteem between husbands and wives.[22] On the other hand, he speculated that spouses may be satisfied because they are self-accepting, competent people who also happen to be husbands and wives. Regardless, whether one is looking at self-esteem and marriage theoretically, experientially, or experimentally, it seems clear that relatively enduring individual characteristics like self-esteem bear a substantial relationship to self-reported marital satisfaction.

IMPLICATIONS

Do we become discouraged with the reminder once again that self-esteem, which is shaped so early and is so resistant to change, is so fundamental to marital satisfaction? We could give up the ship, and nearly 50 percent of all married couples do. Perhaps some have believed that "you can't teach old dogs new tricks." If we were teaching dogs, or teaching tricks, perhaps we, too, would conclude that if two people discover their self-esteem is not high, then they should look for someone whose esteem is high—or bail out until they fortify their self-esteem and *then* search for another mate. Though occasionally this may seem to work, the very act of withdrawing and separating mitigates against the very security that is foundational to the building of self-esteem. James Dobson records an incident that occurred during the early days of the progressive education movement and seems applicable here.[23] One enthusiastic theorist decided to take down the chain link fence that surrounded the nursery school yard. He thought the children would feel more freedom of movement without that visible barrier surrounding them. When the fence was removed, however, the boys and girls huddled near the center of the play yard. Not only did they not wander away, they did not even venture to the edge of the grounds. In other words, without limits we do not maximize the freedom we do have. It appears that just the opposite of that occurs.

In the light of the current emphasis on independence and being "totally free" (which is not possible anyway), we need to reassess theoretically and pragmatically the relationship between security, limits, and experiencing fully what God designed us to be. Dr. Maurice Wagner speaks of the importance of security, along with a deep sense of value and worth, as well as competency in some area to the solid development of self-esteem.[24] He also addresses the relationship of the Trinity to these particular dimensions of self-esteem.

It is interesting to me, as a therapist, that I frequently find people who do not experience the constructive dimensions of limits, often expressing one of two extreme feelings. They often feel overwhelmed with the sense of having to deal somehow with the universe (no human being can cope with the enormity of that) because they have not experienced a more limited or defined world. (One can never experience a cup being "full" unless there is first the limitation of the cup.) Or, having experienced too many confining limits, like a growing hand that is bound over a long period of time and so becomes distorted as it grows, they want to challenge or break free from as many limits as possible in reaction to feeling bound. They discriminate poorly between appropriate and inappropriate boundaries. Just recently, a married man, who had had two affairs already, said to his wife, "I want to remain married to you. I just need to be free. Why can't you let me be free?" Not understanding appropriate limitations affects many dimensions of life, including the marital relationship.

We can benefit personally and professionally from reconsidering freedom and limits from both the theological and psychological perspective to see how these phenomena, which both Scripture and psychology address, affect the self-esteem "set" by which each of us "sees" our own world. It would be well for each of us to be introspective enough (preferably with a significant other) to become aware of what his or her own "set" is and how it has developed. With that foundation, we could more accurately reflect on how it affects our relationship—communication with, appraisal of, responses to—our own mates, our families, friends, counselees.

We also need to examine more closely in Scripture husband-wife relationships from numerous vantage points, such as the marriage relationship in contrast to singleness, attitudes conveyed about each sex, directives (in their contextual setting) to each spouse, roles and what they do or do not imply. We need to check our hermeneutics so that we do not impose on the marriage relationship cultural limitations God never intended (nor accept liberties He may have allowed because of the hardness of man's heart).

Another area we might explore is how we "lump and lock" couples into sameness. Sometimes there is the implication that "look-alikeness" equals spirituality. It appears we are very insecure with difference. Yet God made each of us unique. Not only us, but every plant, animal, snowflake. It seems he has placed in the universe a constant reminder that we are similar enough to be able to understand each other, yet different enough to minimize, rather than emphasize, comparison and competition.

No study of the development of self-esteem can be complete without looking at one's theology of man and the impact of sin. Were only Adam and Eve created in God's image? I like California's bumper sticker interpretation of being created in his image, "God ain't made no junk." Couples may bring "junk" with them into the most intimate and thus most vulnerable of relationships—marriage. But with time and effort invested in knowing and being known, the "junk" can be processed out so that marriages can be strengthened, rather than abandoned.

NOTES

1. T. C. McGinnis and D. G. Finnegan, *Open Family and Marriage: A Guide to Personal Growth* (Saint Louis, Mo.: C. V. Mosby Co., 1976), p. 98.

2. J. Dobson, *What Wives Wish Their Husbands Knew About Women* (Wheaton, Ill.: Tyndale House, 1975).

3. S. Coopersmith, *The Antecedents of Self-Esteem* (San Francisco: W. H. Freeman, 1967), p. 12.

4. Ibid., pp. 5–6.

5. Ibid.

6. P. Pineo, "Disenchantment in the Later Years of Marriage," *Marriage and Family Living* 23 (1961): 3–11.

7. R. O. Blood, Jr., and D. M. Wolfe, *Husbands and Wives* (New York: Free Press, 1965).

8. For an exception to this perspective, see J. Adams, *Christian Counselor's Manual* (Grand Rapids, Mich.: Baker Book House, 1973) p. 144ff.

9. B. I. Murstein, "The Relationship of Mental Health to Marital Choice and Courtship Progress," *Journal of Marriage and the Family* 29 (1967): 447–451.

10. B. I. Murstein, "Self-Ideal-Self Discrepancy and the Choice of Marital Partner," *Journal of Consulting and Clinical Psychology* 37 (1971): 47–52.

11. Robert Winch, *Mate Selection: A Study of Complementary Needs* (New York: Harper, 1958).

12. B. L. Fineberg and J. Lowman, "Affect and Status Dimensions of Marital Adjustment," *Journal of Marriage and the Family* 37 (1975): 155–160.

13. T. Leary, *Multilevel Measurement of Interpersonal Behavior* (Berkeley, Calif.: Psychological Consultation Service, 1956).

14. Fineberg and Lowman, "Affect and Status Dimensions of Marital Adjustment," p. 158.

15. M. Goodman, "Expressed Self-Acceptance and Interpersonal Needs: A Basis for Mate Selection," *Journal of Counseling Psychology* 11 (1964): 129–135.

16. Goodman, "Expressed Self-Acceptance and Interpersonal Needs," p. 133.

17. E. Shostrom and J. Kavanaugh, *Between Man and Woman* (Los Angeles: Nash Publishing, 1971).

18. Shostrom and Kavanaugh, *Between Man and Woman*, p. 24.

19. Ibid., p. 34.

20. B. I. Murstein and G. D. Beck, "Person Perception, Marriage Adjustment, and Social Desirability," *Journal of Consulting and Clinical Psychology* 39 (1972): 396–403.

21. L. R. Barnett and M. T. Nietzel, "Relationship of Instrumental and Affectional

Behaviors and Self-Esteem to Marital
Satisfaction in Distressed and Nondistressed Couples," *Journal of Consulting
and Clinical Psychology* 47 (1979): 946–
957.
22. W. R. Schumm, C. R. Figley, and N. N.
Fuhs, "Similarity in Self-Esteem as a
Function of Duration of Marriage

among Student Couples," *Psychological
Reports* 47 (1980): 365–366.
23. J. Dobson, *Dare to Discipline* (Wheaton, Ill.: Tyndale House, 1970).
24. M. E. Wagner, *The Sensation of Being
Somebody, Building an Adequate Self-
Concept* (Grand Rapids, Mich.: Zondervan Publishing House, 1975).

BIOGRAPHICAL SKETCH

JOYCE HULGUS is currently the director of the Bethany Counseling Center, a member of the Advisory Board, and seminar leader of Life Enrichment in Denver, Colorado. She is also a private marriage, family, and child counselor, and she was an associate professor at Biola College. She received her M.A. in education from Millersville State College and her M.A. in psychology and Ph.D. in Clinical and Counseling Psychology from Rosemead Graduate School of Psychology. She has had articles published in *Psychology for Living*.

SECTION II:
THE CHURCH AND SOCIETY

Introduction

BECAUSE "the church" is composed of people, self-esteem issues are practically relevant. Pastoral attitudes toward self-esteem will govern the kind of preaching and even the kind of leadership that is provided. The need to feel worthwhile will affect the nature of relationships, church politics, conflicts, and volunteer involvement.

Arlo Compaan argues that conflict is unavoidable within the church (because the church is a human community) and that attitudes toward conflict are the key to its impact upon self-evaluation. If conflict is viewed as an indication of immaturity or the absence of love, devaluation and lowered self-esteem will result when conflict appears. On the other hand, Compaan shows that positive self-esteem facilitates creative solutions and a problem-solving orientation, decreases defensive conflict, and lessens the probability of passive resistance. Finally, he argues that conflicts can become occasions for building self-esteem rather than destroying it.

Vernon Grounds suggests that there are both positive and negative factors that influence a minister's self-esteem. As Christians, pastors see themselves as the objects of God's redeeming grace. As pastors, they are set apart and given the special respect due to their spiritual calling. On the negative side, however, pastors struggle with the idealized image expected by their congregations, are faced continuously with the theology of depravity, are called upon to fill multiple and sometimes conflicting roles with few guidelines for evaluation, and are expected to have model marriages and families. Grounds reminds pastors that the heart of self-renewal is spiritual renewal.

Robert Schuller asserts that the deepest of all human needs is that of

The church

self-esteem. As a result, pastoral and evangelistic strategy must address this need. He believes that people are born with a negative self-image that prevents trust in God. Schuller feels that Jesus opens hearts by showing people their worth and beauty, by valuing them, rather than by parading their guilt. He argues that people instinctively know that they are sinners and that they are most receptive when they are approached in terms of affirmation rather than conviction and shame. The gospel is the good news of grace-acceptance, because of God's love.

James Olthuis argues that a healthy society is based upon a population of citizens with positive esteem. He eschews the existence of a choice—self or society. Rather, he proposes a view of the individual and the society that is neither individualistic and self-centered nor collectivistic and self-destructive. Both self and society are to be changed. Olthuis feels that as personal growth and a stable, positive self are encouraged and established, selfless service and sacrifice for the common good become possible. Self-worth frees people from egocentricity and allows them to become self-transcendent. Inner security allows people to take the risks necessary to bring about change and to combat injustice.

Self-Esteem and Conflict in the Church

ARLO COMPAAN

UNFORTUNATELY, the average church is not paradise. Conflict within the church is an unavoidable reality. We may work overtime to avoid conflict, regard it as inherently destructive, consider it to be an indication of failure, but we cannot completely get rid of it. This is because the church is made up of people. People have different goals, varying ideas on how to reach those goals, and have strong individual needs that may not be in harmony with others.

In a sense, then, conflict in the church is normal, not abnormal. The issue thus shifts from attempts to avoid all conflict to ways in which the negative effects of differences can be minimized. Poorly handled conflicts result in damage to the self-worth of the parties involved, and frequently lead to church splits or continuous disharmony that prevents proper functioning. On the other hand, conflict resolution that is satisfying to those involved brings about individual affirmation and mutual appreciation.

Because conflict and self-esteem are so crucially intertwined, and they vitally affect the life of the church, it is important to fully understand their relationship.

EFFECTS OF BELIEFS ABOUT CONFLICT ON SELF-ESTEEM

The conclusions that we draw regarding ourselves are based upon the attitudes we take toward major experiences that we anticipate. When our experience matches our anticipations, we feel satisfied because we have been realistic and we have behaved as we had wanted. In response, our self-evaluation of ourselves improves. When we have inaccurately anticipated the experience and have not behaved as we had wanted, we conclude that we have failed and are inadequate. The beliefs with which we approach conflict are thus very influential on the conclusions that we draw about ourselves and others. These beliefs become the standards by which we assess ourselves. When those standards are not consistent with reality, definite problems follow. With regard to conflict, many of the current beliefs entrenched in church settings are not realistic. Consequently, considerable loss of self-esteem is experienced by many persons within churches. Since they are unable to modify their behavior to conform to the beliefs, and since the beliefs about conflict are strongly culturally and religiously supported, the only possible outcome is that they will draw some negative conclusions about themselves. "Something is wrong with me." Self-esteem is undermined.

Cognitive dissonance theory is helpful in understanding this dilemma.[1] This theory suggests that all persons seek to maintain congruence between their belief systems and their actual behaviors. When dissonance between the two is experienced, people seek to remove that dissonance by changing the belief system, by changing the behavior or by reinterpreting either so the one is consistent with the other. In regard to conflict, this means that people seek to change either their typical ways of acting in conflict or their beliefs about conflict. Because certain beliefs about conflict are strongly supported by a larger group of people within the person's religious and cultural community, the tendency is usually to try to work to change personal behaviors. However, because the sought-after behaviors are often unrealistic, many persons find it impossible to behave in the desired manner. They then draw the conclusion that there is something wrong with or inadequate about themselves. Such loss of self-esteem can be significantly reversed, if beliefs about conflict are changed.

In addition to the fact that these beliefs affect our self-esteem, it is worth noting that the beliefs often affect our management of conflict in such a way that resolution is impossible. Thus they work against the very outcomes that would enable the increasing of self-esteem. Some changes in our beliefs about conflict will thus assist us in arriving at resolution, which increases self-esteem.

A major belief among most religious groups, certainly among most Christian groups, is that *conflict is wrong.* Conflict is viewed as sinful and hence it must be avoided as much as possible. G. Douglass Lewis, in a book on church conflicts, writes:

The Christian faith is usually interpreted as being opposed to conflict. As a result most churches develop norms rejecting behavior that encourages conflict and rewarding behavior that tends to suppress it.[2]

The very occurrence of a conflict thus is an indication to some of the failure of the church or the individuals to avoid wrong behaviors. Such evaluations of failure significantly decrease both corporate and individual self-esteem.

The belief that conflict is wrong and should be avoided stems largely from the fact that the experience of conflict is usually accompanied by feelings of discomfort, rejection, and pain. Since most of us find such feelings unpleasant, and so try to avoid having them, we tend to conclude that conflict is bad. This evaluation is based upon the immediate feelings produced and does not take into account the long-range consequences of either resolved conflict or avoided conflict. The evaluation is also not based upon solid biblical support, since the Bible records numerous examples of conflict[3] and Jesus is presented often as one who deliberately engaged conflict because he had in view some longer range benefits.[4] This is true even with regard to conflict with the Pharisees, which ultimately led to his death,[5] because he knew that there would be long-range benefits from this conflict. That did not mean that he did not experience discomfort, rejection, and pain while in the conflict. He did, and that experience is also recorded for us.[6] It appears, then, that belief that conflict is wrong comes out of our dislike for certain feelings that are generated in conflict, rather than out of an evaluation of biblical material or an assessment of the long-range consequences of conflict resolution.

Indeed, conflict is an unavoidable part of human life. Lewis sees conflict as a result of the natural differences in goals among people.[7] G. Bach, a well-known marriage counselor, says, "Fighting is inevitable between mature intimates."[8] When we so view conflict, then the mere occurrence of conflict does not have consequences for our self-esteem. It happens because it is an unavoidable part of life. At the same time, this frees us to focus upon the manner of moving toward conflict resolution. Our energy and efforts are not aimed at suppression for the sake of avoidance, but at management for the sake of resolution.

A second belief about conflict that affects our self-esteem is that the occurrence of *conflict is an indication of immaturity:* That is, the fewer the fights, the greater the maturity. We often identify conflict with childhood experiences. Children indeed are much freer than adults in our culture to engage in conflict. So we often see adult conflict as an indication that someone has not grown up. When it occurs in the church, we often add to this belief the evaluation that the person is an immature Christian, a baby in the faith. Consequently, we do not elect such a person to church office; instead, we elect the person who suppresses conflict. Maturity is attached to the occurrence of conflict, not to the management of conflict.

If we judge ourselves and are judged to be immature, we devalue ourselves.

A third belief about conflict is the occurrence of *conflict is an indication of the absence of love,* and perhaps the presence of active rejection. Love is seen only as support and affirmation. Conflict must mean that love is gone. When church board members raise issues over which they disagree with the pastor, the pastor often views this situation as an indication that he or she is no longer liked or loved by these people. The same is true in marriages. The marriage in which there is considerable conflict is often the marriage that people believe is in trouble and in which there is no love. Marital therapists, however, tell us that the marriage in which there is no apparent conflict is the one about which they are more concerned.[9] Again, this belief about conflict is based upon an evaluation of the immediate feelings that are present in conflict. To be sure, feelings of anger and rejection are very prominent in the midst of conflict. They are almost unavoidable parts of a conflict. However, researchers in conflict resolution tell us that conflict can be a very strong indication of care for a person.[10] Occasionally a spouse will identify the same when he or she says, "He doesn't love me enough to get angry with me." Here some conflict is viewed as an indication that love is present and that the spouses are important to each other.

An immediate consequence of the belief that conflict means the absence of love is that the relationship's existence is threatened. When couples believe this, worries are activated that the relationship is moving towards a breakup. Such fears escalate the stakes in the conflict, for now they are not just in conflict over an issue, but the existence of the marriage is at issue. Since much more is involved, the individuals will invest more, with the consequence that the outcome will have more effect on their self-esteem. The same is true for conflict within the church. When the pastor is involved in conflict, conclusions are quickly drawn that it is not going well in the church, that the pastor may or ought to leave, or that certain members will or ought to leave. When such partings occur in the midst or as a result of conflict, individuals usually go through a period of self-evaluation during which they view themselves more critically than is warranted. Again, their self-esteem is affected by what may seem like failure.

When these beliefs are present in churches, pastors are most often expected to be the ones who put out the fires of conflict. They are called into a conflict with the hope that they will reduce or help avoid the conflict as quickly as possible. When they are able to avoid the conflict, they are often seen as effective pastors, highly esteemed by the membership. When they use methods of conflict resolution other than avoidance or suppression, they are often evaluated negatively and may consider themselves as ineffective. Here again, self-esteem suffers unnecessarily.

Clearly, the attitudes and beliefs we bring to conflict affect the outcome of the conflict and the evaluation of ourselves as persons and as Christians. When we can view conflict as unavoidable and a necessary part of intimacy, then its occurrence says nothing about our effectiveness, maturity, and love in the situation. The criteria for evaluation shifts to the manner we choose to obtain resolution of conflict. These standards have far greater potential for raising our self-esteem because they are attainable, whereas the total avoidance of conflict is an unattainable standard, guaranteed to produce evaluations of failure.

THE EFFECTS OF SELF-ESTEEM ON CONFLICT

While beliefs about conflict do significantly affect self-esteem, self-esteem also is an important variable that influences the particular behaviors employed by individuals in their conflict styles. Since self-esteem is such a fundamental aspect of human personality and is formed over a period of years, it is not quickly changed. And as self-esteem is one variable that influences a conflict style, we can better understand people and better work with them in conflict if we can see how self-esteem issues are affecting the observed behaviors. Sometimes we tend to attribute to people motivations that involve intentions to harm others or ourselves in the conflict, rather than to see the behavior as a consequence of low self-esteem. When it is seen as the latter, then the nature of interventions or management procedures will be distinctively different from when it is seen as intentionally hostile behavior. Also, the recognition that conflict behaviors are related to self-esteem gives us a sense that change in conflict-management behaviors will take time and will be coordinated with changes in self-esteem. We do ourselves and others a real disservice when we expect the conflict styles to change rapidly.

The higher the self-esteem of a person, the more willing that person will be to consider a number of possible solutions to the problem in addition to those already proposed. Such an openness requires risk, since the total effect of the new solutions has not been considered by the individuals involved. When self-esteem is low, the tendency is to settle quickly on one or two solutions that the individuals see as accomplishing what they set out to obtain. The behaviors in the conflict then become variations of ways to get this one position accepted by the parties to the conflict. As the conflict intensifies, the behaviors increasingly become more power-oriented. Within the church context, this may mean that some outside authority or expert is appealed to as requiring adoption of this one particular solution. The focus of the conflict is placed upon a particular solution, rather than upon the problem or issue to which all parties are seeking a satisfactory solution. This difference is a subtle but very significant one, and the issue of self-esteem is often the underlying factor.

The persons who appear as strong, forceful, and dogmatic parties to the conflict may in fact possess low self-esteem. They may be thinking, "I am not well respected, not understood, not likely to be treated fairly and will lose unless I resort to some behaviors that will force the others to take my side." Thus they appeal to higher and external authorities, such as the pastor, the Bible, traditions, and major religious leaders, in the belief that these will carry the weight that they themselves do not have. Some may also seek to induce guilt in order to be able to manipulate others into accepting the proposed solution. While these behaviors often make others very angry, it is helpful to recognize them as indications of low self-esteem. Interactions with these people must address the self-esteem issue through reassurance of support and love, while continuing to work toward a solution that will be agreeable to all parties to the conflict. Making people feel good about themselves is a critical skill for successful conflict resolution.

Persons with low self-esteem may also approach a conflict with hidden agendas. They have objectives that they do not quite dare reveal, believing that others would reject their objectives while keeping them hidden from others. The resolution thus is difficult to obtain and the conflict may drag on with many wondering why it continues. The higher the self-esteem, the more likely it is that people will acknowledge verbally their objectives so that all parties can include it in the consideration of the final solution.

The lower the self-esteem, the more likely it is that people will become personally involved in the conflict to the extent that particular events and solutions are viewed as either personal victory or personal defeat. When this occurs, resolution is made more difficult, since there is so much personal investment in particular solutions. Underlying this process is low self-esteem. The higher the self-esteem, the more likely it is that individuals will continue to feel good about themselves, no matter what the outcome of the conflict. People with high self-esteem are not greatly affected in their self-evaluation by resolutions to conflict that are different from solutions they had personally proposed, maybe even fought for.

In the church, another style of behavior is also seen that is related to self-esteem. Some individuals choose a passive silence and do not actively declare their preferences until forced to in a vote. These individuals are often afraid to voice their opinions, expecting those opinions and themselves to be rejected. Sometimes in their quietness, they may go along with the more strongly articulated position, while still resenting the solution. As researchers in group dynamics tell us, such individuals often end up sabotaging the solution later on because of their resentment.[11] Again, their passive stance is very much related to their low evaluations of themselves. With such individuals, encouragement and affirmation aimed at supporting their self-esteem will contribute to more active participation and, in the long run, better conflict resolution.

In facilitating good conflict management, an awareness of the fact that low self-esteem is often behind particular behaviors can help one to address this as well as the particular issue. Helping people to feel better about themselves is critical in good conflict management. The same is true at the level of the church. When a church feels good about itself, conflict resolution is a much easier task. Pastors and church leaders can do a great deal to enhance people's assessment of themselves and so contribute to better conflict resolution.

BUILDING SELF-ESTEEM THROUGH CONFLICT RESOLUTION

When individuals realize that conflict is unavoidable and that what is significant is how resolution is obtained, then there is great potential for them to feel good about themselves and to see the competence in their experience. The sense of accomplishment and success that follows resolution is lost because the individuals involved have been upset and sometimes hurt during the conflict. These feelings may overwhelm the solid recognition of the fact that resolution was obtained. In such situations, taking the time to note the resolution and to affirm the fact that the individuals contributed to bringing it about does a great deal to increase self-esteem.

Conflict can also build self-esteem because it helps to identify common commitments among the participants to the conflict. Conflict that is engaged in by all parties because of a commitment to the maintenance of the same values has positive consequences for the relationship.[12] A conflict that is engaged in by a couple because each is concerned for the future existence of the relationship has positive value because it makes clear each person's commitment to the relationship. A church that engages in conflict over the budget may benefit a great deal if it is clear that all parties are concerned about the stewardship responsibilities of the church. Such a conflict helps to make clear the continuing similarity of their commitments, while articulating differences on how this is to be applied in a particular situation. As common commitments are acknowledged, the valuing of each other is also affirmed.

During most conflicts, feelings are intense. Anger can be expected to be displayed and different parties in the conflict will experience their own and others' feelings differently. Often conflict is experienced as hurt and rejection. Sometimes injurious statements are made and rejection does actually occur. When the conflict is resolved, it is significant that some time is taken to heal the emotional wounds that have occurred. Individuals need to take responsibility for having done and said some things that now they wished they had not, if relationships are to be repaired. Clearly acknowledging this and requesting forgiveness will not only heal the wounds, but also lead to improved assessment of self and others. Too often this is not done and individuals leave the conflict harboring resentment about others and guilt about their own behaviors. Both will ultimately reduce their self-evaluation, unless something is done to change the feelings. Openly and directly acknowledging the feelings is an important first step.

Conflict, when it is well managed, has the potential of increasing the self-esteem of all parties in the conflict. Each party will experience the sense of success that comes with having reached an acceptable resolution. Their commitment to each other or to common goals will have been identified again. Respect for each other's feelings will have been exemplified. All this will contribute to increased self-esteem.

Conclusion

Conflict is seldom an experience that we seek and hardly one that we expect to have major effect on our self-esteem. Yet it does affect us greatly. As a result of the faulty beliefs that we hold and that our church cultures affirm, we often experience the occurrence of conflict as a detraction from our self-esteem. We view it as an indication of sin, immaturity, and rejection. Yet conflict holds great potential for enhancing self-esteem when we learn to manage it and accept that conflict is an unavoidable part of our life together in the church.

NOTES

1. Arthur R. Cohen, *Attitude Change and Social Influence* (New York: Basic Books, 1964), pp. 73–80.
2. G. Douglass Lewis, *Resolving Church Conflicts* (San Francisco: Harper & Row, 1981), p. 12. See also Speed Leas and Paul Kittlaus, *Church Fights: Managing Conflicts in the Local*

Church (Philadelphia: Westminster Press, 1973).

3. Acts 15, Exodus 16, Mark 11:27–33 are examples.
4. See Luke 6:6–11; Luke 11:37–54.
5. See Luke 12:1–12; Matthew 21:12–17.
6. See Luke 13:31–35; Luke 22:39–53.
7. Lewis, Resolving Church Conflicts, pp. 8–12.
8. George Bach and Peter Wyden, The Intimate Enemy: How to Fight Fair in Love and Marriage (New York: Aron Books, 1968), p. 26.
9. See Alan S. Gurman and David G. Rice,

Couples in Conflict (New York: Jason Aronson, 1975).
10. See Irving L. Janis and Leon Mann, Decision Making (New York: Free Press, 1977).
11. Marvin E. Shaw, Group Dynamics (New York: McGraw-Hill Book Co., 1976), pp. 390–392.
12. Harold L. Raush, William A. Barry, Richard K. Hertel, and Mary Ann Swain, Communication, Conflict and Marriage (San Francisco: Jossey-Bass Publishers, 1974), pp. 30–33.

BIOGRAPHICAL SKETCH

ARLO COMPAAN is the executive director of the Center for Life Skills in Chicago. He received his Ph.D. from the School of Theology in Claremont in the area of pastoral psychology. He received his B.D. from Calvin Theological Seminary and his A.B. from Calvin College. He is a licensed psychologist in the state of Illinois, an ordained pastor in the Christian Reformed Church, and president of the CAPS Board of Directors. He has pastored a church in Michigan and taught as an associate professor of psychology at Trinity Christian College. He has lectured in many different churches and has had articles published in The Bulletin and CAPS Proceedings.

The Highs and Lows of
Ministry

VERNON GROUNDS

IS THE self-esteem of evangelical Protestant pastors characteristically high or low? Are these ministers, by and large, models of healthy-mindedness, blessed with self-images that are both realistic and positive? Is the clerical self-attitude unique, controlled by criteria that the nonclerical population does not take into account? Is self-esteem a more troublesome problem for religious professionals than for persons who may be adherents of Christianity, but who are not paid to perform ecclesiastical functions? What factors affect the self-esteem of evangelical clergy?

In answering these interrelated questions, we need to consider, first, the influences of religious belief and practice on mental health. We are doing this because it may be hypothesized that strong self-esteem is one indication of psychic well-being. In their exhaustive article, "Religion and Mental Disorder: A Research Perspective," Bernard Spilka and Paul H. Werme summarized hundreds of research projects that include religion and mental disorder as variables, undertaking "to explain why research has been so inconsistent."[1] Evidently, it has been done with "gross measures, nondiscrete categories, and inadequate theory."[2] So the vast amount of research carried on until the beginning of the 1970s, when this article was published, produced no conclusive findings.

With respect to the mental health of clergy, Spilka and Werme report that there appears to be a "higher incidence of mental disorder among clergy and other religious professionals." But in their judgment, this "can be—and has frequently been—explained in terms either of the stress of the professional role or the attractiveness of the role for potentially disturbed persons." Yet having said that, they immediately enter a caveat: "It is still not perfectly clear that there is such a higher incidence to explain."[3] Carl

Christensen expresses a similar opinion: "Any attempt to determine the prevalence of mental disorders among religious personnel can at best, yield only vague approximations."[4] James Dittes of Yale University, who has focused his attention on the interface between religion and psychology, reinforces the conclusions of Spilka, Werme, and Christensen. While he is aware that "personality characteristics of religious professionals has [sic] received a prodigious amount of investigation," he regrets that, "almost nothing is confidently known"[5] as yet regarding these supposedly distinctive traits. Past investigations, his own included, have been rendered suspect by methodological shortcomings and woefully inadequate theory.

Keeping in mind the lack of reliable findings, we may surmise, nevertheless, that pastors are as emotionally healthy as any other segment of our society. The one-time medical director of the American Medical Association, Daniel Blain, himself a child of the manse, declares on the basis of his personal and professional observations that "most ministers have a high degree of mental health," if mental health, in the words of George H. Preston, means that persons "are able to live happily and productively with other human beings within the limits imposed by bodily equipment."[6] Samuel Southard renders the same verdict. Referring to a survey of state mental hospitals throughout our country made by Chaplain Leonard Morgan, Jr., he writes:

Fewer ministers are in hospitals than would be expected from their numbers in our society. Chaplain Morgan reports that only 7 out of every 10,000 mental patients are clergymen, whereas 20 out of every 10,000 persons in the community are clergymen. Again, if hospitalization tells us much about the incidence of illness, the minister is less likely to have a "nervous breakdown" than the people in his congregation."[7]

Against this background, we are now ready to project our specific inquiry: "Is negative self-esteem a significant problem among Protestant evangelical pastors? If so, why?" This issue is obviously inseparable from that of the ministerial self-image. Here we are entering virgin territory, since the trailblazing material is limited and largely anecdotal. "Almost nothing has been done in the early research," laments sociologist Laile Bartlett, "certainly nothing definitive with the self-image of clergy. The search for the missing 'x' goes on, but until we explore this factor adequately, we will not have the picture."[8] Granted that Bartlett is right about the dearth of definitive research, we can still venture to explore the issue of pastoral self-esteem with the help of whatever literature is available, as well as through observations, impressions, and clergy self-reports. After all, as Leonard Small remarks, every one of us is an "inveterate mirror-gazer." Human beings, as introspective animals, scrutinize themselves critically, now from this angle, next from that.

This critical evaluation we call self-esteem—"I am good" or "I am bad"—is the job of the conscience or superego. Frequent and important among the comments about the self are those that concern performance, the competencies of the whole individual, where the sense of doing something well parallels being "good." In fact, to be competent so often is equated with being good. . . . The way in which we work and the kind of work we do are crucial in forming our self-evaluations. It is a question not only of pleasure and skill but of social status, and beyond this the attainment of adult maturity, for work can bring responsibility and independence. Self-esteem, then, is derived from our work as well as from our moral judgments. . . .[9]

How, then, do pastors (if we may be permitted to discuss this generalized abstraction of the pastor as if it were really a flesh-and-blood individual) appraise themselves in the light of their sacred profession with its demands and rewards? What are those factors that contribute to a minister's self-esteem? After we have looked at the positive aspects of this question, we will examine the debit side of the ledger.

Positive Influences

To begin with, pastors are Christians. As such, they are the objects of God's redeeming grace and hence the very apple of the cosmic Eye. From all eternity, the Lord Almighty has been mindful of them. God created the whole order of nature and has guided the entire process of history for the sake of bringing them into a loving and intimate relationship with their Maker. Indeed, that relationship is as intimate as the union between husband and wife, even in its sexual dimension. God and every redeemed human being already live together in a spiritual oneness that, to borrow Tennyson's words, is "nearer than breathing, closer than hands and feet." Planned by God, created by God, loved by God, saved by God, indwelt by God, and destined for a rapturous face-to-face fellowship with God, Christians understandably view themselves as possessing a value that is literally incalculable.

Furthermore, pastors read in the New Testament that, with spellbound curiosity, the angels watch the salvific drama in which they, the pastors, and the Godhead are the protagonists. They read, too, that invisible forces of measureless might and malignity make them the target of unceasing attack.

How, then, can they write themselves off as insignificant nonentities, earthlings worth little more than earthworms? In a most self-reassuring sense, they are the *raison d'etre* of worms, galaxies, everything. If, as the Westminster Shorter Catechism affirms, their chief end is to glorify God and enjoy Him forever, at any rate they glorify God as no other created beings do, and their enjoyment of God is both exquisitely unique and uniquely intimate.

For a second thing, pastors are ordained and thereby lifted to a loftier level of divine/human relationship, regardless of the contrary pronouncements made in some theologies. Set apart from the rank and file of believers, they are God's human creature superlatively, engaged in a task that, unlike medicine or engineering, involves eternal values. Free to devote their time and energy wholly to their sacred profession, they are entitled to willing and generous support by their flock. They are also entitled to a deferential respect and, for that reason, bear the honorific title of reverend, a title that the Authorized Version of the Bible reserves for deity. Besides this, in most denominations they are exclusively entitled to officiate at the central rituals of baptism and eucharist, evidently because their ordination endows them with a kind of unction, stoutly denied in theory, yet subtly acknowledged in practice. In their ministerial role, they are the parson—that is, *the* person, the foremost persons in their spiritual communities. The pastor's head is encircled by a nimbus of piety. "Consider," David and Vera Mace suggest, "the image of the minister that is deliberately presented to the congregation."

When the members gather for worship he occupies the pulpit. Raised high above the congregation, and apart from all others, he is marked out as special, different, the authority. When he preaches, he is delivering the authentic Christian message. Sunday by Sunday, he tells the congregation how to live the Christian life. He has the answers. He is not "one of us"—he is set apart. The very posture required of the congregation, looking up to him from a lower level, emphasized that he is the leader, the teacher, the guide.[10]

The rewards of the ministry are thus enviably rich. It would seem, therefore, that a pastor, of all human beings, ought to be blessed with a solid, secure self-esteem.

NEGATIVE INFLUENCES

Unfortunately, however, there is a reverse side to this shining coin, a side that is less alluringly bright, perhaps somewhat tarnished. Over against the ministry's rewards, we now set its demand.

For one thing, pastors are professional religionists, salaried disciples of Jesus, who are called upon, J. Sidlow Baxter exhorts his fellow-clergymen, to be *"living reproduction[s] of Christ."* According to Baxter, this entails a character that is "1) intensely *spiritual,* 2) perfectly *natural,* and 3) thoroughly *practical."* Nothing short of this ideal, he insists, will qualify a person to serve effectively in the pastoral office. "Each of us who dare to represent Him in the ministry of His church is meant to embody a replica of His character."[11] No doubt Baxter is correctly stating the New Testament ideal that churches consequently expect their clergy to incarnate. Yet, in itself, this demand may produce frustration and guilt. Pastors know, on the one hand, the biblical ideal and their people's expectations. They know, on the other hand, the perhaps dismal reality of their own spiritual experience. Hence pastors may wonder with the apostle Paul, "Who is sufficient for these things?" and may live in persistent psychic discomfort as self-condemned hypocrites. To live like that is scarcely conducive to self-esteem.

A second demand laid upon Protestant evangelical pastors is a concomitant of their theology. They subscribe, let us assume *con amore,* to the doctrine of total depravity. They believe and preach with Isaiah that "all of our righteousnesses are as filthy rags." They quote the ego-shattering words of Jesus, "If any man come to me, and hate not his father, and mother, and wife, and children, and brethren, and sisters, yea his own life also, he cannot be my disciple." They share Paul's conviction that "in me [that is, in my flesh] dwelleth no good thing." They join that apostle in denouncing the finest of human aspirations and the best of human efforts as "dung." They accept John Calvin as a spirit-illuminated expositor of God's truth, and Calvin makes statements like this, scarcely calculated to inflate one's self-esteem: "For nothing arouses us to repose all confidence and assurance of mind on the Lord so much as diffidence of ourselves, and anxiety arising from a consciousness of our own misery."[12]

Subscribing with Calvin—or, perhaps, with Augustine, or Luther—to this sort of self-denigration, evangelical pastors lead their people as they worship in singing a hymn by Isaac Watts:

> Alas, and did my Saviour bleed
> And did my Sovereign die?
> Would He devote that sacred head
> For such a worm as I?

Thus ministers demand of their people, as well as of themselves, what their theology appears to demand of all evangelicals—self-rejection, self-mistrust, self-hatred, self-crucifixion. Confessedly, this demand does not bolster a feeling of self-esteem.

A third demand laid upon each evangelical pastor is that of handling a multifaceted role that calls for a battery of diversified skills rarely found together in any one individual. Pastoral work defies a succinct job description because it is a hodge-podge of responsibilities. Samuel Blizzard in his survey of 690 clergymen concluded that the Protestant ministry is a composite of six overlapping roles:

1. *Administrator.* The supervision of the activities in the local church and parish.
2. *Organizer.* The development of programs in the church and community.
3. *Pastor.* Caring for the needs of church members. This includes counseling.
4. *Preacher.* Proclaiming the gospel.
5. *Priest.* Performing religious functions, such as leading worship, conducting baptisms, weddings, and funerals.
6. *Teacher.* Giving instruction in the Christian faith.[13]

More often than not, therefore, ministers are plagued by role diffusion and role confusion. Are they the ecclesiastical counterparts of efficient executives, or are they stern-visaged prophets who emerge from the book-lined seclusion of their studies on Sunday to deliver their biblical message before retreating again to heaven-consulting isolation? Are they to be the scholars modeled by their seminary professors or are they to be the back-slapping public relations experts able to talk shop with their leading laymen? Gereon Zimmerman highlighted this tension in his report of a research project conducted twenty years ago:

In drawing up a psychological test for seminaries for the Rockefeller Brothers program, the Educational Testing Service sent a questionnaire to 1,100 lay leaders in various denominations, asking them to mention adjectives and to give profiles that represented their own concept of "an outstanding minister." This data was then turned over to another group of psychological testers, who were not told who was being described. These testers were asked, "Who [sic] do you think is being described?" Their answer: "A junior vice-president of Sears-Roebuck."[14]

Today, one suspects, lay people would describe "an outstanding minister" in exactly the same way. How, then, can pastors decide what they are to do and, at the same time, who they are? It is precisely this combination of role confusion and role diffusion that James Gustafson thinks is a major cause of clerical job-dissatisfaction. According to Gustafson, the minister continually struggles to determine *who he is* and *what he is doing* within the complexity of his functions. He frequently lacks, more than anything else, an awareness of what he is about, and therefore he has no central focus for the integration of his various activities.[15]

Because pastors are pulled in a dozen different directions simultaneously, their self-esteem is liable to sag and shrivel. Indeed, this role uncertainty is so acute for some clergymen that it does far worse than gnaw away at self-esteem. It undermines morale, brings on burnout, and may motivate an exodus from the church.

To compound this tension, pastors have no very helpful guidelines as to how ministers function effectively or, for that matter, what constitutes effectiveness. A leading researcher in this field, Allen Nauss, complains:

Despite this apparent general interest, various studies, exhortation, seminary curricula and research have to date very little empirical evidence of what is required of a parish minister to function at a high level of effectiveness.[16]

Educational administrators and denominational officials, aided by vocational psychologists, continue to work on this problem. Yet in his article, "Current Research of Performance Effectiveness Among Religious Leaders," H. Newton Malony drily admits, "Much remains to be done."[17] It certainly does. And meanwhile pastors typically remain unsure concerning their performance. The effect of this on their self-esteem requires no elaboration.

Inseparable from the demand that they serve as ecclesiastical jacks-of-all-trades who have no firm criteria by which to measure their effectiveness is the demand made upon pastors that they, at all costs, are to be successful. This means that they are to be busy enlarging their congregations, increasing their churchs' annual incomes, and expanding the facilities that their flocks use. Pressure comes from multiple sources, including their own peers who apparently delight to indulge in statistical comparisons. Yet pastors read their New Testament and thereby are constantly reminded that success, as Jesus taught it, is not a matter of bodies, buildings, and budgets, but a self-forgetting, sacrificial labor of love that brings people into the life and likeness of God. Espousing this ideal of Christianity, both personally and publicly, they hopefully refuse to water it down or give it up. But at times they may be sorely tempted to do so, manipulating their flocks rather than serving the spiritual needs of those flocks. They come across this prescription for clerical success given by popular psychologist George W. Crane, and they wonder.

Remember names and faces. It inflates the ego of parishioners to have their priest or clergyman call them by name. . . . Name at least three parishioners in your sermon every Sunday, in an incidental but complimentary manner. Urge classes to divide into teams with a captain over each. Schedule short contests every month, with the winning team to be entertained at a picnic or wiener roast by the losers. . . . Praise those who arrange the altar flowers, as well as the ushers, singers, and especially the cooks of the church suppers.[18]

Well, why not? Yes, why not turn people into objects, employing the techniques that work effectively in secular organizations and some burgeoning churches? Pressured to attain more and more statistical success, pastors battle against the temptation to compromise their own convictions. If temptation is resisted, their inner glow of Christian integrity may not compensate significantly for their relative failure as sanctified promoters.

Still another demand typically laid upon pastors is that of giving themselves unstintingly and uncomplainingly to God's work while they somehow manage to be husbands and fathers whose families are model Christian households. John G. Koehler conducted a study of 119 American Baptist ministers whose wives were requested to keep an accurate ledger of the time their husbands spent at home in a week. Here are the results:

At home fewer than ten hours per week—6%
At home ten to nineteen hours per week—39%
At home twenty to thirty hours per week—30%
At home thirty to forty hours per week—18%
At home more than forty hours per week—7%[19]

This indicates that pastors may spend no more than four waking hours a day at home, and those four hours include everything they do—eating, dressing, shaving, watching television, entertaining, the whole gamut of their activities.

Koehler likewise found that less than half of the churches he surveyed seriously urge their pastors to take off a day a week. In general, the pastors, even if they were urged to do so, rarely did. Koehler further discovered that wives of pastors complained because their husbands were "on call twenty-four hours a day." They also complained because their husbands' schedules were frustratingly unpredictable and often necessitated abrupt changes in plans.[20] Busy and preoccupied, however, pastors may selectively ignore the messages that communicate that their spouses, to say nothing of their children, feel neglected and stifled.

In their analysis of these troublesome home realities, Truman G. Esau and Richard H. Cox called attention to the trauma that plagues many self-denying pastors' wives, euphemistically referred to as "shepherdesses." Among the "facts of their lives" are problems of loneliness, forced conformism, life in the goldfish bowl of the manse, exhausting participation in church activities, the threat of periodic uprooting, financial stringency, and worry about rebellious children who deviate from parental and congregational expectations. They point out that these emotional tensions may result in hostile dependency, reactive depression, psychosomatic disorders, a chronic sense of unfulfillment, and, needless to add, disabling guilt.[21] It seems obvious that no pastors who feel their service for God is being psychically underwritten by their spouses and children are likely to enjoy a fulfilling self-esteem.

An additional demand that ministers frequently face is that of maintaining a life-style comparable to the standard of their parishioners, while on a lower salary. The authors of the research project *Ex-Pastors*, an investigation of "Why Men Leave the Parish Ministry," spotlight financial stress as a crucial element in clerical job-satisfaction. "There is little doubt," they assert, "that the ministry is the poorest paying profession. Starting salaries for pastors are even less than starting salaries for teachers in most states." Since, in our culture, money is an important ingredient of job-satisfaction (and hence self-esteem), ministers whose incomes are low may feel inadequate and dissatisfied, and may eventually look for another job. Our society assumes, these researchers comment, that "if a man is a success, he will make enough money. If he is a success, when he changes jobs the new job will pay considerably more."[22]

Yet as God's servants, devoted to transmundane realities, pastors condemn themselves if they are concerned about their insufficient incomes. As followers and proclaimers of a certain homeless Nazarene, they tell themselves, one ought never to complain about money. So if and when they do, guilt feelings arise, and their self-image as God-dependent may be deflated.

On the other hand, if ministers are well paid and enjoy a bourgeoise life-style, they may be guilt-ridden because of their unspiritual affluence—or, more likely, semiaffluence. Daniel Walker, himself a pastor for years, sees no reason to ignore this problem.

We American preachers of the 20th century are in the curious position of preaching the Gospel of the Cross from the comforts of a couch. We declare the superiority of the spiritual while enjoying a life absorbed in the material. Against this background a Gospel of sacrifice sounds hollow. Any sensitive minister is aware of this, and is less comfortable with his conscience than with his car. There is something unnerving about going out to a steak dinner after telling a congregation that for the price of a milkshake you can feed a Korean orphan for a week. . . . Having begun our careers with commendable idealism, many of us wind up in middle life thinking, if not saying, "I'll go where you want me to go, dear Lord, if I can be guaranteed the comforts I am accustomed to." We are not happy with this state of mind, but what can we do about it? Some men simply close their eyes to it.[23]

But the tension does not vanish when shoulders are shrugged and eyes are averted. It remains a persistent ambiguity that may diminish a pastor's self-esteem.

One more demand that the ministry levies is that of necessitating a consistent verbalization of faith in the transforming power of the gospel and hypocritically continuing that verbalization even though confidence in its power has been ebbing. Pastors may realize, with pain and disillusionment, that regardless of their fervor, dedication, and dogged proclamation, the people in their churches are not changing. Somewhat traditional, they can sympathize deeply with the more iconoclastic brother who said he was suffering from "soul fatigue." This is the enervating discouragement that grows from "the hopelessness one feels as he sees everything he believes in compromised or eliminated altogether in the life of the Church." As one Southern clergyman who was fighting to overcome racial prejudice put it in a letter: "I realize that the effort is futile. So what is my attitude now —one of utter hopelessness—despair. I am almost as low as a fellow can get and still keep his cool."[24] Thus what Helmut Thielicke writes concerning the Protestant ecclesiastical scene in Germany applies with appropriate modifications to evangelical ministers in both rural and urban America as well. And this whole long passage—all of it!—merits pondering.

The big city pastor must spend his evenings sitting in meetings of esoteric church organizations where he is always seeing the same faces. During the day he is being chewed up by instructional classes, occasional services, pastoral calls, and the Moloch of his bureaucracy. All this pulverizes him in the mortar of that tiny sector of a pluralistic society which is called a "church"—a sector which the dwellers in the gigantic secularized provinces of life hardly notice. The pastor has the feeling that he is performing this ministry almost to the exclusion of any public notice whatsoever. And as he drives and runs about, carrying with him the commission to proclaim a message that would revolutionize life, he may be oppressed on the one hand by the thought of the tremendous contradiction between the claim and the promise of this message and on the other by the utter immovability of the deeply rutted tracks in which he must move. What is happening? And where is there even the slightest indication that a light is shining in the world and that the salt is at work in the soil, keeping it from going sour? Because a man so harassed is threatened by the onset of melancholia, he may also be oppressed by the institutional unreality and unveracity in the midst of which he does his work: the public and legally privileged consolidation of this ecclesiastical establishment which has no equivalent inner authority.[25]

When ministers look at the discrepancy between the alleged dynamism of their message and "the utter immovability of the deeply rutted tracks in which [they] must move," their morale *and* their self-esteem sink.

Underlying all of these demands, though, is the one previously alluded to: that pastors be somewhat superhuman and so, in effect, less than—and really other than—human. Perhaps at this stage of our investigation, we are able to empathize much more acutely with pastors who love their Lord and people but who yearn nevertheless to be authentically and freely their own selves and their own persons. They may smile at the all-too-accurate stereotype of the pastor in Charles Merrill Smith's *How To Become a Bishop Without Being Religious,* but wince as with mock seriousness Smith ironically counsels his fellow-ministers: "It is absolutely essential to the preacher's image that he hedge in his natural inclinations with a rugged set of custom-made inhibitions."[26] In keeping up their preacher image, and insisting also that their families conform to a parsonage ideal, inhibited pastors are not only being hypocritical; they are likewise running the risk of "a denial and suppression of the true self which may be the beginning of a neurotic trend"[27] for their spouses and children no less than for themselves. They may never have heard of Albert Haversat, who worked extensively with Lutheran clergy, but they would doubtless concur with that researcher's pronouncement: "The major ministerial crisis is self-image, that is, dependency and lack of confidence. He may bitch about inner 'church structure'—but this only helps him to avoid facing himself."[28] How to face oneself honestly and how to feel good about oneself in the presence of God and before the bar of one's own conscience—that is for many pastors the toughest problem they confront. And it is a problem that just does not go away.

Nobody, not even the spouse, may be aware of the battle, but in the pastor's psyche (or—to be theological—in the pastor's soul), the conflict goes on. How can pastors be themselves, their own persons, genuine human beings, expressing human individuality, while living and serving God, playing their clerical role and fulfilling their functions with integrity without simply maintaining a professional *persona?* Is it possible, at one and the same time, for them to be spiritually vibrant, emotionally healthy, and vocationally effective? This triple demand, some pastors may sadly decide, is impossibly taxing. They may, accordingly, choose to leave the church. This has been the route some ministers have chosen to follow. Though Laile Bartlett exaggerates when she affirms that "the most notable defection from the service of the church since the Reformation"[29] has been taking place of late, clerical drop-out has been, if not, to quote the authors of *Ex-Pastors*, "a run-away epidemic," at least "a persistent low-grade infection."[30] Bartlett does not exaggerate when, having listed the reasons that may motivate a pastor to plunge into the maelstrom of a career-change, she singles out "one basic and encompassing issue: *the quest for personhood.* . . . He is leaving because the ministry as he finds it, fails to fulfill his own personhood and blocks his efforts to help others."[31]

Pondering the option of becoming an ex-pastor, a conflicted minister may elect to remain a minister. But the authors of *Ex-Pastors* describe this reaction: "With grim determination, he may redouble his efforts at church ministry in spite of all." Simultaneously, they add, "he may depend more and more heavily on support systems and withdraw from others (we suspect this is why ministers invest their wives with such powerful reference and support functions)."[32] Pastors who decide to remain, however, will find they must overhaul their, to quote William Hulme's insightful phrase, "professional defense systems." These systems are energy-consuming habits and attitudes that serve "as an escape rather than as a solution to . . . inner problems." It is crucial that pastors put at the top of their agendas the difficult but ultimately rewarding task of self-renewal. Whatever resources and methods they utilize, pastors must work prayerfully and persistently on self-change. The pastor must persevere, even if at first the self-image seems "too threaten[ed] to look at directly without upsetting the balance maintained by his compensations and catapulting him into an acute sense of guilt or even despair."[33] Although a pastor may temporarily risk intensified guilt and despair, it is imperative that, with God's enablement, the pastor fight and conquer those and other emotional giants like frustration and hostility. Only by self-renewal, with all its unavoidable stress, can a pastor experience career renewal and, hopefully, church renewal. At the heart of self-renewal is spiritual renewal, and at the heart of spiritual renewal is devotional renewal. Devotional renewal, through which God's enablement can be enlisted, will deepen the pastor's

counseling relationship with God. Combining the openness to receive that characterizes meditation with the cathartic expression of confession, the minister may clear the confusion from his mind regarding his commitment. The feeling of being lost that he at times has, which he cannot express as a leader in prayer, he can express in his room when he has shut the door. Here the feelings that need to come out can come out. . . . The pastor can get his thinking straight concerning what *can* be done and what *cannot.* Through his relationship with God, which is exercised by this experience, he receives the courage to do what needs to be done and the confidence to commit to God what he cannot do. . . . The pastor more often than not finds himself refreshed in spirit and restored emotionally.[34]

In ways such as these, troubled ministers may eventually work through their self-defeating problems and arrive at that level of self-acceptance and self-confidence where, borrowing Paul's self-witness, they sincerely testify concerning themselves and their own church vocation, "I thank God that he counted me worthy putting me into the ministry."

NOTES

1. Bernard Spilka and Paul H. Werme, "Religion and Mental Disorder: A Research Perspective," *Research on Religious Development*, ed. Merton P. Strommen (New York: Hawthorn Books, 1971), p. 475.
2. Ibid., p. 460. This is the editorial comment that introduces the Spilka/Werme article.
3. Ibid., p. 469.
4. Carl Christensen, "The Mental Health of Clergymen," *Clinical Psychiatry and Religion*, ed. E. Mansell Pattison (Boston: Little, Brown and Company, 1969), p. 192.
5. James Dittes, "Psychological Characteristics of Religious Professionals," in *Research on Religious Development*, ed. Strommen, p. 425.
6. Daniel Blain, "Fostering the Mental Health of Ministers," *The Minister's Own Mental Health*, ed. Wayne E. Oates (Great Neck, N.Y.: Channel Press, 1961), p. 19.
7. Samuel Southard, "An Overview of Research on the Mental Illness of the Minister," in *The Minister's Own Mental Health*, ed. Oates, p. 233.
8. Laile E. Bartlett, *The Vanishing Parson* (Boston: Beacon Press, 1971), p. 166.
9. Leonard Small, "Work and Personality Adjustment," in *The Minister's Own Mental Health*, ed. Oates, pp. 271–272.
10. David and Vera Mace, *What's Happening to Clergy Marriages?* (Nashville, Tenn.: Abingdon, 1980), p. 57.
11. J. Sidlow Baxter, *Rethinking Our Priorities; The Church: Its Pastor and People* (Grand Rapids, Mich.: Zondervan, 1974), p. 145.
12. John Calvin, *Institutes of the Christian Religion,* cited by Erich Fromm, *Escape from Freedom* (New York: Rinehart & Company, 1941), p. 84.
13. Samuel Blizzard, "The Minister's Dilemma," cited by Mace, *What's Happening to Clergy Marriages?* p. 62.
14. Gereon Zimmerman, "Help Wanted: Ministers, Priests, and Rabbis," cited by Robert G. Middleton, *Privilege and Burden* (Valley Forge, Pa.: Judson Press, 1969), p. 32.
15. James Gustafson, "An Analysis of the Problem of the Role of the Minister," in Middleton, *Privilege and Burden,* p. 104.
16. Allen Nauss, "Problems in Measuring Ministerial Effectiveness," in H. Newton Malony, "Current Research on Performance Effectiveness Among Religious Leaders," *Research in Mental Health and Religious Behavior* (Atlanta, Ga.: Psychological Studies Institute, 1976), p. 242.

17. Malony, "Current Research on Perform-ance Effectiveness Among Religious Leaders," p. 254.

18. Goerge W. Crane, "The Worry Clinic," in Wesley Shrader, *Anguished Men of God: A Guide to the Crisis Among Today's Parish Clergy* (New York: Harper & Row, 1970), p. 33.

19. John G. Koehler, "The Minister as Family Man," in Mace, *What's Happening to Clergy Marriages?* p. 63.

20. Ibid., p. 64.

21. Truman G. Esau and Richard H. Cox, "The Mental Health of Ministers' Wives and Families," *Clinical Psychiatry and Religion*, ed. Pattison, pp. 202–203.

22. Gerald J. Jud, Edgar W. Mills, and Genevieve Walters Burch, *Ex-Pastors: Why Men Leave the Parish Ministry* (Philadelphia: Pilgrim Press, 1970), pp. 76–78.

23. Daniel D. Walker, *The Human Problems of the Minister* (New York: Harper & Brothers, 1960), pp. 77–78.

24. Cited by Charles Prestwood, *A New Breed of Clergy* (Grand Rapids, Mich.: William B. Eerdmans Publishing Co., 1972), p. 24.

25. Helmut Thielicke, *The Trouble with the Church*, trans. John W. Doberstein (Grand Rapids, Mich.: Baker Book House, 1965), pp. 1–2.

26. Charles Merrill Smith, *How to Become a Bishop Without Being Religious*, cited by Bartlett, *The Vanishing Parson*, p. 141.

27. Daniel Blain, "Fostering the Mental Health of Ministers," *The Church and Mental Health*, ed. Paul B. Moves (New York: Charles Scribner's Sons, 1953), pp. 257–258.

28. Albert L. Haversat, "Statistical Report: Lutheran Church of America Ministers Who Have Been Removed from the Register of Active Ministers" (September 15, 1962–October 10, 1968), cited by Bartlett, *The Vanishing Parson*, p. 157.

29. Bartlett, *The Vanishing Parson*, p. 8.

30. Jud, Mills, and Burch, *Ex-Pastors*, p. 59.

31. Bartlett, *The Vanishing Parson*, p. 25.

32. Jud, Mills, and Burch, *Ex-Pastors*, p. 107.

33. William E. Hulme, *Your Pastor's Problems: A Guide for Ministers and Laymen* (Garden City, N. Y.: Doubleday & Company, 1966), pp. 101–102.

34. Ibid., pp. 127–128.

BIOGRAPHICAL SKETCH

VERNON GROUNDS is the president emeritus of the Conservative Baptist Theological Seminary. He received his Ph.D. from Drew University and an honorary L.H.D. from Gordon College. He has had articles published in *Eternity*, *Christianity Today*, *Christian Herald Magazine*, *Seek*, *Decision*, *Christian Association for Psychological Studies*, and *Leadership*. He is the author of *The Reason for our Hope*, *Evangelicalism and Social Responsibility*, *Revolution and the Christian Faith*, *Emotional Problems and the Gospel*, and *Is God Dead?* He also served as the pastor of the Gospel Tabernacle in Paterson, New Jersey.

Pastoring and Evangelizing for Self-Esteem

ROBERT H. SCHULLER

> I find a restiveness in man, a dissatisfaction of a universal sort. The average human being, as I judge it, is uneasy. He is like a man who is hungry, gets up at night, opens the refrigerator door, and doesn't exactly see what he wants because he doesn't know what he wants. He closes the door and goes back to bed.
>
> —ROBERT ARDREY

WE CAN all identify with that statement, but it only sets the stage for the question, "What is the ultimate hunger of the human being?" For the past fifty years, psychologists and psychiatrists have been trying to answer this bottom-line question.

The will to experience pleasure, according to Sigmund Freud, explains the basic deep-seated hunger of human beings.[1] Beyond a doubt, the pleasure instinct is a very real and very powerful force in human behavior. On the other hand, men and women by the millions have been known to forsake pleasure in favor of work, love, religion, or war. Man craves something deeper than pleasure. The appetites of the eye, the stomach, the ear, and the sex organs can all be satisfied, yet the human spirit hungers for something more.

Alfred Adler came along and argued that Freud's observations were too shallow.[2] To him, the will to achieve power explains everything. The desire to be in control and the exhilaration of being in command illustrate man's drive for power. The bloody pages of history offer horrendous evidence that man will kill, cheat, lie, and betray his own soul in his pursuit of power.

Yet power does not produce ultimate satisfaction. On the contrary, power often produces enormous anxiety and feelings of insecurity. The man on the top is the man who is shot at, threatened, and challenged by those who seek his position of power. The possession of power often leads only to futility and frustration.

The late Victor Frankl detected a deep and powerful undercurrent in human motivational forces when he suggested that the will to find meaning is the ultimate hunger of man.[3] With perception, he has pointed out that man is able to achieve mental and emotional equilibrium when he sees meaning in his life experience. This explains why some people are able to achieve peace of mind in the midst of enormous suffering and misery. He, of course, had experienced the Nazi death camps. His family was exterminated in the holocaust, and he alone survived. When Frankl stood naked before the Gestapo, they made him take off his wedding ring. At that horrible, terrifying moment, the thought came to him, "You can't take away my freedom to choose how I will respond to what you are doing to me." Yet deep inside, man seeks more than meaning.

Abraham Maslow suggests that man's deepest need is for self-actualization. Erich Fromm believes it is the will to love. Rollo May talks about the will to create. All of these men speak to one of the strong subsurface currents within man. But none of them identifies the basic force we are seeking.

The position I have taken is that none of these theorists is totally wrong, and no one is totally right. There is a deeper human hunger that I call self-esteem. Based on my perception of the person of Jesus Christ, the work of Christ, and the teaching of Christ, I submit that the deepest of all human hungers is the need for self-esteem.

Historically, systematic theology has started with the doctrine of man. I agree with this approach, for the people to whom I am trying to talk do not accept the Bible, God, or even Jesus Christ. But they do accept and believe in human beings. So I believe that it is my sincere calling from God to take the systematic approach.

The whole theology of self-esteem is a systematic theological approach. To be systematic in theology is not to be antibiblical. It had better be biblical or it is not going to have integrity. But I chose the systematic theological approach because I feel that is the way to communicate to people who will ask questions, listen to answers, and, if it makes sense, accept it. That's our strategy at Garden Grove Community Church.

From that perspective, then, we have developed a system of theological concepts. I never verbalize them to the television congregation, but they undergird everything we say and do: our substance, our style, our strategy, and our spirit.

Mankind's deepest need is for self-esteem. I consider this to be universal. I have traveled around the world and met Christians and non-Christians in a variety of cultures and nationalities and have found this to be true.

Let me illustrate how this relates to sin, salvation, and fullness of life. I come out of a Reformed theological background. For my thesis at Western Seminary, I made a topical and a scriptural index to *Institutes of the Christian Religion* by John Calvin. I had to read through *Institutes* word for word ten times, until I finished a 285-page index.

A central theme of Reformed theology is that a human being is, by nature, rebellious against God. But this does not go far enough. We must go deeper and ask why. The explanation given is that Adam and Eve disobeyed God and thus sinned in the Garden of Eden. They were expelled from the Garden, and that's it.

Let me illustrate with a cross-section slice of a golf ball. First, the outside of the golf ball is the white, dimpled plastic. Classical theologians look at the golf ball and they see man, by nature, as rebellious against God. He sins, he steals, he kills, and he fights, unless he is born again.

Now when we say that man's nature is to rebel against God, we are looking only at the outside of the golf ball. We must ask the question, "Why is he that way?" or we won't know how to approach him. I contend that the skin of sin is rebellion. But at the very core of the golf ball, there is a hard rubber pea. That is the core with which all human beings are born, and I call that "negative self-image."

Erik Erikson, an authority in child-development theory today, contends that there are several stages of human psychological and emotional development.[4] During the first twelve months, after the traumatic experience of being expelled from the womb and thrown into a world of sound and light and sensations, the child must learn to trust. It is not born with trust. In every premature nursery in America, nurses are taught to stroke and talk to the premature infant. Infants do not, by nature, trust.

If you want to know why Schuller smiles on television, if you want to know why I make people laugh once in a while, I'm giving them sounds and strokes, sounds and strokes. It's strategy. People who don't trust need to be stroked. People are born with a negative self-image. Because they do not trust, they cannot trust God.

So *lack of trust* is the exact opposite of *saving trust.* This is understood in the light of the classical Reformed theological definition of saving faith in Jesus Christ. Faith in Jesus Christ includes three elements:

* Knowledge of the facts surrounding Jesus Christ.
* Belief that the facts are true.
* Personally trusting in Jesus Christ alone for salvation.

We want to see people turn from a negative self-image, or lack of trust, to trust in Jesus Christ. Unless trust is adequate, all kinds of defense mechanisms enter the picture. Because people don't trust, they wear masks; because they don't trust, they are not honest.

Second, around the hard, solid rubber pea in the golf ball there are all kinds of tight, stretched rubber bands. They represent the intricacies and complexities in each person of tensions, worries, fears, guilts, ambitions, and ego trips. Finally, when you come to the outer skin, you have a rebellious person.

I happen to believe with all my soul and being that you don't approach the rebellious person and say, "Hey, buddy, you're rebellious." You're going to get a sock on the chin. But that's been the classical approach. Tell him what a sinner he is, convict him of his guilt. The trouble is that the only people who are getting that message are the Christians who are sitting in church. The sinners stay away like fat people avoiding a bathroom scale.

When this church was being started, I rang doorbells and asked, "Why don't you go to church?" and "What books do you read?" I found the unchurched people were reading Norman Vincent Peale. So I invited Dr. Peale to come and preach in the drive-in theater, and I promised him a big crowd. I told him we had the biggest church parking lot (1,700 cars) in southern California where everybody can have a soft seat near an open window. Dr. Peale said he'd come.

For that Sunday, we advertised in the sports page, the business page, the news section, and the women's page. We really blanketed southern California. The drive-in theater was jam-packed with cars. I'll never forget that Sunday, because a movie was playing on the life of Audie Murphy, the World War II hero, and carried the title on the marquee "To Hell and Back—In Person—Norman Vincent Peale."

Well, that morning I forgot Dr. Peale's biographical sheet. As I walked up to the podium to introduce him I prayed for guidance. This is what came out:

"Ladies and gentlemen, we have with us today the greatest positive thinker in the world. His name is a household word. He is, in my mind, the most beautiful person I have ever known. If you get to know him personally and have a chance to talk to him alone as I have, you'll be born again. His name is Jesus Christ; and here to tell us all about him is Norman Vincent Peale."

Dr. Peale blushed from the collar up. My introduction had intimidated him, although I hadn't intended it to do so. He began, "If Jesus Christ were here today, what would he tell you? Would he tell you what terrible sinners you are?"

I thought, "Yes, he would." But Dr. Peale said, "No, I don't think he'd have to. Deep down in your soul you know it. What he would tell you is 'Follow me and I will make you fishers of men.'"

He started the sermon where I usually ended mine. I must tell you that my preaching strategy up to this time was to make the listeners realize how sinful they were, to generate a sense of guilt within them, and then to give them the Good News that they can be forgiven. I patterned this after the classical formula of the Heidelberg Catechism, question-and-answer number two:

How many things are necessary for you to know, that you in this comfort may live and die happily? Three: the first, how great my sins and misery are; the second, how I am delivered from all my sins and misery; and the third, how I am to be thankful to God for such deliverance.

I don't quarrel with this. I believe it. But as a strategy for mission, it's a lot better just to start with question-and-answer number one:

What is your only comfort in life and death? That I, with body and soul, both in life and death, am not my own, but belong unto my faithful Savior Jesus Christ. . . .

That feeds my self-esteem. If he is mine, and if I belong to him, I am somebody.

Then Dr. Peale made another statement that was really very revolutionary. He said, "In fact, in the Bible, Jesus never called any person a sinner." I knew at that point he was wrong. So I went home that afternoon and I read through the gospels of Matthew, Mark, Luke, and John in the King James Version, red-letter edition. I discovered that Jesus never called any person a sinner! He recognized the reality of sin. He recognized the fact that all persons were sinners, *but* to convert them, he didn't use the strategy of calling them sinners! Jesus did call some people snakes and vipers. Those stern words were used only against the religious leaders, who made it a practice to use their religious authority to deepen a sense of guilt rather than to share the knowledge of God's grace. But Jesus didn't use that language when he was trying to take a person of the world and turn him into a believer.

I don't think there is anything a minister could do that would provoke the wrath of Jesus more than if he failed to communicate to sinners the grace of God. But what is grace? Grace is God's love in action for people who don't deserve it.

Adam and Eve were created, according to Genesis, without sin. Then they fell, which means they had a chance. They knew better. If Adam and Eve were in my congregation, I would not hesitate to say, "Adam and Eve, you are sinners. You both knew better." But their children were born in the bushes, in hiding, and it's not fair to pick on those kids and preach to them as if they were the same as the parents. Those kids never had a choice. They never had a knowledge of the beauty of God. Adam and Eve did. They walked in the Garden. So you take the positive approach with their children, one that has some strokes in it.

If I had to write a book on communication, I think it would be a development of this one sentence: "I am not what I think I am; I am not what you think I am; I am what I think you think I am."

How do you approach people? You don't approach them through battering their self-respect and insulting their dignity. That violates their self-esteem. The worst sinner still is not a monkey. The human creature is a cathedral, not a shack. That's true whether he's white, black, yellow, or red; whether he's rich or poor, literate or illiterate, Mongoloid or genius. He's not a shack; he's a cathedral. He may be a cracked cathedral with the windows destroyed; he may be in ruins because of his rebellion, but he's still a cathedral because he was created in the image of God.

The secret of success is to find a need and fill it. That principle can be applied to communication. The theology of self-esteem produces a theology of communication. One never communicates with people by insulting, manipulating, or intimidating them. In all the churches and denominations, there are people who claim to be Christians; they claim to be born again; they love the Word; they preach the Scriptures; and they know the right answers—but they're mean as the dickens. The love isn't there. And the number one reason is that the seeds of salvation were planted in the soil of some soul's shame, instead of being planted in the remnant of some soul's self-esteem. A person who is converted out of shame still has the same basic uncured problem of a negative self-image. That's different from the person who experiences conversion and who knows out of the reality of what God thinks: "I am wonderful and he loves me, and he wouldn't stop at anything, not even the Cross, to make me his friend again." When you appeal to a person's self-esteem as a strategy for evangelism, a different kind of a Christian will emerge than when you appeal to a person's shame and degradation and insecurity.

That's why I won't be controversial from the pulpit when I'm communicating with unchurched people. The controversial material is better placed in the classroom setting where Christian education takes place. In that setting, there is give and take. Dialogue takes place. Growth through interaction is experienced. This communication approach respects and promotes the dignity of the individual.

A theology of self-esteem also produces a theology of evangelism, a theology of social ethics, and a theology of economics; and these produce a theology of government. It all rises from one foundation: the dignity of the person who was created in the image of God. I see this relating to the central theme of salvation, which is clearly developed in the book of Romans. This is examined and well developed by Professor Anthony Hoekema in his book, *The Christian Looks at Himself*. [5]

Let's suppose a person has a negative self-image. How would you build that person's self-respect? Do you know what Jesus did? He approached Zacchaeus and said, "Let's have dinner together." When he came to Mary Magdalene, he treated her like a lady.

"I'm not what I think I am; I'm not what you think I am; I am what I think you think I am." We become what people expect from us. We will fulfill the expectations that others hold for us.

If somebody with an immoral reputation invited me to have coffee with him, I would be a little ashamed to be seen with him. That would violate my self-dignity. If someone who is my equal invited me to have coffee with him, that wouldn't do anything for my self-esteem. If somebody high up the ladder invited me out—let's say the president of the United States asked me to the Oval Office—that would give my self-esteem quite a boost.

But let's suppose there's somebody above the president whom almost everybody accepts as the Ideal One. In biblical terms, it's the Lamb of God, without spot or blemish. Let's suppose he calls me on the phone and says, "Schuller, I want to meet you." So we meet all alone, and we talk, and he looks at me as if he really respects me. He puts his arm around me and makes me an offer: "I wanted to get together with you, Bob. You know,

I'd like to live my life through yours if I could." And I say, "Wait a minute, I'm not good enough for you." And then he takes his robe of righteousness and puts it around me. "Here, wear this." I'm declared to be righteous by the person of God, and the righteousness of Jesus Christ is imputed, freely given to me as my own.

When you meet this Ideal One, who knows you as you really are but treats you as if you were perfect, you have a psychological, existential, and spiritual encounter with the grace of God at the most profound level. That's when you are truly born again. Now you can also accept yourself. "What is your only comfort in life and death?" You can now say

that I, with body and soul, both in life and death, am not my own, but belong unto my faithful Savior Jesus Christ; who with his precious blood has fully satisfied for all my sins, and redeemed me from all the power of the devil; and so preserves me, that without the will of my Father in heaven, not a hair can fall from my head; yea, that all things must work together for my salvation, wherefore by his Holy Spirit, he also assures me of eternal life, and makes me heartily willing and ready, henceforth, to live unto him.

Real self-esteem now emerges. At this point, I dare to receive the Holy Spirit because I feel worthy to be a channel for the Holy Spirit. And now it becomes possible for the fruit of the Spirit to flow through me in love, joy, and peace. I no longer have to function at the level of my old defense mechanisms: still insecure, defensive, touchy, and angry.

Don Quixote, the Man of La Mancha, beautifully illustrates the gospel of Jesus Christ. Cervantes portrayed the Ideal One as Don Quixote. Any Ideal One is going to be called crazy by the world; and they called the Man of La Mancha crazy. So he asked, "Who's crazy? Am I crazy because I can see the world as it could become? Or are you crazy because you see the world as it is? Who's really crazy?"

I have thought about that question, and I believe the Man of La Mancha is right. I'm not crazy if I'm an idealist. I'm not crazy if I'm a beautiful dreamer. People are crazy who only see the world as it is. They're crazy because they're not creative; they're crazy because they are not uplifting sources. Because they're not part of the solution, they keep the world as it is.

"I am not what I think I am; I am not what you think I am; I am what I think you think I am." If you say we are all sinners, you're right. I agree with you. Your condemnations only reinforce my own rebellion. So don't tell me what I am—tell me what I might become.

The Man of La Mancha sees this harlot, this whore, this Mary Magdalene. Aldonza is her name. She's a waitress by day and a prostitute by night. She serves the drunken camel drivers. The Man of La Mancha says to this whore, "My Lady." She looks at him and exclaims, "Lady?" Some camel driver makes a pass at her and she squeals . . . laughs. The Man of La Mancha says, "Yes, you are My Lady, and I shall give you a new name. I shall call you Dulcinea. You are My Lady . . . you are My Lady, Dulcinea."

Once, in distress, not comprehending him, when they are alone, she says, "Why do you do and say these things? Why do you treat me the way you do? What do you want from me? I know men. I've seen them all; I've had them all; they're all the same. They all want something from me. Why do you say these things? Why do you call me Dulcinea? Why do you call me your Lady? What do you want?" He says, "I just want to call you what you are . . . you are My Lady, Dulcinea."

Later there is a horrible scene backstage. You hear screams . . . she is being raped. She runs onto the stage. She has been insulted with the ultimate indignity and she's crying and hysterical, dirty and disheveled. Her blouse has been torn off and her skirt is ripped. He sees her and says compassionately, "My Lady, Dulcinea, Oh, My Lady, My Lady."

She can't stand it and cries, "Don't call me a Lady. Oh God, don't call me a Lady. Can't you see me for what I am? I was born in a ditch by a mother who left me there naked and cold—too hungry to cry. I never blamed her. She left me there hoping I'd have the good sense to die. Don't call me a Lady. I'm only a kitchen slut, reeking with sweat. I'm only a whore men use and forget. Don't call me your Lady. I'm only Aldonza. I am nothing at all."

As she runs into the night of self-flagellation, he calls out, "But you *are* My Lady." The curtain drops.

The curtain rises again. The Man of La Mancha is dying, like our Lord, from a broken heart, despised and rejected of men, a man of sorrows and acquainted with grief. To his deathbed comes a Spanish queen with a mantilla of lace. She kneels, makes the sign of the cross, and prays. He opens his eyes and says, "Who are you?" She replies, "My Lord, don't you remember? You sang a song, don't you remember? 'To dream the impossible dream, to fight the unbeatable foe, to bear the unbearable sorrow, to run where the brave dare not go. . . .' My Lord, don't you remember? You gave me a new name, you called me Dulcinea." She stands proudly. "I am your Lady."

And the angels sing, and he goes to be with his Father. It is finished. She was born again.

That illustrates for me the gospel of grace in Jesus Christ. There is no philosophy, no psychiatric system, no theology of any religion in the world that can match this for an immortal soul.

NOTES

1. Robert B. Ewen, *An Introduction to Theories of Personality* (New York: Academic Press, 1980), p. 13.
2. Christopher F. Monte, *Beneath the Mask* (New York: Holt, Rinehart and Winston, 1980), pp. 316–317.
3. Victor E. Frankl, *Man's Search for Meaning* (New York: Washington Square Press, 1963).
4. Erik H. Erikson, *Childhood and Society* (New York: W. W. Norton and Company, 1963), pp. 247–274.
5. Anthony A. Hoekema, *The Christian Looks at Himself* (Grand Rapids, Mich.: William B. Eerdmans, 1975).

BIOGRAPHICAL SKETCH

Dr. ROBERT H. SCHULLER is the founder and pastor of the Crystal Cathedral of the Reformed Church in America and can be seen weekly on the internationally televised "Hour of Power," which proclaims the focusing message, "There is Good News in Jesus Christ." He has shared self-esteem and possibility thinking principles through lectures and numerous books, including *Self Love—The Dynamic Force of Success, You Can Become the Person You Want to Be, Move Ahead with Possibility Thinking,* and *Turning Your Stress into Strength.*

This chapter originally appeared in *Leadership* magazine 2/1 (winter 1981), where it was titled "Why Bob Schuller Smiles on Television." © *Leadership,* Winter 1981. Used by permission.

Self or Society:
Is There a Choice?

JAMES H. OLTHUIS

SOMETHING needs to change in our global village—for the sake of survival. We are running out of the basic stuffs necessary for life: clean air, good food, energy, stable currency, warm families, relevant churches. We are all victims surrendering our humanity. Differences only emerge in how we are responding to our common victimization.

For many of us in the affluent West, there is almost an irresistible temptation to retreat into our own small concerns and seek our own little islands of happiness and pleasure. This "cult of subjectivity,"[1] as it has been called, seeks peace, solitude, and inner healing by going inward and attending to the needs of self in communes, personal therapy, and/or Eastern religions. Sometimes it degenerates into a me-first, satisfy-all-my-desires hedonism.

At the same time, faced with the uncertainties of the present, many look askance at this attention to and absorption in self, and promise a return to paradise with its old values and old securities. Many learned liberal and conservative champions of culture and order more sublimely talk of the need for temperance, self-restraint, public interest, citizenship, cultural excellence, and the old, established values.[2]

On the one hand, we hear talk of self-fulfillment and a withdrawal from the societal arena. On the other hand, we are called to do our societal duty and deny self. Self or society—are these the only alternatives? Is the present vacuum of public leadership the result of the seventies' narcissistic absorption with self? Is the way out of the global crisis less attention to self? Does rebirth of public passion and purpose mean the subordination of self to public duty, the closure of the inner life?

Needed: A Marriage of Personal Maturity and Social Justice

In this paper, I want to argue that the self-or-society choice that we are again being saddled with needs to be rejected as wrong-headed and in fact dangerous. Wrong-headed because there is no intrinsic opposition between the individual person and society. Dangerous because acceptance of the dilemma insures that our society will ping-pong back and forth between the extremes of individualism and collectivism, between the orgy of hedonism and the vice of totalitarianism.

The path toward a sane, healthy society, I am convinced, can only be created by healthy, sane people. Not less attention to self is needed today, but more. Social justice can only emerge in tandem with personal maturity. It can only be brought about by people who have genuine self-knowledge. There is no split between the personal and social spheres of existence, between personal growth and societal renewal. You cannot have one without the other. The way to a renewed political vision is via the inward journey. Unless there is a continuous interplay between personal growth and societal renewal, projects for social reform are seriously crippled and almost certainly will not attain their desired ends. Without attention to self as person,[3] its growth and integration, campaigns for change and renewal in society—no matter how noble and just initially—will misfire, derail, and fail. The specific reasons for failure will vary, but I suggest that a significant, overriding factor will come down to lack of personal maturity.[4]

The Individualist-Collectivist Dilemma

My thesis that personal growth and societal renewal belong in tandem means rejecting the individualist-collectivist, self-society dilemma that has become virtually second nature. It is common currency that commitment to institutions can only take place at the expense of personal freedom. The only real question is how little or how much self-interest is permissible if we are still to have a viable society. The needs of the person and the needs of society are at odds. That's the nature of life. All we can do is compromise as best we can. The key to breaking this dilemma of social collectivism and individualistic self-interest is the knowledge that it is based on a wholly inadequate view of the human person as an isolated unit of self-interest and on society as a plurality of such units. In this framework, any concern with self can only be an expression of self-interest. That is true whether or not self-interest is vice (Social Democracy or Marxism) or virtue (Social Darwinism or Capitalism). Attention to self simply amounts to individualism, selfishness, social injustice, and political elitism.

Possessions and performance—what we have and what we can do—are everything. The roles we play, the material goods we acquire, the sexual prowess we manage measure individual importance. "Having" rather than "being" defines the person.

Consequently, attention to public duty and the common good means taming individual desires and relinquishing individual freedom. The individual is not a person with a sense of inherent worth, but an ego of self-interest under pressure to be self-less in service of the public cause. Every individual is in competition with every other individual and exists in that competitive reference and in terms of external status.

The collectivist tradition of social democracy treats the person no better. The intention is high, the "people" are held in honor, the promise is bright. But the people become a behavioristic herd to be conditioned and indoctrinated into virtue.

The heart of the problem for individualists and collectivists is "their common blindness to the demands of the person."[5] Individualism reduces the person to an isolated unit of self-interest lacking personal depth and communal ties. Collectivism politicizes the personality out of existence, abolishing human mystery.

We need, I am saying, a viable alternative that is neither individualist nor collectivist. We need to break from the pernicious dualistic tradition which, reducing the self to an assemblage of needs, sees only two possibilities: self-denial for the good of society or self-satisfaction at the expense of society.

What Is "Human"?

We need a third choice, a choice that begins from a more holistic, socially oriented view of the human person, a view that I take to be the biblical understanding of humankind. I will attempt to capture the heart of such a view in a number of brief paragraphs.

1. *Humanity is cohumanity.*   Communality, neighborliness, is constitutive of the very I-ness of each person. We are all associates. None of us stands alone. We are called by our very natures to be cohuman (as opposed to inhuman); we are to be companions (rather than competitors); we are to realize our interdependence (rather than claiming independence). Being with and for each other is part and parcel of being a human person.

Our very I-ness is a We-ness. We belong to each other.

2. *Humanity is biunity.*   Together, male and female, are in a mutual partnership of belonging and reciprocity. God created Adam (earth creature), male and female, created he them.

3. *Humanity is centeredness, personhood.*   We belong to each other, yet we are individually unique persons. Each of us is called to realize our unity as integral persons. We are to act as subjects active on our own behalf, conscious of the I as the center of awareness, strength, intention, and action. We are to be whole persons of one piece living in singleness of heart before God and neighbour.

4. *Humanity is calling to life-service.*   Humanity is, at core and root, unity of service. As a unified body with many members, humanity is caretaking of self, neighbor, and creation in service of God. The call of life and to life—in its many forms—is inescapable. Life beckons to be unfolded, formed, cared for, enjoyed, analyzed, celebrated.

5. *Humanity is a developmental calling.*   There is a course to each of our lives, a timed course with clearly defined tasks and stages. What and who we are is not given to us ready-made, it is filled (full) as life moves on. Our cohumanity and our integration as whole persons develop in the process of living and growing, a process that for all of us is deeply enmeshed in corporate and individual sin.

At the heart of our search for personal-societal *shalom* is this view of humanity: to be fully personal is to be fully social; to be fully social is to be fully personal. It is not one or the other. Human freedom is not freedom if it is not social; but neither is it freedom if it is not fully personal.

To view concern for self as retreat from the cosmos into some private inner sanctum is to have an inadequate view of self. To love another person is not over against loving self; in loving others, I am loving myself. To commit myself to another person is not the curtailment, but the avenue of my freedom. In this manner, a biblical view of man enables and empowers us to avoid the conflicts between egoism (self) and altruism (others), between freedom (capitalism and individualism) and equality (communism), between freedom (existentialism) and authority (hierarchical institutions); in short, between individual and society.

SELF-KNOWLEDGE IS THE KEY

Each of us faces the communal calling of service in our own unique, personal way. At the center of our personal pilgrimages lies the search for self-knowledge: knowledge of that core or heart of our being that gives us a sense of continuity amid change, that heart to which others appeal and upon which they rely. It is that core that is held responsible, and it is that which we must sense if we are to have the strength to carry out our convictions.

To go deep into one's being is imperative for a grounded awareness of both self and the rest of reality. Not that this turning inward is the end. Rather, it is the beginning. For in turning inward, we confront the question of why we exist at all. We meet the inescapable root of our existence, the God who made us and saves us, the God who invites us and empowers us to be ourselves, fully and socially.

Without going through the depths of our soul, without coming to grips with our own deep-seated illusions and facing our inner core, our self-knowledge remains superficial and illusory. And our outward movements of love and sharing lack depth and authenticity. Without self-discovery, our encounter with God and other persons, even animals and plants, remains external, without inner connection and integrity.

When, on the other hand, we begin to know ourselves in our inwardness, we find ourselves urged to reach out, to meet others, and to contribute to society. Taking our own inner life seriously, we can take the inner life of our neighbor seriously. In encounter with persons and with God, we grow in self-knowledge. And the growing self-knowledge leads to more realistic and grounded journeys outward.

There is a rhythm to this inward-outward movement: increased inner wholeness works for societal health, and societal renewal encourages and promotes inner growth. That rhythm is the ideal we all seek to realize.

But the reality we more often face in our daily struggles is the negative side of this same rhythm: lack of inner security or lack of connection with inner self leads to outward actions that lack solid ground, are based on illusions, and betray inner weakness.

Personal Growth

But we are getting ahead of ourselves. What is personal growth? It has to do with growth in realizing and actualizing our integrality as whole persons. It is achieving an increasing awareness of self as subject, as agent active on its own behalf, bringing often fragmented and unbalanced sides of self into unified and integrated harmony. It is the experience of living rather than "being lived," the experience that I am doing things rather than the things are happening to me.

Neither man nor woman is like a layer cake, an animal layer topped with a special personal layer. Man and woman are human throughout; every apparently animal feature is actually human. There is a wholeness to man and woman. *Anything* they are must be related to *everything* they are—in their entirety. Whatever upsets or affects a person, upsets and affects the whole person he or she is. To concentrate all one's efforts on making a person "spiritual" is in fact to dehumanize that person, just as to stress emotional health above all leads to one-sidedness. The truly spiritual person is at the same time the more human, the healthier, the more developed, the more alive, the more in-touch person. To grow emotionally, confessionally, or physically, a person must grow humanly. Physical health does not make a whole man or woman. Nor does emotional health. Nor does confessional health. Health in each area of life makes for and is conducive to total health. Human well-being is an integrated affair; the faith dimension is inextricably interwoven with the physical, the emotional with the social, the analytical with the truthful, and so on.

However, two dimensions and their interaction play unique and crucial roles in personal integration: the commitment or faith dimension and the emotional or feeling dimension. For identity, a person requires an ultimate purpose or certainty, a deep meaning and commitment in terms of which to integrate all of life. Secondly, a person must be in touch with feelings and have integrated them in the whole self in order to have a *sense* of self-identity. The interplay between these two dimensions is complex and dynamic.

COMMITMENT: THE ANCHOR FOR OPENNESS

Commitment is the secret to wholeness and the anchor for openness. Committed, one has an axis, a centering principle for life, which delivers one from being lost. Being integrated means using one's rooted convictions as to who she or he is and about where certainty is to be found as the guiding framework of life. Commonness of confession is the heart of human fellowship. Committed to Christ, a Christian has self-identity with certainty and perspective.

Not just any vision of life promotes growth and maturity. Wrong beliefs can inhibit growth and promote continued immaturity. Religion can also be an unhealthy and disintegrative force rather than the way to healing. When visions of life—including some emphases within Christianity—no longer serve to integrate the person towards wholeness but become ways of escaping one's humanity, they can give rise to serious pathologies and can foster passivity, immaturity, and inflexibility.

A healthy view of life should encourage the opening up, integrating, and maturing of the human drives and emotions and should not create a split between a "higher" divine soul and a "lower" material body or stress the need to hold down and restrict the "lower" bodily passions. A healthy vision should lead to questioning of the accepted social order and counsel adjustment to the Kingdom of God, not to society. In short, the beliefs we hold need to be life-affirming and not life-destroying.[6]

EMOTIONS: FOUNDATIONAL TO WELL-BEING

A mature person is impossible without a mature faith. But an immature person cannot have a mature faith. Although belief in Jesus Christ is indispensable, it is not enough for maturity. We also need an emotional sense of that new self rooted in Christ. Emotional integration is foundational to human maturity.

Sensing, feeling, and emoting are the second way we come to know the truth about our environment.[7] (Our physical way of being in the world—shivering from cold, sweltering from heat, for example—is the first way). Through our emotional life, we are placed in vibrant touch with our surroundings. Sadness helps us deal with loss, excitement keeps us with the task at hand, joy brings us close. A healthy emotional life knows all the kinds of emotion, and experiences and expresses them in a way appropriate to the situation.

However, emotions always find their full meaning and particularity in a larger human context. There is the joy of surrender, the joy of troth, the joy of discovery, along with many other kinds. Only in such opened-up contexts or full-life situations with their relevant norms can we judge the appropriateness of our emotional reactions.

Emotions, then, are not norms that give direction to human life. However, if a person is closed down emotionally, his or her emotions can easily, unawares and inappropriately, play the role of norms. For a closing down of the immediate emotional openness to reality leads to denial, distortion, and repression of experiences.

We then engage in selective inattention, projection, rationalization, and take shelter in various defensive postures. Such defensive patterns develop in the early developmental stages of our lives, as protection against the hurt of experiences of rejection, deprivation, humiliation, smothering, and the like. Such armoring was then necessary for our survival—but at the same time it did not allow us to experience the love, care, and openness we needed and wanted. Moreover, it did not (and still does not) allow us to flow freely, throwing our full energies into our various tasks. Instead, we become stuck in our emotional patterns, which become engrained and reinforced as we continue to live our adult lives according to the childhood script.

In one way or another, in one degree or another, I believe all of us are so scripted and so stuck. Only when these emotional blocks and disturbances are recognized and dissolved are we able to enjoy a healthy, emotional functioning. All of us, as Laing has so graphically expressed it, need to go through our own hidden forms of madness in order to insure our spiritual maturing.

In fact, if we really believe that our emotional life is also part of our God-given human nature, it is incumbent upon us to seek such healing as an integral part of putting off the old and putting on the new man or woman in Jesus Christ. We will gain a new sense of our inner self, new strength to act on our basic convictions, new ability to open our hearts and be fully involved in life. For until we feel a sense of self as new creatures in Christ, until we feel the reality of God's love, our Christian confession will be thin and heady. That in fact is one of the main reasons why so many Christians plunge into the depths of depression, guilt, and self-doubt.

If we don't feel self-worth, we develop a negative self-image marred by feelings of inferiority, powerlessness, and helplessness. These, in turn, give rise to a basic feeling of inadequacy and discouragement and to various compensatory or neurotic tendencies. Without self and sense of self, we have no self to give either to God or to our neighbor.

CONTAMINATED BELIEFS

A person with sense of self is a person searching for something to commit the self to. Identity leads to commitment; commitment strengthens and roots one's sense of identity.

At the same time, the weaker the sense of identity and sense of self, the less stable the commitment. In fact, out of emotional anxiety we often go along with matters we in fact know are wrong, or resist matters that are right. Thus we can resist changes for the better because we lack the stamina to see the matter through. Often we try to put a good face on a bad thing by searching for confessional justifications, rather than by admitting and dealing with our emotional anxieties.[8]

Indeed, it is not easy to have the inner security necessary to live out personal convictions. It is tempting to accept rationalizations that serve to allay our fears and calm our consciences. Our anxieties can lead our basic beliefs astray, contaminate them, or cause us to abandon them, just as wrong basic beliefs can lead our emotional lives astray and keep us emotionally immature.

In all of this, I can only conclude that not less sense of self is needed, but more. Not too much identity is our problem, but too little. Where true sense of self and personal power grounded in that self is lacking, a person's need for self-esteem is perverted into a need to dominate other things and other people, and a person's need for acceptance is perverted into a need to be possessed by other things and other people. No wonder that we seldom meet each other in the middle, no strings attached, enjoying each other, giving and sharing by just being together. No wonder that we more often only get entangled in each other's needs, forcing ourselves on the other person or holding our inner selves back, mutually fooling ourselves that we are really giving and sharing.

However, when we grow in our sense of self-identity, we are able to give each other more space: I don't need to pull neurotically on you for acceptance and affirmation or, as the case may be, I don't need to pull back from you, fearing engulfment, when you are needy and reaching out. In my growing strength, I can take you in as the person you are, rather than as the person I want you to be. We can have a person-to-person meeting.

The Personal and Social Connect

What now has all this to do with societal renewal? Everything. For social change is, in the end, a mere change of masters, if not in tune with and accompanied by interior growth and integration.

Marx's position on social transformation has its attraction: seize control of the means of production and establish the power of the proletariat. Take power and then move to deeper changes in culture and self. But I think this approach is doomed to failure. Even in countries where Marxism has been established, the second stage of social transformation has not taken place. Transfer of power from one group to another changes little; only the names of the oppressors change. Moreover, the diminished and deprived humanity of the postindustrial society does not have the vision, strength, and personal resources to pull off such a struggle.

Without the journey inwards of personal growth, we will not have the heart for the journey outwards. And I mean heart in two senses: neither we will have the courage and internal strength to stand firm in the struggle and follow through on our convictions, nor will we have the proper motives that make for true healing and authentic shalom. Without the dark night of the soul, as Christians in the mystic tradition have graphically described it, without the self-knowledge gained in self-examination and growth, people will get in their own way in working for societal renewal. Their causes will be, at the critical junctures, betrayed, misled by their own hidden, unresolved fears and needs.

Without personal growth, people engage in causes for all kinds of reasons, mainly wrong, for power, money, applause, acceptance, escape. And they carry out their sacred missions on edge, with messianic zeal, anxious, fearful of being taken advantage of, defensive, projecting their rage hypercritically on society.

We need to have a good feeling about ourselves if we are really to like others. We need to feel cared for in order to care for others. If we only have a headtrip about the poor and needy in the world and lack a sense of injustice, we miss the emotional motivation that leads to healing action.

HEALING SOCIETAL INVOLVEMENT

No wonder that society needs renewal and reformation. For if the persons in the society are not in touch with their deepest selves in their strengths and weaknesses, their societal arrangements can only be superficial, impersonal, and inhumane. And, in turn, these tight boxes and prearranged slots in which we live further discourage taking personal responsibility and initiative. The cultural (dis)order has turned all of us into diminished and compulsive beings called the "modern" human.

The journey inward is essential to a grounded journey outward. Self-transcendence, reaching out to others, healing societal involvement—all start with an esteeming self, not with a negation of self.[9]

Freed from the paralysis of being unable to give oneself to life or from the frenzy of throwing oneself into every project to find oneself, men and women reach out, from personal strength and rootedness, to give and share of themselves in terms of God's intentions. Not neurotic needs, but the issues themselves become the motivation to social action. Inner healing leads to personal involvement in life; it frees a person to surrender to the normativity of life.

Societal renewal carries on into new ways of self-discovery or it falters and dies. Personal growth flows into societal renewal or it dead-ends in self-absorption and self-service. You can't have one without the other. Personal growth provides the courage, strength, and integrity for projects of societal renewal. Societal renewal provides the space and respect for personhood that makes for personal growth. Internal growth of itself leads to external outreach and is the impulse to cultural reform.

In a healthy rhythm of journeying in and out of, of inhaling and exhaling, we will find ourselves open to ourselves, to our neighbour, to our world, and to God. In touch with ourselves, we can be touched by the cry of the poor, the put-down of women, the fear of men, the struggle of adolescence, the horror of oppression.

Growth in personal integration helps us look evil and injustice right in the face and accept its risks and threats to personal security. Personal growth is relief of private burdens and release to focus on more universal hurts.

Today a person who seriously and openly takes the journey inward—without which authentic self-knowledge is impossible—risks being accused of selfishness, neglect of public duty and world-flight. No wonder that the world, clamoring for solutions, mourns the shortage of wise, trustworthy, and caring leaders. Not having done any *inner work*—even failing to understand what these words refer to—how can they renew society by their outer work? Rearrangements of the system will not bring the changes required. Restoration must come from changes within, from a turning around, a *metanoia*.

FINDING THE STRENGTH TO ACT

Where do we go from here—if my analysis is on the right track? Let me offer a few suggestions.

1. We cannot afford to ignore the internal sounds of the self. They will only return to haunt us. We need to try to work out where and why we get stuck; why, for example, we have difficulty giving or receiving or whatever. Perhaps that means counseling.

2. We ought to seek out people who think and feel and struggle much as we do and form small support-groups with them. In the emotional clearance and release that takes place, genuine growth is promoted, personal contact is increased and caring support becomes more real.

3. We ought to look for ways to give more room for the personal in work situations, to make the work place also a people place. Regular sessions sharing personal concerns in addition to the ordinary business meetings would be a good start.

4. We need to encourage each other to give ourselves to projects that offer healing to the world and with which we can identify. Such projects need not be big, and most likely will be small. Societal involvement that is at one with our inner convictions promotes personal integration and helps

develop a sense of personal strength. And in giving ourselves to small, specific projects, rather than avoiding action while waiting for the perfect societal overhaul, we give tangible evidence that we not only talk the faith but do the faith. God asks no more.

Since renewal of the world in which we live cannot advance apart from growth in self-knowledge, we need to deepen awareness of our selves and of the way who we are and how we are affects our work. The quality of our contribution as agents of social change depends upon the quality of our humanity.

NOTES

1. As Russell Jacoby, in his *Social Amnesia* (Boston: Beacon Press, 1975), has named it (cf. pp. 103–105). Cf. also Christopher Lasch's *The Culture of Narcissism* (New York: Norton & Co., 1978).

2. Theodore Roszak shows how critiques of the left (Jacoby adopts the viewpoint of the Frankfurt School) and right (such as Daniel Bell and Robert Nisbet) speak with one mind on this issue because they both work with a view of the self as inherently treacherous and selfish. Cf. his *Person/Planet* (Garden City, N.Y.: Doubleday, 1978), pp. 73–99. Robert Nisbet, *The Twilight of Authority* (New York: Oxford University Press, 1975), p. 144. Cf. also Daniel Bell, *The Cultural Contradictions of Capitalism* (New York: Basic Books, 1976), pp. 13, 245. E. Schur takes the same approach in *The Awareness Trap: Self Absorption Instead of Social Change* (Chicago: Quadrangle Books, 1976). Roszak asks the crucial question that all positions of this kind face (which Bell frankly admits leads to contradiction in such positions): if self-discovery and its journey inward is not to be permitted, "are we not in fact making self-knowledge an impossibility?" p. 78.

3. Theodore Roszak has written a compelling "manifesto of the person" entitled *Person/Planet* as a sequel to his *The Making of a Counter Culture* and *Where the Wasteland Ends.* His basic thesis—that "the needs of the planet are

the needs of person, and, therefore, the rights of the person are the rights of the planet" (p. xxx)—is of one piece with the argument of this essay. Unfortunately, however, Roszak's correct emphasis on personhood is not accompanied by a correlative emphasis on a primal normativity (the Word of God for creation). Richard Shaull in "The Death and Resurrection of the American Dream" (in G. Gutierrez and R. Schaull, *Liberation and Change* [Atlanta, Ga.: John Knox Press, 1977] makes a plea for a view of self-realization that issues in normative social change and need not deviate in individualism or anarchism. (pp. 97–180).

4. It is, for example, our moral lack of good will that is the root cause of much social injustice. "What makes injustices so unacceptable in our time is the fact that we now possess the knowhow to feed the world and provide the basics for all its citizens. What is lacking is the will and the way. What is lacking is compassion." Cf. Matthew Fry, *A Spirituality Named Compassion and the Healing of the Global Village* (Minneapolis: Winston Press, 1979), p. ii. The economist E. F. Schumacher is equally insistent: "There is no economic problem. . . . But there is a moral problem. . . ." Cf. *A Guide for the Perplexed* (New York: Harper & Row, 1977), p. 140.

5. Roszak, *Person/Planet*, pp. 112 and 117.

6. Ernest Becker, *The Denial of Death*

(New York: Free Press, 1973), pp. 202–204.

7. Arnold De Graaff, "Psychology: Sensitive Openness and Appropriate Reactions," *The Bulletin*, Publication of the Christian Association of Psychological Studies VII (1981): 3–11.

8. According to Paul Ricoeur, Marx, Freud, and Nietzsche were the "masters of suspicion" who unmasked the tricks of the ego. Cf. *The Conflict of Interpretations* (Evanston: Northwestern University Press, 1974), pp. 148–149.

9. Esteeming of self ought not to be confused with worship of self. Paul Vitz, in talking of "the selfist self, or the self as subject," fails to see that viewing self as subject and active agent need not end up in worship of self (selfist). The "losing self" of the Scriptures is no downplaying of the self as subject: it points the way to the fulfillment of self in active self-surrender to Christ. Cf. Vitz, *Psychology as Religion: The Cult of Self-Worship* (Grand Rapids, Mich.: Eerdmans, 1977), p. 127.

BIOGRAPHICAL SKETCH

JAMES H. OLTHUIS is senior member in theology at the Institute for Christian Studies, Toronto, Ontario. He holds a Ph.D. in ethics from the Free University of Amsterdam. He is the author of *Facts, Values and Ethics* and *I Pledge You My Troth: A Christian View of Marriage, Family, Friendship,* as well as several articles in books and magazines. He takes an active interest in individual, marriage, and family counseling.

Index